Job

TEACH THE TEXT COMMENTARY SERIES

John H. Walton
Old Testament General Editor

Mark L. Strauss
New Testament General Editor

When complete, the TEACH THE TEXT COMMENTARY SERIES *will include the following volumes:*

Old Testament Volumes

New Testament Volumes

To see which titles are available, visit the series website at www.teachthetextseries.com.

TEACH THE TEXT
COMMENTARY SERIES

Job

Daniel J. Estes

Mark L. Strauss and John H. Walton
GENERAL EDITORS

Rosalie de Rosset
ASSOCIATE EDITOR

BakerBooks
a division of Baker Publishing Group
Grand Rapids, Michigan

Published by Baker Books
a division of Baker Publishing Group
P.O. Box 6287, Grand Rapids, MI 49516-6287
www.bakerbooks.com

Printed in the United States of America

Library of Congress Cataloging-in-Publication Data
Estes, Daniel J., 1953-
    Job / Daniel J. Estes.
        p.   cm. — (Teach the text commentary series)
    Includes bibliographical references and index.
    ISBN 978-0-8010-9206-0 (cloth)
    1. Bible. O.T. Job.—Commentaries. I. Title.
BS1415.53.E88 2013
223′.107—dc23   2012040326

13   14   15   16   17   18   19   7   6   5   4   3   2   1

To Rev. George Hattenfield:
faithful pastor,
wise mentor,
and beloved friend,
who through forty-two years of ministry
at Clintonville Baptist Church and Linworth Baptist Church
has demonstrated what it means
to shepherd the flock of God.

1 Peter 5:1–4
Luke 6:40

Contents

Welcome to the Teach the Text Commentary Series

Why another commentary series? That was the question the general editors posed when Baker Books asked us to produce this series. Is there something that we can offer to pastors and teachers that is not currently being offered by other commentary series, or that can be offered in a more helpful way? After carefully researching the needs of pastors who teach the text on a weekly basis, we concluded that yes, more can be done; this commentary is carefully designed to fill an important gap.

The technicality of modern commentaries often overwhelms readers with details that are tangential to the main purpose of the text. Discussions of source and redaction criticism, as well as detailed surveys of secondary literature, seem far removed from preaching and teaching the Word. Rather than wade through technical discussions, pastors often turn to devotional commentaries, which may contain exegetical weaknesses, misuse the Greek and Hebrew languages, and lack hermeneutical sophistication. There is a need for a commentary that utilizes the best of biblical scholarship but also presents the material in a clear, concise, attractive, and user-friendly format.

This commentary is designed for that purpose—to provide a ready reference for the exposition of the biblical text, giving easy access to information that a pastor needs to communicate the text effectively. To that end, the commentary is divided into carefully selected preaching units, each covered in six pages (with carefully regulated word counts both in the passage as a whole and in each subsection). Pastors and teachers engaged in weekly preparation thus know that they will be reading approximately the same amount of material on a week-by-week basis.

Each passage begins with a concise summary of the central message, or "Big Idea," of the passage and a list of its main themes. This is followed by a more detailed interpretation of the text, including the literary context of the passage, historical background material, and interpretive insights. While drawing on the best of biblical scholarship, this material is clear, concise, and to the point. Technical material is kept to a minimum, with endnotes pointing the reader to more detailed discussion and additional resources.

A second major focus of this commentary is on the preaching and teaching process itself. Few commentaries today help the pastor/teacher move from the meaning of the text to its effective communication. Our goal is to bridge this gap. In addition to interpreting the text in the "Understanding the Text" section, each six-page unit contains a "Teaching the Text" section and an "Illustrating the Text" section. The teaching section points to the key theological themes of the passage and ways to communicate these themes to today's audiences. The illustration section provides ideas and examples for retaining the interest of hearers and connecting the message to daily life.

The creative format of this commentary arises from our belief that the Bible is not just a record of God's dealings in the past but is the living Word of God, "alive and active" and "sharper than any double-edged sword" (Heb. 4:12). Our prayer is that this commentary will help to unleash that transforming power for the glory of God.

The General Editors

Introduction to the Teach the Text Commentary Series

This series is designed to provide a ready reference for teaching the biblical text, giving easy access to information that is needed to communicate a passage effectively. To that end, the commentary is carefully divided into units that are faithful to the biblical authors' ideas and of an appropriate length for teaching or preaching.

The following standard sections are offered in each unit.

1. *Big Idea*. For each unit the commentary identifies the primary theme, or "Big Idea," that drives both the passage and the commentary.
2. *Key Themes*. Together with the Big Idea, the commentary addresses in bullet-point fashion the key ideas presented in the passage.
3. *Understanding the Text*. This section focuses on the exegesis of the text and includes several sections.
   a. The Text in Context. Here the author gives a brief explanation of how the unit fits into the flow of the text around it, including

reference to the rhetorical strategy of the book and the unit's contribution to the purpose of the book.
   b. Outline/Structure. For some literary genres (e.g., epistles), a brief exegetical outline may be provided to guide the reader through the structure and flow of the passage.
   c. Historical and Cultural Background. This section addresses historical and cultural background information that may illuminate a verse or passage.
   d. Interpretive Insights. This section provides information needed for a clear understanding of the passage. The intention of the author is to be highly selective and concise rather than exhaustive and expansive.
   e. Theological Insights. In this very brief section the commentary identifies a few carefully selected theological insights about the passage.

4. *Teaching the Text*. Under this second main heading the commentary offers guidance for teaching the text. In this section the author lays out the main themes and applications of the passage. These are linked carefully to the Big Idea and are represented in the Key Themes.

5. *Illustrating the Text*. Here the commentary provides suggestions of where useful illustrations may be found in fields such as literature, entertainment, history, or biography. They are intended to provide general ideas for illustrating the passage's key themes and so serve as a catalyst for effectively illustrating the text.

Abbreviations

b.	born	NASB	New American Standard Bible
ca.	circa	NIV	New International Version
cf.	*confer*, compare	NJPS	*The Tanakh: The Holy*
chap(s).	chapter(s)		*Scriptures: The New JPS*
e.g.	*exempli gratia*, for example		*Translation according to the*
esp.	especially		*Traditional Hebrew Text*
ESV	English Standard Version	NKJV	New King James Version
KJV	King James Version	*T. Job*	*Testament of Job*
MT	Masoretic Text	v(v).	verse(s)

Introduction to Job

Authorship, Date, and Setting

The book of Job does not identify its author or indicate the date when it was written. The story is set outside of Israel, likely in the land of Edom, so the historical narratives in the Old Testament cannot be used to determine specifically when the action occurred. In addition, the date when the book was composed may not have been the same as the literary setting of the action, because authors often set their texts in historical periods different from their own. Furthermore, the theme of suffering that dominates the book of Job is a common subject discussed by humans in every age.

Because of these uncertain factors, interpreters throughout history have arrived at a wide variety of opinions concerning who wrote this book and when.[1] The Jewish Babylonian Talmud attributes the book to Moses, but various rabbis suggest numerous other alternatives. The early church father Eusebius asserts that the book contains accurate transcripts of speeches that were recorded at the time they were spoken, which he believes was around the time of Abraham. Other interpreters have suggested dates throughout Israel's history, with some dating Job as late as the postexilic period (sixth century BC and later).

Many of the details in the book seem to fit best in the patriarchal age of Abraham, Isaac, and Jacob. For instance, the old divine names El, Eloah, and Shaddai are used throughout most of the book. Also, Job's possessions closely resemble the holdings of the patriarchs, and his life span is comparable to theirs. However, the themes of the book of Job are related best to the Old Testament wisdom books of Proverbs and Ecclesiastes, as Job and his friends wrestle with the traditional wisdom teaching that God blesses the righteous but punishes the wicked.

When all these factors are considered together, it may be best to regard the book of Job as written by an unidentified wisdom teacher, likely during the period when wisdom flourished in Israel, beginning in the time of Solomon (tenth century BC) and continuing at least through the time of Hezekiah in the eighth century BC (cf. Prov. 25:1). Making use of a story set in the ancient patriarchal period but outside of Israel, the writer addresses the age-old, universal issue of human suffering in the context of the infinite wisdom, authority, and righteousness of Yahweh.

Unity and Structure

Many interpreters of the book of Job have argued that it is composed of disparate texts that have been stitched together by one or more editors.[2] In particular, they claim that the portrayal of Job as a model of patience in the prose framework of the book clashes with the defiance of Job in the central, poetic section. Often, the poem praising wisdom in chapter 28 and the speeches of Elihu in chapters 32–37 are regarded as later additions, and some of the speeches in the third cycle (chaps. 22–27) are reconfigured and reassigned to different speakers.

It must be recognized, however, that the actual manuscript evidence supports the arrangement of the book as we now have it, and there is no textual data that corroborates the hypothetical reconstructions of Job. In fact, when the book of Job is read closely, it renders a coherent and profound development of thought. Following numerous examples in both ancient and more recent texts, the book of Job wraps a prose prologue and epilogue around an embedded poetic center. The prose framework refers to data in the poetry. The poetry assumes knowledge of the prologue, and its conflicts are resolved in the epilogue.

In the prologue (chaps. 1–2), Job's righteous character is repeatedly described by the narrator (1:1) and by Yahweh (1:8; 2:3). The challenge by the adversary about the motivation that prompts Job's righteous behavior is disclosed, as well as Yahweh's permission for the adversary to bring calamity into Job's experience in order to test the sincerity of his commitment to Yahweh. The adversary proceeds to wreak destruction on Job's possessions, family, and body.

The lengthy poetic section begins with Job's opening lament (chap. 3), and then his three friends try to explain to Job why he has experienced this adversity and what he needs to do to resolve his miserable condition. Job and the friends go through three

The landscape of the land of Edom, possible setting for the book of Job

rounds of speeches in chapters 4–27, with everyone becoming more agitated, so that at the end of the section their communication falls apart.

At this point, the narrator interjects a poem in praise of wisdom in chapter 28, which serves to refocus attention on the key theme of the fear of the Lord, the foundational principle of wisdom (see Prov. 9:10). Job then speaks in chapters 29–31, culminating with a challenge to God to answer him (31:35). A young man, Elihu, then unexpectedly speaks up in chapters 32–37, in a valiant but vain attempt to provide youthful insight where the older wisdom teachers have failed. Finally, Yahweh breaks his silence, in chapters 38–41. By posing more than seventy unanswerable questions to Job, Yahweh brings Job to the realization that although he is innocent of sin, he is ignorant of the ways of Yahweh. In the final chapter of the book, Job withdraws his legal claim against Yahweh, and then Yahweh restores Job's reputation, his fortune, and his family.

Literature

The writer of Job so masterfully combines grand themes with exquisite language and intricate structure that this book is rightfully regarded as one of the best literary texts ever written. It does not fit any specific literary type; rather, it combines the best of proverbs, hymns, laments, nature poetry, and legal rhetoric into a unique and brilliant composition.

A debated interpretive question for this book is its relationship to factual history. Does it record the literal account of the calamity that overwhelmed a man named Job at a specific time and place, along with transcripts of the actual words spoken by Job and his friends as they endeavored to come to terms with his tragedy? Or, rather, does the book communicate theological truth through the means of imaginative literature? Scholars who hold to the Bible as the inspired and inerrant Word of God have taken different positions on this issue.

The historicity of the book of Job must not be rejected on a priori grounds. The biblical references to Job in Ezekiel 14:14, 20 and James 5:11 refer to him just as a historical figure would be indicated. The question of the historical factualness of the book of Job, then, must be decided by a careful scrutiny of the textual data in the book.

The opening words in the book of Job are similar to the expressions in both 1 Samuel 1:1, which introduces the historical narrative of the birth of Samuel, and 2 Samuel 12:1, when Nathan begins to tell David an imaginary story about a poor man and his lamb that is stolen by his rich neighbor. The setting of the book is outside of Israel, in the land of Uz, and Job is not presented as a member of the covenant family. The narrator proceeds to describe Job and his initial situation in ideal terms, followed by a series of catastrophes that destroy virtually all that Job owns and loves. As Job and his friends dialogue about

Outline of Job

1. Prologue (1–2)
2. Dialogue: first cycle (3–14)
   a. Job (3)
   b. Eliphaz (4–5)
   c. Job (6–7)
   d. Bildad (8)
   e. Job (9–10)
   f. Zophar (11)
   g. Job (12–14)
3. Dialogue: second cycle (15–21)
   a. Eliphaz (15)
   b. Job (16–17)
   c. Bildad (18)
   d. Job (19)
   e. Zophar (20)
   f. Job (21)
4. Dialogue: third cycle (22–27)
   a. Eliphaz (22)
   b. Job (23–24)
   c. Bildad (25)
   d. Job (26–27)
5. Interlude (28)
6. Job (29–31)
7. Elihu (32–37)
8. Yahweh (38–41)
9. Epilogue (42)

his situation, they take turns speaking through three cycles, in language that seems to suggest conscious artistry rather than being the transcripts of real, extemporaneous responses. The resolution in the epilogue neatly addresses and rights many of the conflicts raised in the dialogue.

In the Bible, there are numerous examples of historical narratives that describe actual events in time and space, and this could be the case in the book of Job. On the other hand, there are also frequent uses of fictional stories, such as the parables that Jesus told in the Gospels, and Job could plausibly be read in that way. It is evident that in the Bible the Holy Spirit employed both historical narrative and imaginative literature to teach divine truth; what is not so clear is which kind of literature is represented in the book of Job.

Purpose

The book of Job does not state its purpose in explicit terms, but it does provide several clues about why it was written. Even a cursory reading of the book indicates that it is a supplement to wisdom teaching like that found in the book of Proverbs. The predominant theme of Proverbs is that Yahweh blesses those who are wise and righteous, but he punishes those who are foolish and wicked; this teaching is known as retribution theology. In Job, retribution theology is tested to see how far it can be legitimately applied. Job's friends insist that retribution is a fixed formula that applies to every case, so Job's suffering indicates that he must have sinned. Job is confused, because he is confident that he is innocent, and yet he is suffering terribly. A major purpose of the book of Job is to demonstrate that though retribution is true as a general pattern, Yahweh's sovereign rule of the world cannot be reduced to a rigid retribution formula.

This book is also written to teach that humans are limited in their knowledge of what Yahweh is doing. Most of the book is acted out on the earthly stage, as Job and his friends discuss his adversity and its probable cause. The reader, however, learns from the prologue that there is much more going on than the humans realize. Yahweh has clearly affirmed the righteous character of Job, and the adversary has accused Job of insincere motivations for his pious actions. At the end of the book, Job comes to the realization that what he knows as a human is minuscule compared with what the omniscient Yahweh knows, so Job yields to him.

The book of Job also reveals that Yahweh, as the Sovereign Lord, is free to act in ways that may seem surprising to humans. Even though his standard mode of operation is retribution, as taught in Proverbs, Yahweh is not bound by the retribution formula. He may allow a case like Job's, in which a righteous person suffers adversity, for purposes that are known only to him. On the other hand, Yahweh is also free to act in grace, granting blessing to those who deserve nothing but divine judgment.

The book of Job, then, serves to supplement the traditional wisdom taught in Proverbs by directing the reader to trust in Yahweh, even when he does not seem to act according to his standard pattern. Because Yahweh is righteous, he may be trusted to act according to his holy character. However, his knowledge surpasses what humans can understand, and he is free to act in ways that humans may not be able to comprehend with their finite perspective. Humans can trust Yahweh even when they cannot understand his mysterious ways.

Theme

In its themes, the book of Job touches upon many important subjects. One of its primary topics is the infinite wisdom of Yahweh, which transcends what humans are able to comprehend. Job and his friends discuss Job's condition as though they could understand how Yahweh governs his world. When Yahweh speaks to Job, however, his numerous unanswerable questions demonstrate that his knowledge far exceeds what any human can understand. The book of Proverbs discloses many features in Yahweh's world that are observable to humans, but the book of Job explains that beyond all that can be known there are vast areas that Yahweh knows perfectly but that remain mysterious for humans.

The book also amends retribution theology to account for Yahweh's transcendent knowledge and his sovereign freedom. The blessing that Yahweh restores to Job in the epilogue indicates that retribution is a valid general pattern of how Yahweh rules in his world. In the specific details, however, there are aspects of life in which retribution must not be pressed into a rigid and absolute formula. There are other factors at work that alter the typical pattern of cause and effect in life. For that reason, a good person like Job may suffer adversity, and evildoers may succeed, but Yahweh will bring things to a proper resolution in his own time, way, and purpose.

Although the book of Job does not formally address the problem of evil, which asks why innocent people suffer in a world governed by a God who is all-good and all-powerful, it does provide several insights that relate to the issue. The book teaches that suffering is not always attributable to personal sin. It also indicates that factors beyond human control can intrude, such as the suffering that Job experienced at the instigation of the adversary. Job's final response reveals that suffering can result in instruction and growth, as God brings good out of evil. Ultimately, the book of Job brings the reader to realize that the explanation for why good people suffer must be left in the realm of divine mystery, but that Yahweh can be trusted, even when humans cannot comprehend all of his ways.

Works Based on the Book of Job

Many literary and art works have been based on and refer to the book of Job. Notable among them is the Pulitzer Prize–winning verse drama *J.B.* (1958) by Archibald MacLeish (1892–1982). MacLeish frighteningly recasts the sufferings of Job in the modern world. More crucially, MacLeish's attitude toward what he perceives to be the basic question involved—the question of why humans suffer—is one not confined to Old Testament tradition. MacLeish is not affirming traditional faith; he suggests that a new faith is needed, one that many people in the contemporary world find attractive. A comparison with *J.B.* could be used substantially throughout a study of Job to show the difference in perspective between the traditional view of Job taken in this commentary and MacLeish's. (*J.B.* has been specifically referenced a few times in the "Illustrating the Text" sections.)

A second literary work is a short story by William Humphrey (b. 1924) called "A Job of the Plains" (1965). This story tells Job's account from the perspective of an earthy, hardworking farmer named Dobbs. It contains irony and a touch of cynicism.

Finally, the renowned British poet William Blake (1757–1827) published a book of twenty-two engravings of the book of Job (*Illustrations of the Book of Job*, 1826). They are considered masterpieces.

Teaching and Preaching Job

When the book of Job is taught or preached, it should be communicated in a way that is true to its intended meaning. The book must be read as a complete unit, with the prose prologue and epilogue framing the poetic speeches in the main body of the work. The framework, reinforced by the narrator's interlude in chapter 28, provides the interpretive clues that enable the reader to evaluate what Job, the friends, and Elihu say. Yahweh's speeches are crucial for bringing Job and the present reader to an understanding of the transcendent divine knowledge and the mystery that humans must accept.

It is helpful to begin a study of Job with an overview of the book as a whole. The prologue should be analyzed in detail to provide an interpretive lens through which to view the rest of the book. As the speeches unfold in the long dialogue section, they should be related back to the synthesis of the book. If this is not done, then the faulty statements and arguments by Job and the other speakers can be wrongly taken as truth, when in fact a careful consideration of what the entire book teaches unmasks them.

The book of Job is primarily ancient poetry, which presents some significant challenges for the modern teacher or preacher. Poetry makes use of many figures of speech that may be difficult for the contemporary reader to grasp. A good tool for unlocking the meaning of the images in Job is the *Dictionary of Biblical Imagery* (InterVarsity, 1998). The book of Job also alludes to many ancient customs that were understandable to its original audience but are unfamiliar to people today. Two useful guides to these topics are the *IVP Bible Background Commentary: Old Testament* (InterVarsity, 2000), and the *Zondervan Illustrated Bible Backgrounds Commentary* (Zondervan, 2009).[3]

It is also important to read the book of Job within its larger biblical context, because other passages of Scripture can fill in the picture that is only sketched in Job. While one must not read later New Testament teaching back into Job in uncritical ways (for example, turning Job's words in 19:25 into a clear anticipation of the resurrection of Christ, as in the famous aria in Handel's *Messiah*), it should be recognized that later passages in the Bible may well be relevant in explaining the significance of features in Job (for example, subsequent biblical revelation about the character and career of Satan may illuminate the action narrated in Job 1–2). For assistance in understanding the wider theological dimensions of Job, a helpful resource is the *Dictionary of the Old Testament: Wisdom, Poetry and Writings* (InterVarsity, 2008).[4]

The book of Job has too often been neglected in the teaching and preaching of the church. This is regrettable, because Job addresses important questions that people in the contemporary church are asking. Its powerful literature and compelling story combine to direct the reader to trust the Lord, who alone knows and controls all that affects the lives of humans in his world. This marvelous book is the word of God and by all means should be studied carefully and communicated clearly. The purpose of this commentary is to equip pastors, teachers, and students to do just that.

William Blake's drawing of Job and his family, plate 1 from the *Book of Job* (ca. 1825)

Introduction to Job

Adversity of a Righteous Man

Big Idea *In the face of severe adversity, Job lives up to the Lord's confidence in his character.*

Understanding the Text

The Text in Context

Job 1 and 2 serve as a prologue for the book. The initial chapter introduces the protagonist, Job, as a man of exemplary character. Both the narrator (1:1) and Yahweh (1:8) describe Job as blameless, righteous, and God-fearing. The rest of the book is intended to be read with this introduction in mind. Under the intense pressure that he faces, Job will make some statements that sound harsh toward God, but the prologue makes it clear that Job is a profoundly righteous man.

Both the prologue (Job 1–2) and the epilogue (42:7–17) are written in prose, but the rest of the book is predominantly poetry. The prologue and epilogue, then, function as a literary and interpretive framework for this long and intricate book. In fact, without the prose framework, it would be difficult to read the rest of the book as a coherent story with a beginning, development, and resolution.

Historical and Cultural Background

The ancient Near Eastern religions outside of Israel were polytheistic, and most of these systems of thought pictured a divine council that made major decisions affecting humans.[1] Job 1 depicts a gathering of beings who are called "the sons of God," and this entourage includes a figure called the *satan*, a Hebrew term that refers to an adversary or accuser. Rather than being their equal, however, Yahweh is clearly presented as superior to the sons of God. They all have to answer to Yahweh, and they must work within the limits he places upon them. The *satan*, then, is not independent of Yahweh or equal to Yahweh; he is a heavenly creature subservient to the one true God.

Interpretive Insights

1:1 *This man was blameless.* Usually in the Old Testament when a major figure is introduced, his genealogy is traced. In the case of Job, however, it is his exemplary character that is prominent. In the first verse of the book the narrator describes Job in glowing terms: "This man was blameless and upright; he feared God and shunned evil." Later, in 1:8 and 2:3, Yahweh repeats this description, affirming Job's impeccable character as a man of integrity and piety. As a sterling example of biblical wisdom, Job loves what Yahweh loves, and he avoids what displeases Yahweh. This is not a claim that Job is morally perfect as Yahweh is perfect, but rather, within the bounds of human fallenness, the righteousness of Job is commended by Yahweh.

1:3 *He was the greatest man among all the people of the East.* By every tangible measure, Job is prosperous. When this description is read against the background of the book of Proverbs, Job is indeed living, at the very highest level, the good life that wisdom promises as a blessing from Yahweh (Prov. 10:22).

1:6 *Satan also came with them.* In the New Testament, Satan is the leader of the forces of evil who endeavors to thwart the will of God. Satan is portrayed as unsuccessfully trying to tempt Jesus (Matt. 4:1–11) and as resisting the rule of God (Rev. 12:9; 20:2, 7–8). Elsewhere in the Old Testament, aside from the references to Satan in 1 Chronicles 21:1 and Zechariah 3:1–2, the Hebrew term *satan* is translated as a descriptive expression (e.g., "adversary" in 1 Kings 5:4; "accuser" in Ps. 109:6) instead of as a personal name (Satan) for the enemy of God and his people.

In Job 1–2, the Hebrew expression includes the definite article before the term *satan*, which means an adversary, or in a legal context, an accuser. Because the *satan* here seems to be included in the heavenly group of the sons of God, many scholars have concluded that this is a member of Yahweh's assembly who does not maliciously assault Job but rather only expresses doubt about God's policy of rewarding righteousness. In this view, he functions as a prosecuting attorney who raises concerns about Job's motives in being pious before God.

This could be true, but one should also consider that the same Hebrew term is used frequently in Old Testament narratives and in the Psalms to refer to enemies who make verbal accusations against the righteous. Also, of the thirty-four New Testament references to Satan, twenty-eight use the definite article when they speak of him (e.g., in Rev. 20:2, 7, when the Lord defeats his ancient enemy, Satan, and binds him for one thousand years). In the Old Testament, the definite article is also sometimes used in this fashion, as for example when "the God" refers to God or "the baal" refers to the Canaanite deity Baal. In view of this, there appears to be significant evidence for viewing the adversary in Job as an antagonist to Yahweh and his servant Job.

1:9 *Does Job fear God for nothing?* When Yahweh points out Job's exemplary life, the adversary suggests that Job may be using Yahweh to get the material blessings he wants. Unstated, but perhaps hinted implicitly, is that Yahweh may be using Job to get the worship he craves from humans. If this is the case, then the adversary is making an accusation concerning the motivation that prompts Job's apparently exemplary piety.

1:10–11 *Have you not put a hedge around him?* The Bible often speaks about how God is the protector of his people (cf.

Pss. 91; 121). Here, the adversary asks a question about the motivation for Job's piety, and then he boldly charges that if Yahweh were to remove this hedge from Job and allow Job's perfect life to be touched by calamity, then Job's worship would morph into cursing. Interestingly, the Hebrew term that the adversary uses for "curse" typically has the opposite meaning, "bless"; the same term also has the meaning "curse" in 1:5, when Job offers sacrifices for his children in case they have sinned and *cursed* God in their hearts.

1:12 *everything he has is in your power.* Because Yahweh alone is God and the supreme sovereign over all, he could reject the adversary's challenge outright. As a created being, the adversary is not Yahweh's equal and he cannot compel Yahweh to do anything. Yahweh, however, does not duck the challenge but allows the adversary to touch Job's possessions. At this time, Yahweh prohibits the adversary from afflicting Job's body. Job is totally unaware of this heavenly conversation that prompts the calamity that is to follow.

1:13–19 *I am the only one who has escaped to tell you!* Narrative literature in the Old Testament typically focuses on action and dialogue rather than description, which is certainly the case in Job 1:13–19. In this episode, the report of Job's adversity sounds like a newscast giving the stark facts of the calamity and omitting any reference to Job's feelings in the face of this immense human tragedy. The scene shifts from heaven (1:12) to earth (1:13–19) as four servants come to Job in rapid succession, each with devastating news. In just a few moments Job is reduced from riches to rags, from delight to disaster, from celebration to sorrow. Job knows nothing of the conversation in heaven between Yahweh and the adversary. All he can see is the devastation of his livelihood and his family. If the adversary is correct, then Job's faith in Yahweh will soon collapse as well. On the other hand, if Job's pious behavior is truly rooted in his heart, then his faith in Yahweh will survive amid the rubble of his experience.

1:20–22 *Then he fell to the ground in worship.* Job's response to this profound calamity is twofold. Feeling the full force of grief, he tears his clothing and shaves off his hair, which are customary rites of mourning in the ancient world (cf. Gen. 37:34; Isa. 15:2; Jer. 7:29). At the same time, Job also falls to the ground and humbly worships God. All that he owns has been given by Yahweh rather than gained by his own efforts, and all that he has just lost has been taken away by Yahweh rather than merely by the secondary agents who have inflicted damage on him. He

In 1:17, among the calamities that befall Job are the loss of his camels and the death of his servants by Chaldean raiding parties. This Assyrian relief shows a woman and a herd of camels seized during one of Tiglath-Pileser's military campaigns (central palace at Nimrud, 728 BC).

concludes by blessing Yahweh, not by cursing him as the adversary predicted in 1:11. The narrator puts a final exclamation point on Job's response: "In all this, Job did not sin by charging God with wrongdoing" (1:22).

Theological Insights

Only on rare occasions does the Bible part the curtains so that the reader can catch a glimpse of what is happening behind the scenes of human history. In Ephesians 6:12, Paul says that Christians struggle against the spiritual forces of wickedness in the heavenly realms. The prophet Elisha prays in 2 Kings 6:17 that Yahweh will open the eyes of his servant to see the invisible divine forces protecting Elisha. Daniel 10 speaks of angelic conflict that affects the success of nations.

Although the book of Job may have been written as an imaginative parable rather than as literal historical narrative (see the discussion in the introduction), in either case the reference to the adversary in Job 1–2 may be compared to other biblical passages. If the adversary is a member of the divine council who assists Yahweh in the governance of his world, then he plays a role comparable to the spirit in 1 Kings 22:19–23. On the other hand, if his actions toward Job are malicious, then the concept of the adversary here could be viewed as a precursor to a more fully formed understanding of Satan, whose activity as the accuser of God's people is developed explicitly in the New Testament (Rev. 12:9–10).

Teaching the Text

Even though every person faces a unique set of circumstances, adversity is an experience that runs throughout human history. Some people face medical problems; for others the challenge may be financial, psychological, or interpersonal. Sooner or later, everyone experiences pain. The story of Job resonates with us, because Job walked down the same path of adversity that all humans do. Like Job, we too find ourselves asking why bad things happen in a world in which the good God is in control.

The book of Job sets the scene in chapter 1 by narrating how in the face of severe adversity Job lives up to the Lord's confidence in his character. Job's good character is evidenced by his righteous patterns of life. Both the narrator (1:1) and Yahweh (1:8) describe Job in glowing terms. Even though Job's wealth is impressive, that is not the focus. Rather, his résumé highlights his character more than his possessions, a stark difference from how our contemporary culture measures success and value. In his patterns of life Job demonstrates integrity, commitment to God's moral standards, reverence for God, and an aversion to evil, which in the Old Testament wisdom literature are the essential components of the wise and righteous life.

As the adversary questions God's policy of rewarding righteousness, he also calls into question Job's motives. Many people are interested in appearing generous, kind, thoughtful, and righteous, but they may be prompted by impure motives (compare Jesus's condemnation of practices done to be noticed by others [Matt. 6:1–6]). For example, a generous donation to charity may be given primarily for the tax benefit it provides. An apparently kind gesture may really be part of a marketing strategy to produce a sale. The adversary in the book of Job argues that adversity will prove that Job's reputation for righteousness is only skin-deep, that it is not really Job's character at all but only his response to a flawed divine policy.

The adversities we experience can come from many sources. Some result from our own mistakes and choices. Others are beyond our personal control, such as many medical problems, financial issues caused by macroeconomic factors, or traffic accidents. The book of Job indicates that some adversities that humans experience may be rooted in cosmic issues that extend far beyond one's individual responsibility.

Job's initial response to his calamity reflects deep pain but also unshaken commitment to the Lord (1:21–22). Faith in God does not mean that we face pain with a stoic, unfeeling response. When adversity strikes our lives, we can and should feel the full extent of the pain. Faith does not deny pain, but rather it takes the pain to the Lord. The numerous psalms of lament, such as Psalms 3, 13, 22, 42, and 142, provide us examples of godly people expressing their deep pain to the Lord and then trusting him with their trouble. Like Job and the psalmists learned, our adversity can lead us into new frontiers in our knowledge of and confidence in the Lord.

Illustrating the Text

All humans face adversity in some form or another.

News Stories: Recent statistics about medical problems, financial difficulties, and natural disasters illustrate the principle that all people face adversity. The power of adversity to quickly reduce a person from prosperity to poverty was witnessed in the stock market crash of 1929, when wealthy people lost everything.

While reputation is often based on how one appears to others, character is what one is truly like.

Literature: *Sense and Sensibility*, by Jane Austen. In British writer Jane Austen's (1775–1817) first published novel, *Sense and Sensibility* (1811), Marianne Dashwood perceives John Willoughby as gallant, but in reality his actions prove him to be a man of poor character. Early on (chap. 10) she thinks of him, "When he was present she had no eyes for anyone else. Everything he did was right. Everything he said was clever." Another character, Elinor, finally notes, "The world had made him extravagant and vain—extravagance and vanity had made him cold-hearted and selfish. Vanity, while seeking its own guilty triumph at the expense of another, had involved him in a real attachment, which extravagance, or at least its offspring necessity, had required to be sacrificed. Each faulty propensity in leading him to evil, had led him likewise to punishment" (chap. 44).

Literature: *Paradise Lost*, by John Milton. The craft and malice of Satan are featured in John Milton's *Paradise Lost* (1667) on the grandest scale. In fact, Satan is so grand and larger-than-life in this epic that some critics have called him the hero of the poem, a contention C. S. Lewis seriously disputes in *A Preface to Paradise Lost* (1942). Nevertheless, few works anywhere so powerfully display Satan in all his demonic, fallen glory. Many passages bear reading; one suggestion would be from Book I, which describes the fall of this huge, powerful being who chose to compete with God.

> Who first seduced them [Adam and Eve] to that foul revolt?
> Th' infernal Serpent; he it was, whose guile
> Stirred up with envy and revenge, deceived
> The mother of mankind, what time his pride
> Had cast him out from Heav'n, with all his host
> Of rebel angels, by whose aid aspiring
> To set himself in glory above his peers
> He trusted to have equaled the Most High,
> If he opposed; and with ambitious aim
> Against the throne and monarch of God
> Raised impious war in Heav'n and battle proud
> With vain attempt. Him the Almighty Power
> Hurled headlong flaming from th' ethereal sky
> With hideous ruin and combustion down
> To bottomless perdition, there to dwell
> In adamantine chains and penal fire,
> Who durst defy th' Omnipotent to arms.[2]

Art: Gustave Doré. French illustrator, sculptor, artist, and engraver Doré (1832–83) has illustrated *Paradise Lost*. Doré's images can reinforce the power of Satan to destroy and deceive.

Illustration of Satan being cast out of heaven (by Gustave Doré for John Milton's *Paradise Lost*, 1866)

Job 1

Turning Up the Pressure

Big Idea *Despite increased adversity, Job reasserts his complete commitment to the sovereign Lord.*

Understanding the Text

The Text in Context

Job 2 completes the prologue, which sets the scene for a thorough discussion of a godly response to adversity. Much of the language of 1:6–22 is repeated and intensified in 2:1–10, as the writer uses the technique of repetition with variation to build suspense and interest. When Yahweh's words in 2:3 are compared to his earlier description of Job in 1:8, it is evident that the first round of adversity has not subverted Job's righteous character.

The arrival of Job's three friends in 2:11–13 serves as a literary bridge to the extended dialogue section in chapters 3–31. As these wisdom experts sit in silence with Job for seven days, the dramatic tension builds, until Job breaks the silence with his brokenhearted lament in chapter 3. It is evident that Job's pain is very great (2:13), which is an ironic echo of 1:3, where Job is described as the greatest of the sons of the East.

Historical and Cultural Background

The literary technique of repetition and variation was often used by ancient storytellers (cf. 1 Sam. 3:1–14; 2 Kings 1:1–16 and 2:1–8), and it may well have been cultivated by the practice of telling and retelling stories orally. In the prologue of the book of Job, the narrator in 2:1–10 repeats with significant variations what he has previously related in 1:6–22.

In 2:8, Job scrapes his sores with a potsherd as he sits in the ashes of the garbage dump, which was a place that outcasts such as beggars and lepers frequented in the ancient world. This graphic picture of Job's brokenness reveals that he is rejected and destitute, isolated from community life.

In 2:12, Job's friends weep, tear their robes, and throw dust over their heads, all traditional expressions of grief and mourning (cf. Josh. 7:6; 1 Sam. 4:12; 2 Sam. 13:19; Ezek. 27:30). By these visual symbols of burial and decay, they identify with the dead person, or in the case of Job, one who appears as good as dead. Similarly, silence (2:13) was often a traditional act of mourning (Lam. 2:10; cf. Isa. 3:26; Ezek. 8:14), and seven days was a typical period of mourning after a person had died (Gen. 50:10; 1 Sam. 31:13; Sir. 22:12; Jud. 16:24).

Interpretive Insights

2:1 *On another day.* The narrative in 2:1–3 is nearly identical to that in 1:6–8, but it includes three subtle and significant changes. In 2:1, the adversary comes among the sons of God with apparent eagerness to continue his dispute with Yahweh about Job. In 2:3, Yahweh says that Job still maintains his integrity, even though he has been ruined "without any reason," using the same term that the adversary stated in 1:9 ("for nothing"). Also in 2:3, Yahweh says that the adversary has incited him to ruin Job.

2:3 *you incited me against him.* The Hebrew verb *sut* that Yahweh uses here

Key Themes of Job 2

- The adversary increases his challenge of Job's character.
- Job endures physical, social, and emotional pain.
- Job accepts his adversity with submission to God.
- Job's friends come to comfort him in his time of great need.

for "incited" has the nuance of prompting someone to act in a way that is different from what that person would have chosen to do without the provocation. In 2 Kings 18:32 and Jeremiah 43:3, humans are the subject of the verb, but in 1 Samuel 26:19 and 2 Samuel 24:1 Yahweh is presented as inciting people to do what is wrong. The parallel in 1 Chronicles 21:1 is instructive, because it indicates that although Yahweh does permit evil actions within his overall sovereign plan, he is not directly responsible for causing evil to occur. It is not Yahweh's pleasure that Job be afflicted, but Yahweh has allowed the adversary to pursue his strategy against Job in his attempt to demonstrate that Job does not have the sterling character that Yahweh thinks he has.

2:4–5 *Skin for skin!* Rejecting Yahweh's favorable evaluation of Job, the adversary retorts with a proverbial expression insisting that Job will not feel the affliction until his own health is in danger. In other words, the adversary alleges that Job values his own physical well-being more than

In 2:12, when Job's friends observe his suffering, they begin to weep aloud, they tear their robes, and they sprinkle dust on their heads. These are typical ways to publically express grief and mourning in the ancient Near East. In this Egyptian tomb painting, a mourning woman puts dust on her head as a sign of her sorrow (tomb of Nebamun, ca. 1350 BC).

his possessions, his servants, or even his children.

2:6 *you must spare his life.* Even though the adversary instigates the affliction upon Job, he is not free to work independently of Yahweh's control. It is clear that Yahweh is sovereign over the adversary and that he puts limits on how far the adversary may go.

2:7 *So Satan . . . afflicted Job with painful sores.* Wasting no time, the adversary goes out from Yahweh's presence and strikes Job with a serious skin disorder, likely a burning rash. This painful ailment (cf. Exod. 9:9–11; Lev. 13:18–20; Deut. 28:27–28) brings overwhelming discomfort to those whom it afflicts. Hints in Job 7:5; 16:16; and 30:30 suggest that it gives Job both intense pain and a hideous appearance.

2:9 *Curse God and die!* Job's wife speaks only this one time in the book, and her words have prompted a wide range of interpretations. Augustine regarded her negatively as an agent of the devil, because without realizing it she takes the adversary's stance in challenging Job to turn against Yahweh (cf. 1:11; 2:5). Some construe her question, "Are you still maintaining your integrity?" as a statement ("You are still maintaining your integrity"), but that does not explain Job's sharp reply to her in 2:10. It may be best to view her words as proceeding from her understandable sympathy for her husband, and as expressing her desire that he not have to suffer longer. Nevertheless, even if this is what has prompted what she says, she is then willing to have

Job surrender his commitment to do what is right, so that his pain can be relieved. Job refuses to do that. At the time when Job has already lost so much, he now feels that he has lost the support of his wife as well.

2:10 *Job did not sin in what he said.* Job replies to his wife that she is speaking like a foolish woman, that is, her speech does not adhere to God's path of wisdom. By contrast, Job's speech, which is a window into his heart, demonstrates his unshaken integrity, just as Yahweh has anticipated in his challenge to the adversary. In literary terms, Job's wife articulates the temptation for Job to act contrary to his integrity.

2:11 *Job's three friends . . . heard about all the troubles.* The Hebrew term

In 2:9, Job's wife exhorts him to "curse God and die!" This scene from the sarcophagus of Junius Bassus shows the suffering Job with his wife and friend (AD 359).

for "friend" (*rea'*) refers to a neighbor, a friend, or a colleague. From their subsequent speeches, it seems evident that these three men are Job's intellectual peers as wisdom teachers. However, their primary intent in meeting with Job is not scholarly but pastoral, for they come to sympathize with him so that they can bring comfort to him.

2:13 *No one said a word to him.* The initial instincts of the friends are on the mark. Realizing that words cannot explain Job's tragic situation, they choose to identify with Job in his pain as they sit with him for seven days, their silence likely a part of their mourning for Job. Only after Job breaks his silence will they attempt to explain why he has experienced such a severe loss.

Theological Insights

The predominant theme of traditional biblical wisdom as taught in the book of Proverbs is that God blesses righteousness and punishes wickedness. However, even in Proverbs there are hints that this general pattern, often called retribution theology, should not be pressed into a fixed formula in which good things always happen to good people and bad things always happen to bad people. The book of Job tests the legitimacy of the retribution formula by presenting the case of a thoroughly righteous man who endures unthinkable adversity. In other words, bad things are happening to a good person. The three friends represent the best efforts of traditional wisdom to explain Job's situation. Job realizes that both good and evil lie under Yahweh's sovereign authority (2:10). When the text states that Job "did not sin in what he said" (2:10), this must be read as a statement of Job's

character, because in wisdom teaching what one says is a reflection of who one is (Prov. 13:3; 18:4; 21:23). This does not suggest that while Job gives the right verbal answers, he is actually sinning in his heart.

Teaching the Text

Adversity often comes as a series of cascading blows that wear a person down physically, emotionally, financially, and spiritually. In Job 2, Job reels under the blows of increasing adversity, but he is fortified by his faith in the Lord. An important lesson of this chapter is that despite increased adversity, Job reasserts his complete commitment to the sovereign Lord. As the rest of the book will teach, God can be trusted even when humans cannot understand all that transpires in their lives.

As the adversary converses with Yahweh in 2:1–6, he intensifies his challenge of Job's character. Job's faith was not toppled when his world collapsed around him in chapter 1, but the adversary cynically insists that like any human, Job is motivated ultimately by self-interest. The adversary receives permission from Yahweh to move beyond touching what Job possesses to afflicting his person, confident that if Job feels personally the heat of affliction, then he surely will abandon his commitment to Yahweh and will curse him. It is when adversity zeroes in on us personally that we demonstrate the quality of our commitment to God.

The pain Job endures as a result of his affliction by the adversary has physical, social, and emotional dimensions. The physical aspects are the most obvious, as his skin is disfigured by sores that cover him from head to toe. Socially, he is consigned to live with the outcasts among the ashes of the city dump, cut off from the honor and esteem he has previously enjoyed in the community. Emotionally, he feels abandoned even by his family. Finally, his wife, perhaps speaking from sympathetic motives, calls into question Job's persistence in holding on to God, as she exhorts him to curse God and die. Adversity often strikes us on several fronts simultaneously. To respond to it successfully, we must trust in the Lord with all our heart (Prov. 3:5), that is, with our whole inner being, rather than allowing adversity to undermine our commitment to the Lord.

Job does not let his adversity blind his spiritual perception, but instead he accepts his pain with submission to God. Genuine faith does not hold on to God only when the weather is beautiful, the stock market is up, our health is robust, and the children are behaving. Rather, true faith holds on to the Lord during both good and bad times, recognizing that he is sovereign over all life's experiences. Like us, Job cannot control what happens to him, but he chooses to honor God in how he responds to his circumstances.

The purpose of Job 2 is not to teach how to minister to friends in pain. However, for all their subsequent faults, Job's three friends come with good intentions to comfort him in his time of great need. Although they soon become frustrated and harsh, they begin well. By sitting with Job in silence for seven days, they seek to salve the person, even though they cannot solve the problem. Their silent presence is far more helpful to Job than the words they speak to him later. In the New Testament, Christians are called to comfort one another, and in doing that they incarnate the love of God as they identify with and encourage their brothers and sisters in need. The initial sympathy shown by Job's friends suggests some of what genuine Christian comfort should entail.

Illustrating the Text

When we cannot control circumstances, we can honor God with our spirit.

Film: *The Elephant Man.* In this 1980 drama based on the true story of Joseph Merrick (played by Anthony Hopkins) in nineteenth-century England, a hideously disfigured man is treated by others as though he is not a human. So deformed that he must wear a hood and is ultimately placed in a Victorian freak show, he is managed by a brute who thinks he is an imbecile. Merrick is, in fact, brilliant and a man of good and gentle character. In the film—some discrepancies exist between the film and the actual story—Merrick has a profound effect on his rescuers. Also, Merrick addresses a crowd of mockers in a deeply moving scene, saying, "I am not an elephant. I am not an animal. I am a human being. I am a man."

Adversity often strikes on several fronts, requiring great trust in the Lord.

News Story: The news provides current examples of people overwhelmed by a series of afflictions. In 2011, Japan suffered a great disaster in the form of an earthquake, including aftershocks, a series of tsunamis, and the meltdown of nuclear reactors. Thousands of people were killed, and thousands of others were displaced or injured.

Adversity leads to new knowledge and strengthens our confidence in the Lord.

Biography: *Something Beautiful for God*, by Malcolm Muggeridge. In his little book *Something Beautiful for God* (1971), on the work and life of Mother Teresa (1910–97), English journalist, author, media personality, and satirist Muggeridge (1903–90) recounts his conversion from atheism to Christianity, attributing the changes largely to the influence of Mother Teresa. He tells a bit of her story, writing that without the grace of God she might have been hard, even "grasping." After she visited the misery-ridden streets of Calcutta, she realized she belonged there, not in the pleasant convent where she had been working. Relinquishing everything, she went to the most wretched quarter of the city, gathered up a few abandoned children, and began her ministry. She chose to live her life within the slums of Calcutta. Muggeridge witnessed horrors in Calcutta he had to turn away from, but he writes that Mother Teresa stayed and reached out, seeming to grow stronger every year.

Adversity can strike at any time. This photo was taken while the US Navy was surveying the damage to Sukuiso, Japan, a week after the 9.0-magnitude earthquake on March 11, 2011. This aerial view shows the destruction caused by the tsunami.

Job Shatters the Silence

Big Idea *Job brings his most troubling thoughts and deepest pains to words and views his adversity in the light of his commitment to God.*

Understanding the Text

The Text in Context

Job 3 begins an extended section of poetry in which Job and his three friends speak in turn. After the prose prologue in Job 1–2, the narrator fades from view, and we hear the voices of the individual speakers. Without the narrator, the readers have no interpreter to explain what is being said, so they have to listen attentively to the threads of the dialogue.

After a seven-day silence, Job releases his pent-up emotions, cursing the day he was born (3:1–10). He does not directly curse God, as the adversary has predicted (1:11; 2:5), but his turgid language evidences that he feels as though the whole created order of the world has come apart. Job turns from cursing to questioning in 3:11–26, using a series of rhetorical questions that all of the speakers will attempt to answer. His key word throughout this section is *why*. Job concludes his initial lament with four rhetorical knife stabs expressing his pain and frustration: "I have no peace, no quietness; I have no rest, but only turmoil." Only when Yahweh reappears with his own set of questions in Job 38–41 will Job find the peace that now eludes him.

Historical and Cultural Background

In his opening lament, Job several times makes use of concepts familiar to his setting in the ancient Near East. His reference to Leviathan in 3:8 calls to mind the Babylonian Canaanite myths about a seven-headed sea monster (see, in the unit on Job 41, the sidebar "Mythological Language in the Bible"). This beast was often used as a symbol of chaos, but in the Old Testament Leviathan was created and controlled by Yahweh (cf. Job 41; Pss. 74:14; 104:26; Isa. 27:1).[1]

The "morning stars" in 3:9 are probably Venus and Mercury, which often appear before sunrise, and perhaps the fainter, more distant planets as well.

As Exodus 1:15–19 illustrates, in Old Testament times children were typically delivered by midwives. In his anguish, Job wishes that no midwife had been kneeling by his mother to receive him when he was born (3:12). Alternatively, this verse could also refer to the custom of a child being placed upon the knees of its nursing mother (Isa. 66:12) or its father (cf. Gen. 50:23, where Joseph's grandsons are placed on his knees).

The ancient world typically viewed death as a place of gloom and darkness (see the sidebar). Job's pain is so great, however, that he inverts this concept, so that he hopes for death as peace, sleep, and rest (3:13), a great improvement upon the horrors of his life in the face of intense adversity.

Key Themes of Job 3

- In the face of extreme adversity, Job does not deny his pain but expresses it honestly.
- Job's questions indicate his ignorance before God.
- Job's pain blurs his perception of God.

Interpretive Insights

3:1 *Job . . . cursed the day of his birth.* Instead of cursing Yahweh, as the adversary has predicted (2:5) and Job's wife has exhorted (2:9), Job in his first speech curses and laments the day he was born. His days of pain have given time for the full enormity of his loss to sink in, and in this soliloquy Job discloses the extent of his anguish and isolation. He is not an unfeeling stoic, but rather his honest, deep feelings emerge. The transparency he displays is similar to the language of many of the lament and imprecatory psalms, as well as of the confessions of Jeremiah (e.g., Jer. 20:14–18).

3:4 *That day—may it turn to darkness.* Job uses the antonyms light and darkness as metaphors for life and death. In contrast to the creation narrative in Genesis 1:3–4, in which God says, "Let there be light," as he separates the light from the darkness, Job now wishes for something

that is impossible, that somehow the day of his birth might be turned back into darkness, that is, that it could be undone. Job's language, with its unrealistic desire for an action that he cannot accomplish, reflects the intensity of the pain that he is feeling.

3:5 *utter darkness.* The Hebrew phrase is a superlative expression that means literally "shadow of death," as in Psalm 23:4 (see NIV footnote there). Here, Job refers to an especially dark shadow that would overwhelm and obscure from sight the day of his birth, just as a total solar eclipse turns the daylight into darkness.

3:6 *may it not be included among the days of the year.* Job wishes that the night of his conception be absent from the calendar, similar to February 29 in years that are not leap years. Of course, if that were to happen then he never would have been born, and consequently he would not have experienced the painful adversity that has afflicted his life.

3:11–12 *Why did I not perish at birth?* In 3:11, Job launches into a series of rhetorical questions beginning with "why?" These questions are fraught with deep

The custom of a child being placed on the knees of its mother for suckling is visualized in this bronze statuette of Isis nursing Horus (Egypt, 664–332 BC). Job 3:12 may refer to this custom.

emotion, as Job reveals the frustration in his spirit. Also, by posing questions, Job unintentionally implies there are aspects of his experience that he does not understand. Later in the book when Yahweh at last speaks and poses his own questions to Job (Job 38–41), Job comes to realize how ignorant he is of the ways of the Lord.

3:14 *with kings and rulers of the earth.* As Job views death, he perceives it as a step above his present condition. Job feels isolated from his community as he sits at the ash heap (2:8), but he regards death as the great social leveler. Death, he supposes, liberates all humans from the inequities of life, because in death all people are equally devoid of possessions, power, and prominence.

3:18 *they no longer hear the slave driver's shout.* As Job perceives death though the lens of his adversity, he sees former captives enjoying their ease far from the oppression of their previous taskmasters. He uses the same term for "slave driver" as is employed in Exodus 3:7 to describe the harsh Egyptians who mistreat the Israelite slaves.

3:21 *those who long for death.* Although Job clearly views death as preferable to the kind of life he is experiencing, he does not take the next step toward ending his own life. His wife has come close to recommending suicide by urging him to curse God and die (2:9), but there is no clear evidence that Job ever contemplates or attempts suicide.

3:23 *whose way is hidden . . . whom God has hedged in.* In Old Testament wisdom literature, the term "way" (*derek*) frequently refers to God's path of wisdom that leads to life. For example, Proverbs

4:18 states that the path of the righteous grows clearer and clearer until the perfect day. By contrast, Job asks why life is given to a man whose way is hidden, who cannot understand where his painful path of life is proceeding.

In 1:10, Satan says that Yahweh has placed a protective hedge around Job by blessing him so generously. Job here uses the same picture to express his feeling that God has trapped and restricted him. This metaphor may well refer to the practice of a shepherd constructing a thorny hedge to enclose and protect his flock from intruders (cf. 1 Sam. 25:16). As Job considers his unceasing adversity, he feels that God has confined him, not for his protection, but so that he cannot escape his restrictions (cf. Hosea 2:6). Job feels trapped and imprisoned by God.

3:26 *I have no rest, but only turmoil.* Job concludes his initial lament by focusing on his personal crisis. He does not lament the possessions or even the people that he has lost, but rather he is intent on the inner turmoil that consumes him. In contrast to Yahweh's created order that is in evidence in the prologue, Job 3 ends with *rogez*, turmoil or agitation. Job in this way discloses that he faces more than just tragic circumstances. At its heart, this is a spiritual struggle within him, as Job tries to reconcile what has happened with what he believes about Yahweh and his rule.

Theological Insights

The narrative of Job is set in a time long before the New Testament teaching about resurrection. Passages such as Paul's explanation of the significance of Christ's resurrection in 1 Corinthians 15 provide details about what comes for humans after their present temporal existence. That revelation of the future is a source of great hope for Christians who are now suffering adversity. In the Old Testament, however, the few hints about hope after death (Pss. 49:15; 73:24) are oblique and debatable, and only Daniel speaks of a future resurrection (Dan. 12:2–3). Old Testament believers viewed death as a shadowy existence, in which all the dead were gathered in the underworld (Deut. 32:22; Ps. 89:48), so their focus was centered on enjoying God's blessing in the land of the living (Ps. 27:13).

Teaching the Text

The language of Job's initial speech is startling in its intensity, and for that reason it can be troubling to readers. How do strong emotions and incisive questions like this fit into the life of faith? Viewed within the larger context of the book of Job and the entire Bible, Job 3 raises some key theological and practical themes. Overall, this chapter pictures Job as bringing his most troubling thoughts and deepest pains to words, so that he can seek to understand his adversity in the light of his commitment to God.

Job does not deny or dilute the pain that he feels but rather expresses it honestly. In this chapter, Job does not address his lament to God, but his candid recognition of his pain is a necessary first step in the direction of faith. Job's language is emotional and not coldly analytical, and it echoes the same level of intensity as found in some of the psalms and in Jeremiah. As these biblical examples of the speech of

Sheol and the Afterlife

In ancient Near Eastern thought, Sheol was viewed as the shadowy underworld, which was a pale imitation of genuine life on earth and a place of no return. When Job says in 7:9 that "one who goes down to the grave [Sheol] does not return," he is reflecting the limited conception of the afterlife found in much of the Old Testament. Before the resurrection of Jesus and the New Testament teaching that expounded on its theological significance for God's people, human death was viewed as final and irreversible (e.g., 10:22; 16:22). There are a few Old Testament intimations of the afterlife in passages such as Psalms 49:15; 73:24; and Daniel 12:2, but these are not nearly as clear as what is disclosed later, in the New Testament.

godly individuals indicate, feeling deeply and speaking from pain are not inherently sinful. Just as parents understand when their children are speaking out of frustration and hurt, and they want their children to turn to them at these difficult times, so God desires that we be open and honest in our dealings with him. We do not have to wait until we have calmed down and gotten things under control before we can speak to God. He knows perfectly what is in our hearts, so he understands how to listen even to our shrill tones when we cry out of an embittered spirit. Our pain and frustration may tempt us to avoid God or to be angry at him, but what he wants is for us to rush into his arms, where we can receive his comfort.

Job's questions indicate his ignorance of God. Although Job's questions are undoubtedly rhetorical as he expresses his agitation, in the context of the book they imply how much he does not understand about his situation. When God later asks seventy unanswerable questions of Job, Job at last recognizes and admits that he is in no position to call God to account. Like Job, we need to learn and remember that God's knowledge is infinite, far above our finite human understanding, so we will never be able to comprehend all that he is doing in our lives. Instead of viewing God through the lens of our limited understanding, we need to learn to trust him humbly, even when we cannot understand what he is doing, remembering that the Bible teaches that God is always great, good, and in control.

The pain that Job endures blurs his perception of God. In 3:23, Job views God as entrapping him rather than remembering that God's hedge around him is intended to protect him. In doing this, Job looks at God through the wrong end of the binoculars. By perceiving God through the lens of his experience, Job sees God as uncaring. If he would view his experience through the lens of the character of God, he would see things in a far different way. In our lives, we are prone to diminish God when we let our feelings about what is happening in our lives become the measure by which we evaluate God. We need to remember that whatever our circumstances, God's character is unchanging.

The metaphor of a hedge of protection in 3:23 may come from the shepherd's practice of creating hedges of rocks or sticks and thorny branches to make an enclosure in which to keep sheep safe from predators and prevent them from wandering. Shown here is a sheepfold with rock walls for protection.

Illustrating the Text

Job expresses his pain honestly; pain sometimes blurs his perception of God.

Poetry: #50, by Gerard Manley Hopkins. In these lines, Hopkins (1844–89) expresses honest pain over God's dealings with him:

> Thou art indeed just, Lord, if I
>   contend
> With thee; but, sir, so what I plead
>   is just.
> Why do sinners' ways prosper? And
>   why must
> Disappointment all I endeavor end?
>   Wert thou my enemy, O thou my
>   friend,
> How wouldst thou worse, I wonder,
>   than thou dost
> Defeat, thwart me?

Though full of pain, the last line of the poem is a statement of belief in the midst of the pain as Hopkins says, "O thou lord of life, send my roots rain."[2]

Bible: Psalm 109. The language of Psalm 109, one of the most prominent imprecatory (cursing) psalms, is even more jarring than Job's lament in this chapter. It is a candid expression of the psalmist's anguished feelings.

Film: *Fiddler on the Roof.* This film (1971) is based on an earlier Broadway musical, which was based on *Tevye and His Daughters*, a book by Sholem Aleichem. In the story set in Tsarist Russia in 1905, Tevye attempts to raise his family of daughters in the Jewish religious traditions in the face of cultural influences pressing in on him and his community. Tevye maintains a running conversation with God as he calls into question why God has brought so much adversity into his life. In one of the scenes from the movie, he says to God, "I know, I know. We are Your chosen people. But, once in a while, can't You choose someone else?"

Whatever our circumstances, God's character is unchanging.

Philosophy: Existentialism. "Existentialism" is a term applied to a set of attitudes, philosophical, religious, and artistic, starting around the time of World War II and continuing after. It is a viewpoint that sees the inadequacy of human reason to explain the enigma of human existence and the universe. As a result, what becomes important is what an individual feels, does, and thinks and what he or she takes responsibility for. While there are substantial differences between existentialists, their emphasis is subjective rather than objective. Such subjectivism can lead one to a feeling of absurdity and purposelessness. In contrast to such pervasive thinking, the Christian understands that he or she can find mooring in the unchanging character of God.

One example of a well-known literary piece by an existentialist is the four-character drama *No Exit* (1944) by French author Jean-Paul Sartre (1904–80). As the play begins, a valet brings a character named Joseph Garcin into a room that, it soon becomes clear, is hell, windowless and equipped with only one door. Two other characters join Garcin, and together they beleaguer one another with questions about one another's sins, passions, and painful memories. Left to their own designs, they make their world a torture chamber. But Christians are not left to their own designs; the circumstances of their lives are about something that transcends feeling; there is meaning because of who God is.

How Eliphaz Explains Job's Adversity

Big Idea *Eliphaz explains Job's adversity as a standard case of God's retribution for sin.*

Understanding the Text

The Text in Context

Job's three friends, who arrived on the scene in 2:11–13, wait until after Job's opening lament in chapter 3 before they speak. From chapter 4 through chapter 27, the friends and Job speak alternately, as they all try to explain Job's adversity. Eliphaz is the lead speaker in each of the three cycles of speeches, and his words introduce the key points that are developed later by Bildad and Zophar. For this reason, in the epilogue Yahweh specifically addresses Eliphaz and tells him that his explanation is wrong (42:7–8).

The three friends represent the major teaching of traditional wisdom, which is often called the retribution principle or retribution theology. This principle, expressed in passages such as Proverbs 28:10 and Psalm 1, teaches that because Yahweh is just, in his ordered world the righteous will be blessed and the wicked will suffer adversity. All of Job's friends agree that the retribution principle is true, and that it is applicable to Job. In fact, they go so far as to conclude that those who prosper are pious and those who suffer are necessarily sinners. However, they are ignorant of what the reader knows from the prologue, that in Job's case there are other factors involved. Eliphaz argues for his position in chapters 4 and 5, and then Job replies to him in chapters 6 and 7.

Historical and Cultural Background

Although other ancient Near Eastern religions discussed the problem of human adversity, they moved in quite different directions from that taken in the book of Job. Because the deities in ancient cultures outside of Israel were not regarded as necessarily just, and often they had the same vices as humans, those who worshiped false gods did not attempt to present them as just in their treatment of humans. Many times, injustice was regarded as being perpetuated by the inconsistent behavior of the gods, by demons, or by evil humans, or even as how the world was. In the Old Testament, Yahweh's just character and his sovereignty over all the world mean that the answer to the problem of a righteous sufferer like Job must in some way involve Yahweh.

Interpretive Insights

4:3–4 *Think how you have instructed many.* As the leader of the friends (cf. 42:7, where Yahweh singles him out), Eliphaz begins with a positive, and almost apologetic, tone, commending Job for his past instruction of others in their times of need. Later in the book when Job utters his final confession of innocence, he too recalls how he has counseled the afflicted (29:21–23). Taking the same conciliatory tone of voice, Eliphaz tries to counsel Job to listen to his advice rather than dismiss what he has to say. Eliphaz's initial intent seems to be constructive, to do for Job as Job has done for others. Unfortunately, the tone of the conversation deteriorates very quickly into accusation.

4:5 *But now trouble comes to you.* After his first words commending Job, Eliphaz shifts his tone to condemn his friend. Eliphaz assumes that what Job is experiencing is simply another routine case with a standard explanation. According to Eliphaz, Job has not followed the counsel he has given to others, and he is unwilling to apply the truth he taught to others to his own situation. In essence, Job needs to practice what he preaches.

4:6 *Should not your piety be your confidence and your blameless ways your hope?* In this verse, Eliphaz uses language that

Key Themes of Job 4

- Eliphaz's counsel starts well but falters quickly.
- In Eliphaz's observation, good always comes to good people and bad always comes to bad people.
- Eliphaz views all created beings as unable to please God.
- Eliphaz leaves no room for Job to hope.

must be painful to Job. The Hebrew word for "piety" is the key wisdom term for the fear, or reverence, of Yahweh in Proverbs 1:7; 9:10. The term "blameless" is from the same Hebrew root that is used for God-honoring people like Noah (Gen. 6:9), Abraham (Gen. 17:1), and the righteous who are blessed by Yahweh in Psalm 84:11 (84:12 MT). What makes Eliphaz's question ironic is that these very descriptions have been used of Job in 1:8 and 2:3, when Yahweh commended him to the adversary. In addition, the term "confidence" is related to a term that refers to folly in Ecclesiastes 7:25 (cf. Prov. 9:13), but to reliance (NIV: "trust") in Job 8:14 and 31:24, so Job may hear a mixed message in what Eliphaz says to him.

4:7 *Who, being innocent, has ever perished?* Eliphaz is so convinced of the validity of the retribution principle that he applies it absolutely. According to Eliphaz, there are no exceptions to this ironclad moral rule. Without considering the specifics of Job's situation, he treats it

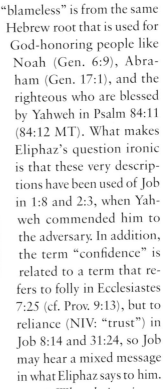

The pagan societies of the ancient Near East often attributed calamity and injustice to the activities of demon deities. This amulet from Mesopotamia features the demon goddess Lamashtu, who caused illness and disease.

as a generic case that can be adequately explained by retribution theology alone. His rhetorical question assumes the answer is "No one." However, later in the book Job will adduce numerous counterexamples that undermine Eliphaz's absolute claim (see chap. 21).

4:8 *As I have observed.* Here and in 5:3 Eliphaz appeals to personal observation as the source of his knowledge. By this he is employing the predominant procedure of traditional wisdom, which scrutinized the world in order to discern its embedded divine order (e.g., Prov. 6:6–11). Eliphaz assumes that what he has observed provides the key for explaining what Job has experienced. What the reader realizes is that beyond the observation available to Eliphaz is the conversation between Yahweh and the adversary in the prologue. Because Eliphaz's observation is limited, the conclusions he draws are flawed.

4:8 *those who sow trouble reap it.* Eliphaz is firmly committed to the validity of the retribution principle. Echoing verses such as Proverbs 22:8, and anticipating Paul's teaching in Galatians 6:7, he contends that those who act wickedly bring trouble on themselves. His implication is that Job is receiving from God only what his sinful actions deserve. Although retribution is valid as a general principle, Eliphaz inaccurately insists that it can be pressed to apply to every particular situation without exception, including Job's.

4:9 *At the breath of God they perish.* In Genesis 2:7 the breath of God gives life to Adam. Here, as in Isaiah 40:7 and Hosea 13:15, God's breath is compared to a destructive wind that destroys those who are wicked.

4:10–11 *The lions may roar and growl.* In the Psalms, the lion is often a metaphor for a wicked person (Pss. 7:2; 17:12; 22:13). By using multiple references to lions in 4:10–11, Eliphaz tries to employ colorful language to support his point and make it convincing. However, since he implies that Job's passionate words in chapter 3 were merely the growling of a toothless lion, Eliphaz's rhetoric sounds more pompous than persuasive.

4:12–16 *A word was secretly brought to me.* After arguing from observation (4:7–9) and by rhetoric (4:10–11), Eliphaz appeals to a secret divine revelation that he has received in a dream (4:12–21; compare God's revelation by dreams to Pharaoh in Gen. 41 and to Nebuchadnezzar in Dan. 2). By this means, he maintains that God has substantiated his assessment of all humans as falling short of God's righteous standard. To the reader, however, the bizarre language that Eliphaz uses sounds more eerie than convincing, and it actually sounds much like a parody of the traditional method of revelation to the prophets that enabled them to say confidently, "Thus says the Lord."

4:17 *Can a mortal be more righteous than God?* Eliphaz contends that no human, including Job, can be considered righteous when measured against the standard of God's own righteousness. By this reasoning, Eliphaz actually obliterates the distinction made in wisdom literature between the wise, who are righteous, and the foolish, who are wicked (Ps. 1), and he replaces it with a single category of sinful humanity. To justify his assessment of Job as guilty, Eliphaz paints with too broad a brush, and thus he implicates all humans as hopeless before God. Once again, Eliphaz does not comprehend or appreciate God's commendation of Job in the prologue, since he is unaware of it.

4:18 *he charges his angels with error.* Eliphaz enlarges the scope of his argument to include even the angels, God's messengers (see, e.g., Gen. 18; Zech. 1–2). Since God scrutinizes all of his creatures and finds even the exalted angels guilty (cf. 2 Pet. 2:4; Jude 6), then humans, who are made of dust (Job 4:19; cf. Gen. 2:7; 3:19) and therefore are inferior to the angels, cannot withstand divine examination.

4:19 *who are crushed more readily than a moth!* The term Eliphaz uses for "moth" (*'ash*) is used elsewhere in the Old Testament as a picture of weakness and frailty. For example, in Job 27:18 the accomplishments of sinful humans are as flimsy as a moth's cocoon. By contrast, Psalm 8 celebrates the exalted place of humans in God's ordered world.

4:21 *Are not the cords of their tent pulled up?* Eliphaz states that before the holy God humans are as vulnerable as a tent held up by frail cords, or perhaps, by tent pegs. As soon as adversity blows on them, humans are prone to collapse, before they acquire wisdom.

Theological Insights

The book of Job is often regarded as an example of theodicy, which is the attempt to defend or explain the ways of a good

> Eliphaz asserts that life is short and fragile, like a tent that will quickly fall when its pegs are pulled out of the ground, loosening the cords (4:21). In this register of an Assyrian relief where an Arab encampment is being attacked, the tents are collapsing and in flames (north palace at Nineveh, 645–635 BC).

Theodicy and the Book of Job

Theodicy asks how bad things can happen in a world that is controlled by a good God (cf. examples in Hab. 1 and Jer. 12). However, the book of Job does not actually answer this question, because it leaves Job's situation in the realm of mystery, in which humans must maintain faith in God even when they cannot fully understand his ways. To complicate the problem, the Old Testament does not present a well-developed theology of the afterlife, so the retribution principle is employed in passages like Psalm 27:13 in an attempt to bring a satisfying closure within the confines of human life upon the earth. In the New Testament, Jesus's explanation about the man born blind (John 9:1–3) points away from the retribution principle to God's larger purpose at work in the life of the blind man.

God in light of the existence of evil. At the end of the book, Job is not given an explanation about his adversity, but he does come to the realization that Yahweh is all-wise and all-powerful, and above all that he can be trusted for situations that humans cannot understand (see the sidebar).

Teaching the Text

After Job's opening lament in chapter 3, chapter 4 begins the major section of the

book of Job, in which Job and his friends attempt to explain why Job is suffering adversity. All of the speakers share some common ground, but they each have individual emphases. In his first speech, Eliphaz explains Job's adversity as a clear-cut case of God's retribution for Job's sin.

For people who want to help others who are enduring difficulties, Eliphaz offers both positive and negative examples. His counsel starts well enough, as he affirms Job for his past ministry to those who are hurting. However, Eliphaz falters quickly when he jumps to conclusions without knowing the full facts of Job's situation. Although the primary purpose of this chapter is not to be a manual for counseling people in pain, what Eliphaz says does provide a cautionary tale about the damaging consequences of speaking beyond what one knows when trying to minister to a person who is suffering adversity. In addition, his negative example challenges us to follow the admonition of James 1:19 by being "quick to listen, slow to speak and slow to become angry." Rather than jumping to judgment, true compassion feels with the pain of those who are suffering.

Drawing from what he has observed, Eliphaz determines that good always comes to good people and bad always comes to bad people. By viewing life as so black and white, Eliphaz is compelled to conclude that Job must have sinned, since he is suffering. Eliphaz assumes that the general pattern of retribution that he has observed is a necessary absolute law in God's moral order. He fails to realize that there is relevant information about Job that is beyond his observation. Because the reader already knows about the exemplary character of Job and the conversation between Yahweh and the adversary in the prologue, it is apparent that Eliphaz's conclusion about Job is flawed. By misjudging Job, Eliphaz only adds to his friend's pain.

In order to substantiate his conclusion about Job, Eliphaz resorts to linear reasoning that backs him into a logical corner. By insisting that God charges both his angels and all humans with error, Eliphaz is just one logical step from a conclusion that he likely does not intend, that no human can ever please the holy God. His logic, then, leads to a conclusion that contradicts God's affirmation of humans in Psalm 8 and his commendation of biblical figures such as Job and Enoch (Gen. 5:22, 24).

In counseling people who are suffering adversity, one of the initial goals is to maintain or rebuild a sense of hope. Those who can see nothing except their present overwhelming pain need to regain a vision that things can get better, that a new day can replace the storms that have overwhelmed their lives. Eliphaz leaves little room for Job to hope; instead he adds to the feeling of hopelessness. It is no wonder that Job's response to Eliphaz expresses his bitterness as he feels that he has been kicked when he is down. Rather than leading Job to hope in God, Eliphaz pictures God as implacably against sinners like Job.

Illustrating the Text

Damage can result from speaking beyond what we know about another's suffering.

Quote: *Escape from Loneliness*, by Paul Tournier. Tournier (1898–1986) was a Swiss physician and writer who had a worldwide following based on his eloquent and wise books and because of his pastoral counseling. He writes the following about how we should approach each other in love, particularly when the one approached is troubled. "In the fellowship of faith we all stand at the same crossroads, but we have come there by different routes. A spiritual ministry does not mean saying to people, 'Take the same pathway I took; it's the best one.' It means rather following them through all the turns of their twisting pathway with love and patience, never losing hope even when they seem to be going in the wrong direction."[1]

A goal of counseling is to maintain or rebuild a sense of hope.

News Story: During natural disasters like Hurricane Katrina (2005) and the Haiti earthquake of 2010, some people respond with heroic and selfless compassion to minister to people in great need, just as Job has done. This stands in contrast to the news story about a prominent television personality who declared that the Haiti disaster was the result of years of occult practice and therefore something that was bound to happen eventually. This is an illustration of criticism that, in a moment of crisis, was deemed highly inappropriate and not constructive for helping people who were suffering.

Hymn: "Be Still My Soul." The beautiful words of "Be Still My Soul," a popular revival hymn written by Katharine von Schlegel (1697–ca. 1768) and translated into English by Jane L. Borthwick (1813–97), could be quoted in this context. The music was composed by Jean Sibelius, from his symphonic poem *Finlandia*. The Scripture reference of this hymn is found in Psalm 46:10: "Be still, and know that I am God; I will be exalted among the nations, I will be exalted in the earth." Some of the appropriate words are as follows:

> Be still, my soul—the Lord is on thy
> side!
> Bear patiently the cross of grief and
> pain;
> Leave to thy God to order and
> provide—
> In ev'ry change He faithful will
> remain.
> Be still, my soul—thy best, thy
> heav'nly Friend
> Thru thorny ways leads to a joyful
> end.

The thinking of some people today is still guided by the retribution principle. This is illustrated by the declaration that the 2010 earthquake in Haiti was the result of years of occult practice (illustrated by this Haitian voodoo altar). We cannot know the mind of God sufficiently to draw such conclusions with any confidence.

Eliphaz Thinks He Knows the Answer

Big Idea *Eliphaz knows much truth about God, but he misconstrues Job as foolish and sinful.*

Understanding the Text

The Text in Context

In Job 5, Eliphaz continues his first speech from the previous chapter. Eliphaz sticks to the retribution principle, arguing that Job's sin must be genuine, because it has brought God's intense punishment upon him. Eliphaz's riff on the fool in 5:3–7 is clearly directed at Job personally. Even

Eliphaz may be borrowing imagery from the Egyptian god of pestilence, Resheph, whose image is inscribed on this stela (Egypt, Nineteenth Dynasty, ca. 1200 BC).

though Eliphaz began his speech with sensitivity toward Job, by this point his language has become critical and even hurtful. In fact, his insensitive references to Job's children in 5:4, 25 must feel like daggers to Job's heart.

The corrective to what Eliphaz says does not come until Yahweh at last speaks in chapters 38–41. In the larger context of the book, much of what Eliphaz says is highly ironic (see the discussion of 5:26 below). Many times, Eliphaz thinks he knows more than he actually does, but at times he speaks more truth than he intends.

Historical and Cultural Background

When Eliphaz refers to sparks (literally, "the sons of *resheph*") flying upward (5:7), he likely borrows his imagery from Resheph, the Ugaritic (Canaanite) god of pestilence. This allusion does not necessarily mean that the writer accepted that this Canaanite god actually existed. Rather, he used this well-known image to picture the damaging but inevitable effects of disease on humans.[1]

In the Near East, both in ancient times and today, rain is always a concern. For example, in 1 Kings 18 Elijah challenges the prophets of Baal to a contest to determine which deity can send rain to break the drought and thus demonstrate that he is the true God. Eliphaz rightly says that it is God who gives rain to the earth (5:10).

One of the key offensive weapons for the ancient soldier was the sword, so this was often used as a metaphor for evil, and especially for the malicious words of wicked men (5:15). Additional examples are found in Psalms 57:4; 64:3; Proverbs 12:18.

Interpretive Insights

5:1 *but who will answer you?* The implied answer to this rhetorical question is "No one," and there is a hint of sarcasm in Eliphaz's tone. Eliphaz indicates that it is futile for Job to call out for an intercessor in heaven to intervene and help him, because his sin has disqualified him from assistance. None of the holy angels (see 4:18; cf. 1:6; 2:1) will take up Job's cause. Later, Job expresses his desire for such a mediator to present his case before God (9:33; 16:19–21).

5:2–3 *Resentment kills a fool.* Eliphaz uses two familiar categories from traditional wisdom (fool, simple) to imply that Job is not wise, so he will be destroyed by his foolish attitudes. Eliphaz suggests that Job resents the adversity he has received from God, for his agitated response in chapter 3 evidenced his folly. Eliphaz also implies that Job envies others who do not have to experience pain as he does, and thus Job does not accept what God has brought into his life. Apparently, Eliphaz equates wisdom with a serene and stoic attitude,

Key Themes of Job 5

- Eliphaz jumps to the false conclusion that Job is foolish.
- Eliphaz recognizes the great and gracious acts of God.
- Eliphaz realizes that God's discipline can result in blessing.
- Eliphaz is overly confident that he knows the answer to Job's problem.

and Job's passionate reaction in chapter 3 did not fit that profile.

5:4 *His children are far from safety.* Eliphaz desires a world with no moral complexity or ambiguity. His reference to the vulnerable children of the fool, if intentionally directed at Job, is a cruel jab. Even if unintentional, it is insensitive and hurtful, because it makes the death of Job's children (1:19) his fault.

5:7 *as surely as sparks fly upward.* According to Eliphaz, just as sparks naturally fly up from a fire, so the kind of trouble that Job has experienced is a natural consequence of human sin. To be human is to be corrupted, and therefore born for trouble. Taking this fatalistic position, Eliphaz indicates that what Job has experienced is no surprise or accident, for trouble is part of the human condition that afflicts all people, even Job. This observation is consistent with the scriptural teaching that when sin entered into the human race it brought corruption to human nature.

5:8 *I would appeal to God.* Eliphaz speaks of himself, but he clearly intends to instruct Job with these words. According to Eliphaz, Job's only hope is to seek God, so that God will either grant him mercy or make known what offense Job has committed. Later in the book, Job places his legal case in God's hands (31:35), not confessing his sins, but instead calling on God

Eliphaz speaks about God's discipline, but he also speaks about God's rescue. For example, in 5:20 he says, "In famine he will deliver you from death." Famine was a real concern in the ancient Near East, as shown on these Egyptian reliefs (Saqqara, Egypt, 2375–2345 BC). Here people are depicted in a state of starvation, with ribs showing and emaciated arms and limbs. At the upper left a child begs for something to eat, while at the lower left a woman eats the lice she picks from her head.

to vindicate his innocence (27:5–6; 31:6). Yahweh's legal judgment in 42:7–8 exonerates Job, in contrast to the charges raised against him by Eliphaz and the other friends.

5:9 *wonders that cannot be fathomed.* By praising the incomprehensibility of God, Eliphaz actually undercuts his conclusion that was based on observation (4:8). God's ways are beyond human comprehension, as will become even more evident when Yahweh speaks in chapters 38–41. Eliphaz has good theology, but he does not apply it properly to Job's situation.

5:11–16 *The lowly he sets on high.* God is as sovereign over the human realm as he is over the natural world (5:9–10). Many of the lament psalms plead for God's intervention against powerful enemies. As Eliphaz notes, one of God's wonders is that he reverses social inequities as he comes to the aid of the needy, transforming their adversity into blessing. But if this is what God does, then he should be on Job's side!

5:17–18 *do not despise the discipline of the Almighty.* Eliphaz now changes from a lecturer to a counselor, speaking directly to Job. Using the standard wisdom phrase "Blessed is the one" (e.g., Ps. 1:1), he urges Job to accept divine discipline, for as Proverbs 3:11–12 teaches (cf. Heb. 12:5–11), discipline is an expression of God's love and a means for growth. However, to accept correction Job will have to admit that he has sinned, which he does not believe. This is the first of thirty-one times in Job that the title Shaddai (NIV: "Almighty"; see NIV footnote) is used for God. This title is used later in Job to speak of God's transcendent power (37:23) and of his just rule over humans (8:3–6).

5:19 *From six calamities . . . in seven.* Old Testament wisdom literature several times uses numerical sequences like this one to present a comprehensive list with common features (e.g., the things that Yahweh hates in Prov. 6:16–19). The sense here is that God will completely rescue the one whom he corrects (5:17–18), so Job should not despise his discipline.

5:24–25 *your tent is secure.* In 4:21 and 18:6 the tent is a picture of human vulnerability. Eliphaz wants to assure Job that if he submits to God's correction, then he will regain the secure prosperity (*shalom*) of his former life under God's blessing (1:1–5). However, by referring to Job's possessions that have been destroyed and to Job's children, who have been killed, Eliphaz is untactful and thoughtless. His supposed solution blinds him to the deep suffering that Job has experienced and leads him to say things that rub salt in Job's wounds.

5:26 *You will come to the grave in full vigor.* Ironically, the epilogue will describe Job in similar terms as Yahweh blesses him with a long and good life (42:12–17). However, that blessing does not come because Job confesses his supposed sins, as Eliphaz insists is necessary.

5:27 *We have examined this, and it is true.* Speaking in the plural on behalf of the three friends, and probably as the voice of wisdom in general, Eliphaz says emphatically that his assessment of Job's condition is accurate. Sounding like a confident prosecutor concluding his opening statement, Eliphaz patronizes Job by suggesting that what he has said is the only answer that Job need consider, so Job needs to hear what Eliphaz has said and apply it to himself.

Theological Insights

Eliphaz's words in chapter 5 connect with other biblical passages at several points. His hymn in 5:9–16 sounds much like a psalm of descriptive praise, and in particular it is comparable to nature psalms such as Psalm 29 and Psalm 104. The emphasis in Eliphaz's song on God's intervention on the side of the needy is echoed in the Song of Hannah (1 Sam. 2:1–10), the Magnificat of Mary (Luke 1:46–55), and Jesus's beatitudes in Matthew 5:3–12. Eliphaz's statement in 5:13 that God "catches the wise in their craftiness" is quoted by Paul in 1 Corinthians 3:19, as he argues that the wisdom of humans is insufficient for their salvation.

Eliphaz's portrayal of God both wounding and healing is reminiscent of Yahweh's self-description in Deuteronomy 32:39. In fact, the theme of God's correction and discipline is predicted in Deuteronomy, carried out in Judges, threatened in the prophets, and applied to Christians in Hebrews 12:5–11.

Teaching the Text

All the human speakers in the book of Job grasp some aspects of God's truth, but they also have blind spots in their understanding. As Eliphaz completes his first speech in Job 5, it is evident that he knows the truth about God, but he misconstrues Job as foolish and sinful. When reading this chapter, one needs to distinguish clearly between where Eliphaz is right in his theology and where he is faulty in his application.

Although Eliphaz at this point does not come right out and call Job a fool, his description of the demise of a fool in 5:3–7 alludes to Job and his adversity. By measuring Job's experience by the retribution principle, Eliphaz jumps to the conclusion that Job must have been foolish and sinful to deserve such an outcome in his life. He does not consider the possibility that there are additional relevant factors that need to be understood to evaluate Job's situation accurately. Too often we follow the haste of Eliphaz in criticizing others rather than taking the time necessary to comprehend the facts fully.

Eliphaz's hymn in 5:9–16 evidences his high view of God. He has observed God's great and gracious works as God cares for the natural world and intervenes on the side of needy people. Even though Eliphaz misjudges Job and is reproved by God for that (42:7–8), Eliphaz does see clearly many of God's wonderful attributes and activities. Thus, there is much truth to be learned in what he says, along with some tragic errors in how he applies his knowledge to Job's situation.

Eliphaz is wrong when he urges Job to confess his sins, but he is right in extolling how God's discipline can result in blessing. In both the Old Testament (Prov. 3:11–12) and the New Testament (Heb. 12:5–11), the Bible teaches that God's discipline is a mark of his fatherly care and nurture of his children. Job's adversity is not prompted by his sin, as Eliphaz wrongly supposes, but God does use this hard experience to increase Job's faith in him, even when Job cannot understand God's ways. This is not the kind of punitive discipline that Eliphaz is talking about in Job 5, but God does transform Job's affliction into blessing.

As Eliphaz concludes this first speech, he is overly confident that he knows the answer to Job's problem. The reader of the book realizes that Eliphaz is in error in his analysis of Job, but Eliphaz himself is blind to

what he does not know. He preaches a theological principle that is valid in many cases, but then he extrapolates it to an ironclad rule that does not account for the specific nature of Job's adversity.

Illustrating the Text

God's wisdom matches the right truth to the right situation at the right time and in the right Spirit; humans often fail to do so.

Humor: Pick a common saying of popular wisdom or common sense like "Don't put off until tomorrow the things you can do today." Acknowledge the clear truth and wisdom in the statement. Then ask listeners what might happen if a person tried to force that truth to fit the following types of situations in his or her life: "I feel so alone and am considering packing up and leaving this town forever." "I get so mad at work, and I sometimes feel like I'm going to strangle my boss." The obvious mismatch between the advice and the situation will create humor and highlight the way in which we as humans are often so inept at matching wisdom to our circumstances. In contrast, God desires to work in our lives by his indwelling Spirit and help us to properly discern which truths fit the times we are facing.

Object Lesson: Suggest a common household task that requires some delicacy, such as changing a light bulb or removing a sliver from skin. Then state that you need help from listeners in choosing the tool that would best fit the job. Display a series of clumsy and extreme tools (like a chainsaw, sledgehammer, bolt cutter, etc.) and play dumb about why they wouldn't work. Use the incongruity of the tools with the task to show how very useful, legitimate tools (truths) can still fail to fit the needs of a given task (finding meaning and direction in times of struggle). Reflect with listeners about how only the Holy Spirit has the wisdom to match the tools to the task.

Hurting people need to hear good news about the God who cares and intervenes in real time.

Testimony: You most likely know someone who can give a testimony about the way

"the Lord is close to the broken hearted and saves those who are crushed in spirit." (Psalm 34:18) Approach such a person and ask that he or she share briefly (either live or via video) about the way God met and comforted them in a time of suffering. Specifically, ask them to focus on how the comfort of his presence made the experience distinctly constructive and substantially different from discipline or chastisement. Conclude with a brief commentary that ties what has been shared back to the passage and the good news that, regardless of what humans like Eliphaz may say, God hears their cries and knows their afflictions, and he desires to give them the gift of himself in the midst of their sufferings.

> Some of the themes from Eliphaz's praise to God in 5:9–16 are included in the hymn "All Creatures of Our God and King" by Saint Francis of Assisi. This painting of Saint Francis by Carlo Crivelli is from an altarpiece at San Francesco (Montefiore dell' Aso, Italy, ca. 1470).

Job's Frustration with His Friends

Big Idea *Job's adversity shapes how he views God, his friends, and himself.*

Understanding the Text

The Text in Context

After Eliphaz's first speech in Job 4–5, Job responds in chapters 6 and 7. In chapter 6, Job indirectly refers in a few places to what Eliphaz has said, but he does not actually refute him point by point. Job's speech, rather, is an emotional outburst in which he defends himself and attacks his friends. Job is clearly frustrated with his painful situation (6:1–13) and with what he sees as the disloyalty of his friends (6:14–23). He demands that they speak honestly and kindly to him (6:24–30).

Like the friends, Job assumes the general validity of the retribution principle. He cannot understand why his life has turned so dramatically from blessing to adversity. In contrast to his friends, who insist that he is sinful and deserving of punishment, Job maintains that he is as righteous as he ever has been. Consequently, he feels that he is under attack by God, and that makes God seem unjust to him.

Historical and Cultural Background

Merchants in the ancient world used scales to weigh commodities for sale. Job says in 6:2–3 that he wishes to put all the sand of the seas on one side of the scales to measure against the pain of his misery. The ox (6:5) was a vital part of ancient Near Eastern agriculture (Prov. 14:4), and Job's five hundred yoke of oxen (1:3) were a measure of his vast wealth. The meaning of the final line in 6:6 is debated, but it may refer to the mallow plant, which had edible foliage but little flavor.

The intermittent streams, or wadis, that Job describes in 6:15–20 are streambeds that were dry during most of the year, but after storms they could become raging torrents. These wadis were like Job's friends, because they could not be counted on as a reliable source of support. Caravans crossing the Arabian Desert from Tema in the northwest or Sheba in the southwest too often were disappointed by potential water sources they glimpsed at a distance that turned out to be dry wadis.

Interpretive Insights

6:2–3 *If only my anguish could be weighed.* The Hebrew term translated "anguish," *ka'as*, has the sense of vexation or despair. In the lament psalms, people in adversity turn to God in their *ka'as* to plead for his intervention on their behalf (Pss. 6:7; 10:14), but the same term is used in Proverbs 12:16

to warn that "fools show their annoyance at once." Eliphaz warned in 5:2 that *ka'as* kills the fool, but Job here contends that his despair compels him to speak impetuously (6:3). The reader must therefore take into account his strong emotions, because they sometimes cause Job to express his feelings at the cost of seeing things clearly. While Job's words accurately disclose his pain, they do not always reflect what God is actually doing in his life. Thus, not all that Job says should be taken as an example for how we should respond to adversities in our lives.

6:4 *The arrows of the Almighty are in me.* The Old Testament often pictures Yahweh as a divine warrior who fights for his people (Zeph. 3:17),[1] as he does notably in the exodus when he defeats Pharaoh and the army of Egypt (Exod. 15:1–18). Job, however, feels that instead of being his faithful protector, God has been his fierce enemy. Bending the familiar Old Testament image of God as the divine warrior fighting for the benefit of his people, Job pictures him instead as an enemy attacking

Key Themes of Job 6

- Job keenly feels the pain of his adversity.
- Job's view of God is distorted by his pain.
- Job cannot depend on the loyalty of his friends.
- Job maintains his righteousness despite the rejection he feels.

him with poisoned arrows that penetrate both his body and his spirit. He feels that he has become target practice for God. Job does not view this as the kind of beneficent wounding prompted by the discipline of the Almighty that Eliphaz described in 5:17–18.

6:6–7 *Is tasteless food eaten without salt?* With this rhetorical question, Job implies that Eliphaz's words are insipid. His friend has not nourished him with life-giving instruction; what he said is worthless, tasteless, and totally unappetizing to Job. Consequently, Job refuses to accept it (6:7).

6:8–10 *Oh . . . that God would be willing to crush me!* Job wants clear resolution to his situation, whatever that might be,

The streams that Job speaks about in 6:15–17, which are known as "wadis," are dry stream beds most of the year, but they become channels of fast-churning water when rain comes. This wadi is part of the Nahal Zaror system in the Negev.

so he calls on God either to bless him or to crush him, but not to leave him in the miserable condition he is in. Like Moses (Num. 11:15) and Elijah (1 Kings 19:4), he desires God to take his life, because that will provide great relief from his pain. However, he does not express the option of suicide but leaves his life in God's hands. All that matters to Job is his integrity before God (6:10), and he does not want to get to the breaking point where he denies God.

6:14–15 *Anyone who withholds kindness from a friend.* Using the proverbial form typically employed by wisdom teachers, Job denounces his three critics as false friends who have shown their true colors by their disloyalty to him. By misconstruing the situation and accusing Job of sin, they fail to fortify Job with faithful kindness when he is struggling physically and spiritually.

6:21 *you see something dreadful and are afraid.* Both Job and the three friends believe in the validity of the retribution principle. Job's confidence in his integrity causes him to begin to question if the retribution principle truly holds for all cases. By speaking of his friends' fear, Job may be suggesting that they are afraid to rethink what they previously believed and taught. They find it hard to consider the possibility that the retribution principle is not adequate to explain all of life. Alternatively, Job may be saying that the friends have seen his adversity so they rush to speak against him, lest something terrible happen to them as well.

6:22–23 *Give something on my behalf.* Despite his overwhelming financial losses, Job is never recorded as asking the friends for their monetary support or for them to ransom him from an enemy, but he does expect and desire their faithful devotion (6:14).

They, however, are not willing to pay the price to help him. Job views them as curious to observe but not committed to assist him.

6:25–26 *But what do your arguments prove?* Eliphaz spoke only about how all humans are corrupt before the just God, but he has not shown that to be the specific case in Job's life. Through the speech of Eliphaz the friends have made a lot of accusations against Job, but they have not proved anything. Job insists that they do not have evidence to make their indictments against him stick. Therefore, he contrasts his own painful but honest words with their glib and baseless charges.

6:27 *You would even cast lots for the fatherless.* Feeling frustrated and insulted, Job directs a barb of his own at the friends. Their treatment of him, Job says, reveals what they truly are like. They are so heartless that they would even gamble for orphans, treating helpless humans as mere commodities to be sold as payment for debts (see, e.g., 2 Kings 4:1; see the sidebar). This charge indicates how tense the situation has become already. Later, in 22:5–9, Eliphaz will use even harsher language as he accuses Job of mistreating powerless people.

6:28 *But now be so kind as to look at me.* Job feels that they are talking *about* him as an object, rather than *to* him as a person. He pleads with them to look at him instead of averting their eyes from his hideous appearance, to acknowledge that he is indeed Job, their friend, a real person with genuine needs. There is also the implication that since the friends know their accusations are false, they do not dare look Job in the eye.

6:29 *my integrity is at stake.* Job appeals to their sense of justice, because he feels wrongfully accused by his friends. He calls on them to evaluate his character rightly as innocent, not to rush to condemn him as guilty. The term translated "integrity" here is not the word used earlier of Job in 2:3; rather, it speaks of Job's righteousness. In 6:29 the term may well have the nuance of Job's vindication, that is, the public declaration that he is in the right. Applying the retribution principle, Job's friends construe his adversity to be evidence of his guilt, but Job contends that their conclusion is unjust and not true to the facts.

Theological Insights

The reason why Job struggles theologically with his suffering is that he views all of life as under God's sovereign control, and Job cannot fathom why the just God would treat him as he has. Job perceives his afflictions as the arrows of God (6:4), language that echoes Psalms 38:2 and 120:4. Job is expressing what has been called the dark night of the soul, and his sentiments closely parallel those in Psalm 88:13–18.

When Job says that a person in despair needs the devotion of his friends (6:14), he uses the term *hesed* (NIV: "kindness"), a term that is frequently employed in the Old Testament for the faithful kindness of Yahweh (Exod. 20:6; 34:6–7; Jer. 9:24). The wisdom instruction in Proverbs 3:3 exhorts, "Let love and faithfulness never leave you," but Job's friends fail to do that in their response to Job.

Teaching the Text

Adversity often reveals what a person is really like in the heart. But adversity can also shape and change one's attitudes. In the prologue, Job's initial humble response to adversity clearly substantiated Yahweh's

Orphans and the Marginalized

Throughout the Old Testament, "the fatherless" refers to orphans, who, like widows and foreigners, are vulnerable, defenseless, and powerless. Yahweh shows a special concern for these classes of marginalized people, and he insists that they be treated with kindness and generosity. Deuteronomy 24:17–18 makes this care explicit: "Do not deprive the foreigner or the fatherless of justice, or take the cloak of the widow as a pledge. Remember that you were slaves in Egypt and the Lord your God redeemed you from there. That is why I command you to do this." (See also Exod. 22:21–24; Lev. 19:9–10; Deut. 24:19–22.)

commendation of his blameless character. By the time we get to Job 6, however, the persistent pain is beginning to affect how Job views God, his friends, and himself. Although not all that Job says is a positive example of how we should handle pain in our lives, he does help us to think through how to respond to God and to others in times of adversity.

Job's opening words in this speech express the weight of his despair. He keenly feels the pain of his great adversity, and he is open and vocal in stating how he feels. In this, Job follows the pattern of lament psalms, in which the psalmists give voice to their feelings as they pour their hearts out before the Lord. In imprecatory psalms (e.g., Pss. 7, 58, and 137), pious worshipers express their feelings even more vividly, turning to God with their rage. These biblical patterns demonstrate that God wants us to be candid and honest as we bring our most ragged emotions before him, which Job will do as he addresses God directly in chapter 7. This is not a license to lash out in retaliation toward others, but it does give us permission to put words to what is in our hearts as we bring our petitions to God. Just as a loving father wants his hurting children to turn to him with their deepest pains, so God wants his people to bring their torn hearts to him.

At the same time, Job's adversity is beginning to distort his view of God. Rather than remembering that the Lord is the divine warrior who fights for his people, Job views God through the lens of his suffering. From this perspective, God looks like an enemy combatant whose poisoned arrows penetrate Job's spirit. Although the Lord is indeed sovereign over all of life, Job extrapolates this truth into an erroneous sense that God is the culpable, or blameworthy, agent for the evil he is experiencing. In this, he speaks beyond his knowledge, because the prologue tells the reader that these adversities have come upon him at the instigation of the adversary.

Job learns from his adversity that he cannot depend on the loyalty of his friends. No doubt this has come as a surprise and a deep disappointment to him, for he supposed that in his despair he could count on their support. Even the best of friends can let down those who trust them, but as Lamentations 3:22 teaches, the Lord's loyalty never ceases. One of the primary lessons of the book of Job is that Yahweh can be trusted, even when his ways cannot be understood. By contrast, humans too often prove to be untrustworthy despite their best intentions.

Even though Job feels rejected by God and by his friends, he maintains a sense of his own righteousness before the Lord. He does not crumble under the pressure, even when it seems like God is using him for target practice and when his friends hurt him more than they help. Job is humble enough to be willing to be taught where he is wrong, but he is not willing to surrender his integrity just to silence the unfounded criticisms of others when he cannot understand why he is suffering such affliction. He knows where he stands with God, and he does not let his adversity alter that conviction. Nevertheless, his experience calls into serious question the retribution theology that he believed previously, producing significant confusion in his thinking. Throughout the rest of the book, Job will wrestle with these difficult questions as he seeks to resolve the dissonance between his piety toward God and God's apparent treatment of him.

Job pictures God as aiming arrows at him rather than offering divine protection against an enemy. This is in contrast to the usual view of deity as a divine warrior fighting on behalf of his people, which is a common motif in the ancient Near East. Shown here is the Assyrian god Assur with bow drawn, going before King Ashurnasirpal in battle (northwest palace at Nimrud, 865–860 BC).

Illustrating the Text

God wants us to be candid before him and to put words to what is in our hearts.

Bible: Two of the most autobiographical books in the Bible are Jeremiah and 2 Corinthians. In both of these books, godly men express honestly their feelings in the midst of deep pain.

We must correct any distortions in our view of God that adversity has caused.

Literature: *Moby Dick*, **by Herman Melville.** Melville's (1819–91) knowledge of Job appears to have been significant. *In Moby Dick* (1851), the protagonist is Captain Ahab, a man filled with rage against the great white whale, Moby Dick, because the whale has destroyed the captain's ship and bitten off his leg. Though he has been warned about his jaundiced view of an experience that could befall any whaler, Ahab pursues the whale—which many critics believe is a symbol of God—believing him to be utterly evil. In response to a warning about his blasphemy, Captain Ahab cries out for vengeance, "The white whale is that wall, shoved near to me. . . . He tasks me; he heaps me; I see in him outrageous strength, with an inscrutable malice sinewing it. That inscrutable thing is chiefly what I hate. . . . I will wreak that hate upon him."[2] In contrast, Job's experience with loss points to his faith in a God who fortifies him.

We must depend on God when friends are disloyal or fail us.

Literature: *The Count of Monte Cristo*, **by Alexandre Dumas.** In *The Count of Monte Cristo* (1844), Dumas (1802–70) tells the story of a man who is betrayed by a friend whom he trusted, and who then spends great effort exacting vengeance on him. Job has a similar experience of disloyalty from those on whom he has depended, but he does not retaliate against them.

Poetry: "Invictus," by William Ernest Henley. This often-cited stoic poem (1888) by English poet William Ernest Henley (1849–1903) provides a great contrast to Job's attitude. At the age of twelve, Henley contracted tuberculosis of the bone. As the disease progressed to his foot, physicians determined that to save his life they must amputate directly below the knee, an event that occurred when he was twenty-five. Victorian textbooks espousing stoicism were popular at the time and inspired Henley's stoic ideal of indifference in the face of suffering. The poem reads as follows:

> Out of the night that covers me
> Black as the pit from pole to pole,
> I thank whatever gods may be
> For my unconquerable soul.
>
> In the fell clutch of circumstance
> I have not winced nor cried aloud.
> Under the bludgeonings of chance
> My head is bloody, but unbowed.
>
> Beyond this place of wrath and tears
> Looms but the Horror of the shade,
> And yet the menace of the years
> Finds and shall find me unafraid.
>
> It matters not how strait the gate,
> How charged with punishments the
>   scroll,
> I am the master of my fate:
> I am the captain of my soul.

Job's faith in God sustained him, something profoundly different from this stoicism.

Job's Complaint to God

Big Idea *Job brings his feelings, fears, and frustrations before God.*

Understanding the Text

The Text in Context

After speaking directly to his three friends in 6:24–30, Job turns away from them in chapter 7. In 7:1–6, Job discloses his inner feelings by speaking in a soliloquy, much as an actor in a play might address the audience in an aside so that they can understand what the character is thinking or feeling. Although Job does indeed have issues with his friends, his overriding complaint is against God (7:7–21), whom he thinks has not treated him rightly. Throughout the remainder of the book, Job more and more will turn away from the friends to address God, and by the end of the book just Yahweh and Job are left speaking.

> Job alludes to a battle between God and chaos (7:12). The similar battle between Marduk and Tiamat in Babylonian mythology is recorded in a series of cuneiform tablets known as the Epic of Creation. This tablet describes the celebratory banquet where Marduk is appointed champion of the gods (Neo-Assyrian, seventh century BC).

Historical and Cultural Background

As in 3:17–20, in 7:9 "the grave" refers to Sheol, the place of the dead. In ancient Near Eastern thought, this was viewed as the shadowy underworld (see the sidebar, "Sheol and the Afterlife," in the unit on Job 3).

In 7:12 Job alludes to the familiar motif of the battle between the creator God and chaos (see also 3:8; 9:8, 13; 26:12–13; 38:8–11; 41:1–34). In Canaanite mythology, the sea (Yamm) and the sea monster (Tannin) are suppressed by Baal and Anath respectively, and their victory establishes order on the earth. Similarly, in Babylonian mythology, Marduk defeats Tiamat and imprisons her. In the biblical creation account in Genesis, God makes the sea monsters (*tanninim*; Gen. 1:21), demonstrating his power and authority over them.

Interpretive Insights

7:1–2 *Do not mortals have hard service on earth?* Job uses the language of military conscription (see Num. 1:3; 1 Chron. 5:18; 7:11) to complain that to live is to be a slave. This same language is used in 1 Kings 5:13–14 to refer to the forced laborers under Solomon who cut timber and quarry stones for the temple. The picture of humans toiling for long days to earn meager wages is a stark contrast to the exalted position of humans made in God's image (Gen. 1:26–27). From Job's perspective, which is distorted by his pain, God seems to use humans as though they are mere agents of labor, a concept also found in the Mesopotamian Epic of Atrahasis.

7:3 *I have been allotted months of futility.* For the most part, the focus in the book of Job is on the intensity of Job's pain rather than on its length in time. The term "months" may be a general marker for the duration of Job's distress as his life feels totally empty and useless. In the *Testament of Job* (a later, pseudepigraphical work), Job's ordeal is said to last forty-eight years (*T. Job* 21.1), but that is likely a speculative embellishment of the biblical text.

7:5 *My body is clothed with worms and scabs.* The worm (*rimmah*) is an image of decay, because worms feed on decomposing corpses (Job 21:26; cf. Isa. 14:11). The same term, which Job uses here to describe his physical affliction, is later employed by Bildad (25:6; NIV: "maggot") in his final derogatory description of the human beings, whom he dismisses as a maggot and a worm.

7:6 *My days . . . come to an end without hope.* The Hebrew term *tiqwah* is a pun meaning both "thread" and "hope." Job feels as useless as the small ends of the thread that are snapped off a loom after the weaving is completed (cf. Josh. 2:18, 21). Thus Job's life is fragile and precarious. Because his life

Key Themes of Job 7

- Job gives words to what he feels in his adversity.
- Job turns to God in his pain rather than turning away from him.
- Job expresses to God the fears that have emerged in his mind.
- Job states the frustrations in his spirit about how he perceives God is treating him.

is at the end of its thread, he is without hope (cf. 1 Chron. 29:15; Isa. 38:12). Job's friends, reflecting the wisdom instruction of Proverbs 10:28, insist that the righteous are those who have hope (4:6; 11:18), but the wicked

have no hope (8:13; 11:20). Although Job readily admits his feeling of hopelessness, he strongly argues against their deduction that he then necessarily must be wicked.

7:7 *my life is but a breath.* In Genesis 2:7, God breathes into Adam his breath or life force, but Job uses the language of breath in a very different way as an image of the transitory nature of human mortality. Later he repeats that life is fleeting (9:25–26; 14:1–2), a sentiment that parallels the psalmist's prayer in Psalm 39:4–5.

7:11–12 *I will speak out in the anguish of my spirit.* Like the psalmists of the imprecatory psalms, who call down divine condemnation on those who afflict them (e.g., Pss. 58:6–8; 59:3–5), Job does not hold back when he expresses his bitter feelings to God. This, however, is a risky move, because the wisdom tradition teaches that the prudent person is restrained in speech (Prov. 10:19; 17:27). Job, however, refuses to be muzzled, as the mythological Yamm and Tannin were (corresponding to the "sea" and the "monster of the deep," respectively; 7:12).

7:14 *even then you frighten me with dreams.* As in verse 4, Job hopes that sleep will bring relief from his painful adversity, but it does not. When he is tossing and turning until dawn, he is also frightened by nightmares and visions. In ancient thought, nightmares were often regarded as the work of demons or divine agents,[1] but here Job attributes them to God himself. It is possible that he also is taking a sideward glance at the disturbing nighttime revelation that Eliphaz described in 4:12–16. In any case, what Job endures is the opposite of the comfort that he has expected (7:13).

7:15 *I prefer strangling and death.* Earlier, in his opening lament (3:11–16), Job expressed his wish that he had died at birth rather than living to experience his adversity. Here, Job's pain is so severe that he views a violent death by strangling as preferable to continued life in his painful condition. His thinking has become clouded and dominated by his desperation to be freed somehow from his pain.

7:16 *my days have no meaning.* Using a term familiar from Ecclesiastes, Job complains that his days are *hebel*. This term, which in its literal sense means breath, was typically used to refer to what is fleeting, futile, or enigmatic. In this context, Job likely intends the negative sense of futility as he speaks of the life he has come to despise. He just wants God to leave him alone (cf. 10:20). What is ironic is that Job has no awareness that at the end of the story he will be restored to live many years (42:17).

7:20 *you who see everything we do.* In addressing God in these words, Job expands on how he views God in verse 8, as "the eye that now sees me." The psalmists frequently appeal to Yahweh to watch protectively over Israel (Pss. 12:7; 25:20; 40:11; 61:7), and in Psalm 139:1–6 God's omnipresence is a great comfort. Job, by contrast, does not feel comforted by God's watchful eye on him but rather badgered by God's unceasing scrutiny. As in 6:4, Job feels attacked and wounded by God, so God's constant surveillance of him produces in Job a sense of distance and tension rather than closeness and safety. Job, therefore, wants God to stop looking at him, in contrast to the psalmist who pleaded with Yahweh, "Look on me and answer" (Ps. 13:3).

In 6:4 Job complained that the arrows of the Almighty pierced him, and now he asks why God has treated him in this way.

Assuming the basic validity of retribution theology, which says that punishment comes as a result of wickedness, Job inquires what sin of his has justified divine punishment on him. From the prologue, the reader knows more than Job does as he endures his pain. In fact, within the context of the whole book, Job never receives an answer from God to this question about the reason for his adversity.

7:21 *Why do you not pardon my offenses?* Job is not conscious of any unconfessed sin in his life, or he would admit it to God. He is not willing to follow the counsel of his friends and confess to sins that he has not committed. Speaking hypothetically, Job asks that if he has sinned, why is God unwilling to forgive him? In verses 20–21, Job uses the three major Old Testament terms for sin (cf. Ps. 32:1–2, 5) as he refers to missing the mark of God's will ("sinned"; v. 20), resisting God's rule ("offenses"; v. 21), and distorting God's desires ("sins"; v. 21).

Theological Insights

Job's view of life as futile (7:3) is broadly parallel to the sentiments found in the book of Ecclesiastes, which views life "under the sun" (see Eccles. 1:3). This perception of human life on earth as harsh toil (Job 7:1) contrasts with the original dominion that God gave to humans in Genesis 1:26–28 and 2:15. It views life as under the curse (Gen. 3:17–19).

In 7:17–18 Job parodies the words of the psalmist in Psalm 8:4 (cf. Ps. 144:3–4). Instead of humans enjoying an exalted status under God, in which they exercise rule over his creation, Job says that they are scrutinized and examined perpetually by God. Whereas the psalmists exulted in wonder and worship as they reflected on the God-given status of humans, Job at this place in the book explodes in bitter anguish and aggravation. Job's negative view of humanity will be intensified by Eliphaz (15:14–16) and Bildad (25:4–6).

Teaching the Text

When people are in pain, they often, but not always, find it relatively easy to vent to other people about their problems. They also frequently talk *about* God and how they perceive his part in what they are enduring. But many times during adversity people find it more difficult to speak directly and honestly *to* God about their reactions to what they are experiencing. Job in this chapter provides an example of courageous candor as he brings his feelings, fears, and frustrations to God. He by no means exemplifies a perfect pattern to imitate, but he does challenge us to turn to God with our problems. As the lament psalms demonstrate, this is a necessary first step on the path from pain to praise.

This chapter is agonizing to read, because Job gives words to what he feels in his adversity. Unlike many of us who routinely say "I'm fine" when we are not at all doing well, Job describes in specific terms and incisive images the depth of his physical, emotional, psychological, and spiritual pain. In his soliloquy in 7:1–6, Job opens up his heart to reveal the depths of his intense emotions. He does not try to maintain a false, stoic appearance, but instead he is candid in expressing what he feels. By taking this risk, Job opens up the opportunity for others to understand and help him. Unfortunately, his friends do not respond with the compassion and assistance he needs from them.

Job does not keep his feelings to himself or content himself by talking to other people. Rather, he takes the full force of his pain to God. Job does not worry that he might offend God by being honest with him, so he articulates the full measure of what is in his heart and mind. In doing this, Job casts himself completely on God, expecting that God will not reject him for his honest, hard questions and deeply troubling fears. Job recognizes that the omniscient God knows and sees all things, so what he says is known by God already. But his very act of saying these things directly to God indicates that Job is confident that his relationship with God is intact. This continuing relationship means that Job can and should share freely and fully from his heart. In a similar way, Peter later challenges his readers to cast all of their anxiety upon God, confident that God cares for them (1 Pet. 5:7).

As Job shares what is in his heart, he includes even the frustrations in his spirit about how he perceives God is treating him. Job recognizes that while adversity often has physical, emotional, social, and financial aspects, it also inevitably has a theological dimension as well. Because God is sovereign over his world, somehow adversity must be understood within that theological framework. Job does not soft-pedal his frustration when speaking to God but raises hard, probing questions for him. Although Job does not get the specific answers that he wants, the rest of the book does go on to provide a broad theological framework for addressing the issues that he raises. By shifting the discussion from "why?" to "who?" Yahweh at the end of the book will point Job out of his frustration and back to faith.

Illustrating the Text

The watchful eye of an all-seeing God can be oppressive if we do not trust in him.

Literature: *The Lord of the Rings*, by J. R. R. Tolkien. Sauron is the titular character and the primary antagonist of this epic fantasy novel by Tolkien (1892–1973). The evil eye of Sauron (which is vividly depicted in Peter Jackson's film version of Tolkien's novel) casts its gaze in all directions. To be under the scrutiny of Sauron was terrifying, and it parallels the feeling Job expresses in 7:20.

Literature: *The Great Gatsby*, by F. Scott Fitzgerald. The novel *The Great Gatsby* (1925), by Fitzgerald (1896–1940), has as one of its prominent images a billboard with an eye, that of Doctor T. J. Eckleburg, which appears to unblinkingly watch the characters of the book. The key description can be found in chapter 2.

Because of his suffering, Job perceives God's watchfulness negatively, as close scrutiny. In the ancient world, however, for the god to watch you usually meant you were offered protection. In Egypt, the eye of Horus became a symbol of protection used for amulets, like the one shown here.

We must take our full pain to God, articulating it honestly and specifically.

Christian Living Book: *Abba's Child*, **by Brennan Manning**. In this eloquent book, subtitled *The Cry of the Heart for Intimate Belonging*, Brennan Manning urges the reader to "come out of hiding." This decision, he asserts, "is our initiation rite into the healing ministry of Jesus Christ. . . . We stand in the Truth that sets us free and live out of the Reality that makes us whole."[2]

Music: Country music, African American spirituals, and the blues are renowned for their lyrics that disclose the deep feelings of people in pain, in contrast to so many contexts in life where people mask what is in their hearts. Suggested blues songs are "Nobody Knows You When You're Down and Out" by Ida Cox (third verse) and "Worried Life Blues" by Bessie Smith. Recommended country music songs are the songs from Johnny Cash's album *Hurt*. A suggested spiritual is "Nobody Knows the Trouble I've Seen." Also good to look at are the lyrics of and the story behind "Precious Lord, Take My Hand" by Thomas A. Dorsey.

Bildad Has the Answer (He Thinks!)

Big Idea *Bildad so focuses on God's justice that he is blind to Job's blamelessness.*

Understanding the Text

The Text in Context

In contrast to Job's passionate speech in Job 6–7, Bildad's first speech, in chapter 8, is calm and analytical. With an almost unfeeling tone, Bildad is more the lecturing professor than the comforting pastor. Unlike Eliphaz, who at least began by affirming Job (4:3–4), Bildad is caustic from the start, dismissing Job's words as a "blustering wind" (8:2). Bildad intensifies the retribution principle that Eliphaz stated into a rigid formula of double retribution, in which God always prospers the righteous (8:20) and always destroys the wicked (8:13). Bildad uses logic (8:3–7), tradition (8:8–10), and analogies from nature (8:11–19) to argue his position, and he refuses to consider evidence that contradicts his formula of how God maintains justice in the world. Zophar, in chapter 11, and Eliphaz, in chapter 22, will assume the validity of Bildad's teaching on retribution and then develop additional implications from it.

Historical and Cultural Background

Throughout the ancient Near Eastern world, the wisdom of prior generations was especially valued, because it represented the accumulation of wisdom over time. This assessment of ancient wisdom is reflected in Deuteronomy 4:32, when Israel is exhorted to ask about what God has done in former times since the day he created humans on earth.

The wisdom of previous generations was highly valued in the ancient world. In Mesopotamia, the primeval sages, known as the the apkallu, brought wisdom to humankind; they are represented on this cultic water basin by the figures wearing fish-type garments (704–681 BC).

Bildad's analogy of the papyrus plant (8:11–12) refers to a plant that grew profusely in the Nile delta in Egypt and also in some parts of the land of Israel (see Exod. 2:3; Isa. 18:2). It was used for a variety of products, including baskets, boats, and writing materials. The papyrus plant can grow up to nearly twenty feet tall, but it requires a constant and ample source of water in order to thrive. Without abundant moisture, the plant quickly withers and dies.

Interpretive Insights

8:3 *Does God pervert justice?* Bildad's rhetorical question clearly expects a negative answer. Distorting Job's complaint against God in 7:7–21, Bildad implies that Job has maligned God's righteous character and his rule (cf. Pss. 89:14–15; 99:4). Bildad is as much as saying that if God cannot do what is unjust, then Job necessarily must be sinful. From Bildad's total commitment to retribution theology, only this could account for the divine punishment that Job has suffered. Toward the end of the book, Yahweh poses the same question to Job (40:8), but the divine assessment of Job is different from what Bildad alleges. Bildad indeed asks the right question, but he gives an incomplete answer to it.

8:4 *When your children sinned.* Because Bildad has come from a distance to comfort Job, it is likely that he did not personally know Job's children. Nevertheless, he is so confident of the legitimacy of the retribution formula that he reasons backward from the observable effect to what he considers the necessary cause. Compelled by his logic, Bildad concludes that Job's children must have sinned. Bildad's insensitive

Key Themes of Job 8

- Bildad's logical analysis desensitizes him to Job's pain.
- Bildad builds his case through logic, tradition, and analogies.
- Bildad prescribes Job's cure without first diagnosing his disease.
- Bildad mixes good theology with inaccurate application.

reference to Job's children evidences that he is looking at Job's case with a cold, analytical eye. His abstract theology without pastoral sensitivity and compassion must pain Job terribly.

8:6 *if you are pure and upright.* Even though Bildad does not really understand what has prompted Job's calamity, he speaks as though he understands it completely. To Bildad's thinking, if Job's life had been marked by moral purity (cf. Ps. 119:9), then God would have come to his defense already. What is ironic is that the prologue has made it clear that Job is indeed upright, because Yahweh himself said so twice (1:8; 2:3).

8:8 *Ask the former generation.* Taking the condescending tone of a teacher scolding a recalcitrant pupil, Bildad instructs Job to review the lessons of past wisdom that he as a wise teacher should have mastered. Traditional wisdom viewed God as the ultimate source of all wisdom (Prov. 8:22–31). God had revealed some of his wisdom, and he had imbedded other aspects of his wisdom in the universe so that humans could access them through the process of observation (e.g., Prov. 6:6–11). Because individual humans are limited in what they themselves can observe directly, they need to make use of the accumulated observations passed down by those who came before them (Deut. 32:7; Prov. 4:1–9).

Although many Bible versions have translated "former generations" as a plural in 8:8, the Hebrew expression is the singular, "former generation." It could well refer to the original wisdom possessed by God from the beginning (Deut. 4:32; Isa. 40:21).

8:9 *our days on earth are but a shadow.* It is crucial to listen to tradition, because an individual lifetime is too fleeting for individuals to accumulate substantial wisdom on their own. Using the image of a lengthening shadow to picture one's brief days on earth (cf. 1 Chron. 29:15; Pss. 102:11; 144:4; Eccles. 6:12; 8:13), Bildad declares that one short life span is too small a lens through which to view wisdom. It needs to be supplemented by the aggregated experiences and insights of past generations.

8:10 *words from their understanding.* The term translated "understanding" is the Hebrew *leb*, which is often rendered as "heart." In Old Testament thought, the *leb* is the center of the whole person, and it incorporates the thinking, feeling, and deciding aspects of the personality. In this verse, the intellectual sense is most prominent.

8:13 *Such is the destiny of all who forget God.* Forgetting God here means more than merely a lapse of memory. Instead, it has the sense of conscious opposition to God that causes one to exclude him (see the sidebar). For that reason, it is parallel to "the godless" in the next line.

8:14–15 *what they rely on is a spider's web.* Bildad compares the trust of the godless in their possessions to the fragile web of a spider. By using this image, Bildad states that human resources are incapable of providing reliable confidence. He likely uses this language to allude to Job's loss of his vast possessions, with the implication that Job placed his trust in what he owned rather than in God.

8:16–19 *They are like a well-watered plant.* In verses 16–19 Bildad develops an extended picture of a luxuriant plant that thrives but then is uprooted and withered. This image seems to build on the previous analogy of the spider's web to demonstrate that the joy of the prosperous will be short-lived if their trust is in their own resources rather than in God. In fact, the test of what one trusts is how it holds up under the heat of adversity. Bildad's implicit point in this image is that Job has been uprooted because he did not place his trust in God.

8:20 *Surely God does not reject one who is blameless.* In verses 20–22 Bildad summarizes his argument and appeals directly to Job. By insisting that God does not reject one who is blameless, Bildad ironically argues against himself, because Yahweh has already described Job as blameless (1:8; 2:3). Bildad correctly predicts Job's restoration to God's blessing (42:7–17), but he completely misses how this restoration will come about. Bildad has no place in his

Bildad uses the image of a shadow to describe the shortness of life (8:9). This sundial from Egypt marked time by measuring the length of the sun's shadow cast by the small upright piece when the sundial was aimed at the sun (1540–1075 BC).

rigid retribution theology for exceptions, such as the good who die young, the wicked who get away with murder, or a blameless person like Job who experiences adversity.

8:21–22 *He will yet fill your mouth with laughter.* At the end of his first speech, Bildad leaves the door open for hope for Job, but only if he will repent of his sin (cf. 8:5–7). Suggesting that Job's situation can be redeemed, Bildad paints a hopeful picture of what Job's life restored to God's blessing would look like.

Theological Insights

Bildad takes the general retribution pattern taught in traditional wisdom (e.g., Prov. 26:27), and he reduces all of life to it. By doing this, Bildad leaves no room for God to work outside the standard pattern, thus making divine action thoroughly predictable and automatic. The book of Job, however, will go on to demonstrate that there is mystery in God's working in the world and that the retribution principle, though valid in general, must not be pressed into an inflexible formula for how God *must* act in every case.

Bildad's emphasis on the justice of God agrees with the theology of the Old Testament, in which Yahweh is presented as just and righteous (Deut. 32:4). Because he is just, Yahweh rules by justice and righteousness (Pss. 89:14; 97:2; 99:4).

Bildad's appeal to tradition in 8:8–10 fits well the approach of traditional wisdom. Because wisdom is rooted in the observation of life, those who have accumulated many observations are wise. The wise teacher learns from the observations made by others in the past, adds personal observations, and then teaches all of this to the

Forgetting and Remembering God

The Mosaic law calls on Israel not to forget Yahweh (Deut. 4:23; 6:12; 8:11) but to remember him and his deeds (Deut. 5:15; 7:18; 8:2). Just as forgetting is an active concept, so remembering also includes activity. For example, in Genesis 8:1 God remembers Noah after the flood, and therefore he brings Noah out of the ark. Similarly, Ecclesiastes exhorts young people to remember their creator by fearing him and keeping his commandments (Eccles. 12:1, 13). Unfortunately, the Old Testament frequently traces the sad pattern of Israel's forgetting the God who has blessed them (Judg. 2:8–19; Pss. 78; 106).

next generation. Although this approach is valid in general, Jesus criticizes the teachers of his day who value their traditions above the revealed word of God (Matt. 15:1–9).

Teaching the Text

It has often been observed that error frequently creeps in when one aspect of the truth is emphasized to the detriment of other aspects. This can happen in theology when, for example, God's sovereignty is exalted to the exclusion of any human responsibility, or when human will is focused on to the point that it diminishes God's plan and control. This also occurs when people try to understand and respond to human experiences, as Bildad's first speech (Job 8) demonstrates. In this chapter, Bildad is so focused on arguing for God's justice that he is blind to Job's blamelessness. His application of rigid retribution theology to Job's situation causes him to make judgments about Job that later on will be proved false.

Bildad's strength is his logical analysis, by which he can develop arguments that are convincing, at least to him and the other friends. However, his strength also proves to be his weakness, because his logic causes him to view Job merely as a case to be solved

The hope of those without God perishes as quickly as a papyrus plant without water. This is one of the analogies from nature that Bildad uses as he presents his case to Job (8:11). The papyrus plant, which requires large amounts of water to survive, grew abundantly in the marshy areas along the Nile delta in Egypt. Papyrus is pictured in this Egyptian painting of a hunting scene from the tomb of Nebamun (ca. 1350 BC).

argument deal with general patterns of life, but Bildad fails to consider that Job's case could be an exception that does not fit within the standard explanations. Because Bildad begins with the faulty assumption that Job's experience can be understood solely within the formula of retribution theology, and the arguments he uses substantiate that assumption, he succeeds in building a logical case, but it does not apply to Job. In effect, Bildad is like a doctor who confidently prescribes Job's cure without first taking care to diagnose correctly his disease. No wonder Job is so frustrated with him! In trying to give the right answer to others, we must be careful to give answers that are truly relevant to their situations.

It might be tempting to write off Bildad and the other friends as worthless because they fail to understand Job's special situation. Nevertheless, it must be acknowledged that Bildad does present a lot of good theology in what he says, particularly when he expounds on the justice of God. Bildad's problem is that he takes good theology and mixes it with inaccurate application. As readers, we need to value the truth he teaches, but at the same time recognize where he slips from truth into error. His theological truth does not mean that he is accurate in what he counsels Job to do, but neither does his faulty advice negate the

rather than as a person in pain who needs support. As a result, Bildad comes across with a condescending tone that only makes Job hurt all the more. In his enthusiasm for stating the correct answer, Bildad overlooks his original purpose, which was to comfort his friend (2:11). Similarly, when we minister to people in pain, we must remember that though we may not be able to solve the problem, we can always salve the person.

Bildad builds his case through three means: by the application of rigorous logical thought, by an appeal to traditional teaching, and by the use of analogies from the natural world. These kinds of arguments can sound very convincing, but to be accurate they need to be relevant to the situation that they address. All three lines of quality of his teaching about God's commitment to justice.

Illustrating the Text

Even a logical analysis of a situation may fall short of the whole picture of God's truth.

Literature: *Hard Times*, **by Charles Dickens.** In British author Dickens's (1812–70) novel *Hard Times* (1854), he was concerned with pointing out, in ironic ways, the flaws of the extreme utilitarians of his day. He described them as "see[ing] figures and averages, and nothing else."[1] Mr. Gradgrind, the infamous schoolmaster in the story, is described as "eminently practical." In fact, Gradgrind wants practically nothing but data; he is obsessed with facts and statistics and so seems "square" both personally and physically. Much like Bildad in Job, Gradgrind focuses exclusively on the facts, leaving no room for the more human aspects of the education of his students, those things that would connect them to their souls and spirits and to the relationship-filled world in which they must live. God's truth is whole and round, not square and truncated, to continue the metaphor used above. It includes reason as well as imagination, and incorporates mind, body, and spirit: it is multidimensional.

Book: *Unchristian*, **by David Kinnaman and Gabe Lyons.** The recent study by Kinnaman and Lyons of the Barna Group, *Unchristian* (2007), documents the great disconnects between what Christians believe and how they behave. Their research is on the thoughts, attitudes, and beliefs of sixteen- to twenty-nine-year-olds on issues of faith, theology, and morality. What is particularly striking is that outsiders perceive these Christians to be "unchristian." Like Bildad, Christians often articulate good theology but then fail to apply the theology accurately to life.

Quote: *Reflections on the Psalms*, **by C. S. Lewis.** In this series of reflections, Lewis writes about Christ's teaching that it is "not given us in that cut-and-dried, fool-proof, systematic fashion we might have expected or desired. . . . We cannot reduce them to a system. . . . His teaching cannot be grasped by the intellect alone."[2]

Good theology may be mixed with inaccurate application, prescribing a cure before diagnosing the disease.

Medical Stories: Many stories exist of doctors who have operated improperly or who have administered the wrong medicines because of misdiagnosis, mistakes that can have dire consequences. Such an illustration is not used to point the finger at the medical profession but to make this point: the diagnosis—physical, emotional, or spiritual—must be made astutely before prescribing the cure.

Military History: Both the Bay of Pigs invasion of Cuba (1961) under President John F. Kennedy and the Battle of Mogadishu (1993) during President Bill Clinton's presidency ranged from unsuccessful to partially unsuccessful because of incomplete knowledge or problematic diagnosis. The result was loss of life for many. The Battle of Mogadishu inspired a book (1999) by Mark Bowden and a film (2001), both named *Blackhawk Down*.

Job Considers a Legal Dispute with God

Big Idea *Job wants God to declare him righteous, but he cannot envision how to bring this about.*

Understanding the Text

The Text in Context

In chapters 9 and 10, Job takes up the challenge made by Bildad in 8:5 to plead with the Almighty. As he contemplates this possibility, Job focuses on his legal status before God. In this speech he begins to work out in his mind how he might approach God with his situation, and how God might respond to him. In his soliloquy in chapter 9, Job turns over in his mind whether he should enter a legal complaint as a plaintiff against God (cf. Jer. 12:1–4), because God appears to be almost arbitrary in his treatment of humans. As he thinks this through, Job finds himself left with three unsatisfying alternatives. Job could drop his complaint against God (9:27–28), but then he would not have the opportunity to be declared innocent by God. Job could try to purify himself (9:29–31), but he senses that this would still not satisfy God's requirements. Or Job could find an impartial arbiter to mediate the case (9:32–35), but where could he find a suitable person to fill this role? Throughout the book, Job considers other legal strategies, until he finally uses the tactic of negative confession as he places his case in God's hand in chapter 31.

Historical and Cultural Background

Job's hymn extolling the wisdom and power of God (9:5–10), followed by his reflection on that theme in the next few verses, alludes to several familiar ancient Near Eastern mythological motifs. The description of God treading on the waves of the sea (9:8) pictures God subjecting his enemy by stepping on its back, as in the Ugaritic literature Baal breaks the power of Yamm (the sea). The reference to four constellations in 9:9 parallels the advanced study of astronomy in ancient Mesopotamia and Egypt, where the stars were thought to represent fate, but in the Bible Yahweh is superior to the stars, because he was the one who created them and who calls them by name (Isa. 40:26). In 9:13, Rahab, as Leviathan and Tannin in other passages in Job, is cited as a symbol of chaos that was conquered decisively by Yahweh (Job 26:12; Ps. 89:10; Isa. 51:9).

Interpretive Insights

9:2 *how can mere mortals prove their innocence before God?* As he begins this speech, Job acknowledges that what Bildad just said in 8:20–22 is true, but then he poses again Eliphaz's question in 4:17. Whereas Eliphaz made the point that no human can be regarded as just by God, Job's personal experience prompts him to ask a somewhat different question: How can an innocent man like himself be legally vindicated before God if God is unwilling to bless him as the retribution principle insists he should?

9:3 *they could not answer him one time out of a thousand.* The language of this phrase is ambiguous, and commentators have taken it in two opposite ways. The NIV reading suggests that human finiteness puts one who disputes with God at a decided disadvantage. Later on, in Job 38–41, Job cannot answer a single question posed by Yahweh. Alternatively and perhaps better, the subject could be taken to refer to God rather

- Job acknowledges the transcendent wisdom and power of God.
- Job realizes he cannot summon God to clear him.
- Job's experience prompts him to question how God treats humans.
- Job can see no good alternative to resolve his situation.

than to Job. In that case, God as the defendant would not answer Job, the human plaintiff, one time out of a thousand. In this interpretation, Job is lamenting that God would refuse to answer his questions, and Job could not compel him to do so.

9:5–6 *He moves the mountains without their knowing it.* As the psalmist does in Psalm 46, Job here portrays God as towering over the natural world (see also Job 26:7–14). The mountains represent the most impregnable feature of nature, but God can move them at will. The description in 9:5–6 may well refer to volcanic eruptions (cf. Pss. 18:7; 97:5; 104:32; 144:5). Similar language is used in Psalms 18:6–15 and 29:3–11 to speak of Yahweh's powerful intervention on behalf of his people in their affliction, but here Job derives no such comfort from the awesome power of God over nature.

John Walton has suggested an alternative to the NIV reading "moves the mountains."[1] He argues that the Hebrew expression is better rendered "traverses the mountains," and that in the second line of this verse God overturns those who resist him (v. 4), even if it requires that God surprise them by passing over what seem to be impassable mountain regions. Both of these readings fit well into the teaching of the book of Job, but the second alternative is more closely aligned with the theme of divine judgment in Job 9.

9:10–12 *He performs wonders that cannot be fathomed.* Job agrees with Eliphaz (5:9) that God's power is beyond measurement. Therefore, if Job were to lodge a legal complaint against God, he would have to contend with the transcendent sovereign of the universe, which is an intimidating prospect indeed! This thought stands behind Job's question in verse 2, "How can mere mortals prove their innocence before God?" It is ironic that Job is endeavoring to fathom the unfathomable work of God in his personal experience.

9:14 *How then can I dispute with him?* Job is convinced that he is innocent (v. 15), but he cannot envision how he could win in God's court. He feels that he would not be able to answer God's questions (9:15), secure a legal hearing (9:16), or maintain his stand under the barrage of God's words (9:17–18). Like a first-year law student arguing a case before the Supreme Court, Job is not up to the challenge of that high level of judicial proceedings.

9:15 *I could only plead with my Judge for mercy.* Job's insistence on his integrity and his recognition of God's supremacy leave him with few alternatives. He could not consider admitting to sin, because that would mean abandoning what he knows to be the truth. He could not compel God to declare him righteous. All he could do would be to plead to God against God, knowing that God is judging his case. In this strange legal case that Job is contemplating, God in effect is functioning as prosecutor, defendant, judge, and jury at the same time.

9:17–18 *He would crush me with a storm.* In the prologue, a storm killed Job's children (1:19). As Job looks to the future, he can envision only more of the same treatment by God, because he feels that he is under divine attack (6:4; 7:20). Although Job anticipates that the situation will only get worse for him, when the storm he fears actually arrives at last, Yahweh speaks from it to Job (the Hebrew term for "storm" in 9:17 is nearly identical to the word in 38:1 and 40:6). What Job here views with anxiety eventually will become the setting for the restoration of God's blessing to him.

9:19–20 *who can challenge him?* Job reasons that he has no possibility of successfully litigating his complaint against God. Even if he is in the right, he cannot force God to vindicate him. Because humans are not equal to God, they have no leverage to compel him to appear in court.

9:21 *Although I am blameless.* Using the same term as in 1:1, 8; 2:3, Job insists that he is blameless. In contrast to his friends, who demand that he confess his sin, Job consistently maintains that his sin is not the issue prompting his catastrophe (10:7; 13:23; 23:11–12). Job, however, cannot prove his innocence or get God to clear his name. He resigns himself to what appears inevitable, even though it is unsatisfying to him.

9:22–23 *He destroys both the blameless and the wicked.* Job rejects the simplistic assertion by Bildad in 8:20 that God does not reject the blameless person or support evildoers. To Job, it appears that God destroys humans regardless of their moral condition, and this may be why Yahweh later describes Job as one who obscures his plans (38:2). Job longs for life to run according to just standards; he, like the others, wants the retribution formula to work! However, his personal experience does not fit the retribution principle. The tension between God's sovereign and just rule and Job's apparently arbitrary experience of adversity produces deep dissonance in Job's mind, because he cannot reconcile those two conflicting realities.

9:24 *If it is not he, then who is it?* Job cannot conceive either how the just God could treat the blameless and the wicked alike, or how anyone else could thwart God's justice. Because Job has no awareness of the dispute between Yahweh and the adversary in the prologue, God appears to him as arbitrary and capricious in his treatment of humans.

9:25 *My days are swifter than a runner.* In one respect Job's pain seems to slow his life to a crawl (7:4). But his life also seems to be slipping away quickly without any progress. Job has the bitter sense that his life will soon be over without any resolution to his adversity or answers to his questions.

9:26 *They skim past like boats of papyrus.* Boats constructed from papyrus were very light and fast (cf. Isa. 18:1–2), but they were also fragile and easily destroyed. Job's life under affliction bears both of those traits.

9:30–31 *Even if I washed myself with soap and . . . with cleansing powder.* The terms "soap" and "cleansing powder" indicate two very strong cleansing agents, soapwort and lye (cf. Isa. 1:25; Mal. 3:2). Using these rather than the typical water or oil is like cleaning up with ammonia and bleach. Even such extreme measures, however, would not be sufficient to make

Job feels that no amount of scrubbing will make him acceptable to God (9:30). Washing to make oneself ritually pure was an important practice in the ancient world. Here is a bath with an interior seat that was found at Tel Dan, Israel (ninth century BC). It may have been used for ritual immersion and purification.

Job clean before God (cf. Jer. 2:22), because Job feels that nothing would be able to render him acceptable to God (9:31).

9:33–34 *If only there were someone to mediate between us.* Job and his friends all share similar conceptions about the heavenly beings. Eliphaz refers to the holy ones (5:1), and Elihu speaks of a mediating angel to deliver humans (33:23–28). In 16:19 Job will contemplate a heavenly witness who could advocate for his cause. Here in 9:33, Job longs for a third party, likely a heavenly being, who could listen both to him and to God, and then make a judgment as an umpire between the two disputants. In effect, this mediator would function like a referee breaking up two boxers who are clinched together in a bout.

9:35 *Then I would speak up without fear of him.* Job feels intimidated by God, because God seems to be hostile in his punishment of Job. Job fears additional divine disapproval if he were to speak his mind. Only if God's affliction were to be removed from him (9:34) would Job feel free to speak fearlessly about God.

Theological Insights

The legal language and the image of a trial that permeate Job 9 are found frequently in the Old Testament prophets as well. In most cases, Yahweh initiates a lawsuit against his sinful people (cf. Isa. 1:2–26; Mic. 6:1–4). Here, however, Job contemplates taking

Job acknowledges that God made and rules over the world when he says that God is the "Maker of the Bear and Orion, [and] the Pleiades" (9:6). The Pleiades is a very bright cluster of stars in the constellation Taurus. It is depicted by the seven circles in the top left of this modern impression from a Mesopotamian cylinder seal.

the role of the plaintiff filing a legal complaint against God, just as Jeremiah does in Jeremiah 12:1–4.

The description of God's wisdom and power in Job 9:5–10 parallels closely the psalms of descriptive praise (e.g., Ps. 145), and in particular the nature psalms (e.g., Ps. 104). Throughout the Bible, God is presented as both the creator of and the sovereign over the world of nature. Nature, then, does not function independently of God but is subject to his control. God both made the world and rules over it.

Teaching the Text

In teaching this chapter, one must take care to explain that Job's candid words reflect accurately what he feels and thinks, but they do not necessarily provide a pattern for how godly people should respond to their adversities. In the context of the whole book, Job's perceptions of God in chapter 9 are later corrected when Yahweh at last speaks to Job and restores him to blessing. Nevertheless, at this point in the action, Job wants God to declare him righteous, but Job cannot envision how to bring this about.

The conflict in Job's mind emerges when his theology and his experience collide. On the one hand, his theology correctly teaches that God is transcendent in his wisdom and power. But on the other hand, Job's experience of adversity, even though he is blameless, prompts questions he cannot answer. Like many Christians who experience pain, Job cannot resolve in his mind how God could be all-wise and all-powerful and yet could allow a righteous human to suffer so badly. Those who experience great physical and psychological pain often struggle with deep theological doubts as well.

Part of Job's frustration is that he cannot compel God to clear his name from the false accusations of his friends. As a human, Job cannot force Almighty God to fulfill his personal agenda, even though he desperately wants God to act on his behalf. In fact, Job can see no good alternative to resolve his situation. As the rest of the book will go on to indicate, the resolution he desires will come only at God's time and in God's way. Job has to learn to live in humble dependence on God, even though he cannot understand or appreciate what God is doing in his life. We, too, must learn to trust God when we cannot understand what he has brought into our experience or how he will answer our questions and calm our fears.

Illustrating the Text

Our spirits are conflicted when our theology and our experience collide.

Quote: *Disappointment with God*, by Philip Yancey.

I found that for many people there is a large gap between what they *expect* from

their Christian faith and what they actually experience. From a steady diet of books, sermons, and personal testimonies, all promising triumph and success, they learn to expect dramatic evidence of God working in their lives. If they do not . . . they feel disappointment, betrayal, and often guilt.[2]

Literature: *The Trial*, by Franz Kafka. In *The Trial* (1925), German writer Franz Kafka (1923–84) draws the portrait of a character called Joseph K., who is imprisoned and then prosecuted by an authority who is detached and incommunicative. Furthermore, what crime Joseph K. has committed is never made clear to him or the reader. Joseph K. feels totally unable to get a just hearing, a reality that leads him to despair. Even his uncle, who is initially sympathetic, grows apathetic, and an individual who is supposed to be his advocate eventually mocks him. This might be the way Job feels in chapter 9.

Poetry: Saint John of the Cross (1542–91) was a Spanish mystic and a Carmelite friar and priest who learned from his mother and father the beauty and significance of sacrificial love. In fact, John's father abandoned riches and reputation when he married out of his social class, which caused his family to disown him. John experienced much poverty and suffering growing up, but he gave his life for others. In his poems, he is always honest and sometimes expresses the hiddenness of God in his life.

What Job Wants to Tell God

Big Idea *Job wants to tell God how he feels wrongfully judged.*

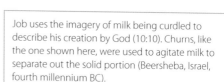

Understanding the Text

The Text in Context

Job is continuing the response to Bildad that he began in chapter 9. In chapter 10, Job speaks out of the bitterness of his soul (10:1), and he expresses what he would say to God if given the opportunity (10:2–19). Job, however, is pessimistic that God would acquit him, because God's treatment of Job seems to have turned the retribution principle on its head. Because Job perceives the character of God through the lens of his personal experience, what he sees in God is distorted, leading Job to question if God is good after all. Discouraged by this thought, Job just wants God to leave him alone, if only briefly, before he dies (10:20–22). When Job is finally granted the opportunity to speak directly to God in 40:3–5 and 42:1–6, his answer is profoundly different from what he envisions here in Job 10.

Historical and Cultural Background

As Job discusses how God fashioned his body, in 10:10 he uses an image that is also employed in part in the apocryphal

Job uses the imagery of milk being curdled to describe his creation by God (10:10). Churns, like the one shown here, were used to agitate milk to separate out the solid portion (Beersheba, Israel, fourth millennium BC).

Wisdom of Solomon 7:1–2. Job pictures God as pouring out semen like milk and then causing it to congeal like cheese to form the embryo from which Job developed. In 10:21–22, Job once again (cf. 3:4–9) pictures death as a place of gloom and darkness, an image found in many ancient Near Eastern texts.

Interpretive Insights

10:1 *I loathe my very life.* In chapter 10, Job intensifies his rhetoric as he gives full rein to his complaint. Echoing his earlier description in 7:11, Job speaks to God out of his deep and painful emotion. In contrast to Bildad, who clinically analyzed Job's suffering as punishment for sin, Job expresses himself in highly emotional language. Bitterness has penetrated his *nepesh*, his inner being, causing Job to feel fearful, frustrated, angry, and disappointed. He now determines to take all of these strong emotions to God as he presents his legal case to him.

10:2 *tell me what charges you have against me.* In chapter 9, Job envisioned being a plaintiff against God, not realizing that the prologue has revealed that the adversary is the prosecutor in this situation and God is the defendant. In this chapter, Job views God as the prosecutor and himself as the defendant. He feels condemned by God, and he cannot understand why God would condemn him. Job, therefore, rehearses what he wants to say to God should he have the opportunity. Because Job cannot fathom why God has condemned him to suffering, he pleads with God to state explicitly how he is guilty.

10:3–4 *Does it please you to oppress me . . . while you smile on the plans of the wicked?* Job's questions to God in 10:3–4 anticipate Yahweh's inquisition of Job in chapters 38–41, but what Job asks is paltry by comparison. Elsewhere in the Bible, "oppress" is used to refer to the harsh mistreatment of people God condemns (Ezek. 22:29; Amos 4:1). Similarly, Psalm 5:4 states that God does not take pleasure in evil. However, in Job's case God seems to violate his own righteous character, not to mention the retribution principle that Job previously accepted. Job senses that God has spurned him, and this calls into question all that Job believes about the character and conduct of God.

10:7 *you know that I am not guilty.* Mere humans, like Job's three friends, can make wrong judgments (10:4–6), but the all-knowing God cannot. Job is confident that the omniscient God knows full well that Job is not guilty. Nevertheless, God has not treated Job as though he is innocent. In Deuteronomy 32:39 and Isaiah 43:13 the expression "no one can deliver out of my hand" refers to the finality of God's judgment. By using the same Hebrew phrase here ("no one can rescue me from your hand"; 10:7) Job reflects his own feeling of hopelessness before the divine judge.

10:8–12 *Your hands shaped and made me.* Job acknowledges that God has fashioned him with great care and skill (10:9–12; cf. Ps. 139:13–16; Jer. 18:5–12). What should have been a great comfort actually causes Job to feel threatened by God, because God seems to be destroying what he has crafted so expertly. Job cannot comprehend why God would turn so diametrically against him. He has no knowledge of the fact that it is the adversary who has incited Yahweh to destroy Job without cause (2:3).

10:13–14 *But this is what you concealed in your heart.* In these verses Job takes a sharp turn away from God's past beneficent action that providentially made and protected him and instead focuses on the pain that he is experiencing in the present.

Job reasons that God's treatment of him demonstrates that behind God's apparent care he has a hidden, sinister agenda. While appearing to show Job kindness, God actually is scrutinizing him in order to dig up incriminating evidence to justify destroying him. Job suspects that God's past blessing does not indicate how God really feels toward him. By these words, Job reveals that his adversity has seriously distorted how he views God.

10:15–16 *Even if I am innocent, I cannot lift my head.* Despite his blamelessness, Job feels full of disgrace and robbed of all his dignity. He senses that regardless of his guilt or innocence, God would be against him all the same. Even if he were to stand tall and unashamed in the face of his adversity, God would hunt him like a lion (10:16; lion hunting was a common sport of ancient Near Eastern kings).

Job feels as though God is stalking him like a lion (10:16). This Assyrian relief shows a lion pursuing the chariot of King Ashurnasirpal (palace at Nimrud, 865–860 BC).

10:18–19 *Why then did you bring me out of the womb?* The emphasis of this rhetorical question is on "you." Job asks why God, the one who so carefully crafted him (10:8–11), would bring him out of the womb only to experience such shameful suffering. With these bitter words Job expresses his deep frustration with how God has treated him. He wants to keep holding on to God, but his confidence in God has been severely shaken. As in 3:11–16, Job wishes that he had been stillborn rather than born only to endure adversity.

10:20 *Turn away from me so I can have a moment's joy.* Job feels that the intimidating presence of God has destroyed his capacity for joy. Like a prisoner on death row granted the final delight of a special meal before his execution, Job calls on God to relent and give him a few days of peace before his death (cf. 7:16).

10:21–22 *the land of gloom and utter darkness.* In the concluding two verses of this chapter, Job uses five parallel terms to emphasize the darkness of death. The

expression "utter darkness" is the same Hebrew term used in Psalm 23:4 to speak of an intense shadow that cannot be penetrated by light. As far as Job can tell, there is nothing inviting or pleasurable in death (see the sidebar). Nevertheless, as gloomy as is the prospect of death, Job considers it far preferable to the misery and frustration that his life under adversity offers to him.

Theological Insights

Job's extended portrayal of God's shaping of his body (10:8–11) can be compared with Psalm 139:13–16. In the psalm, God's intimate care for the person he has fashioned prompts the psalmist to turn toward God to appeal for his intervention during a time of affliction (Ps. 139:19–22). By contrast, Job's experience of adversity has caused him to recoil from the God who fashioned him but who now seems bent on destroying him.

Teaching the Text

When people are upset about an injustice, they may well rehearse in their minds what they would say if given the opportunity to speak to someone who could make a difference. That is what Job does in chapter 10, as he expresses his inner thoughts of what he wants to say to God (10:2). In this chapter it is clear that Job wants to tell God how he feels wrongfully judged by him. As we read this chapter, we are able to overhear what is going on in Job's mind and heart as he endures his severe adversity.

Job feels condemned by God, but he cannot understand what charges God has against him. Many people are blind to their own sins, but this is not the case for Job, for

> ### Death and Hope
>
> In the Old Testament, death is regularly described as a place of gloom and darkness (cf. Job 38:17). Death is full of sorrow (Ps. 116:3) and inactivity (Eccles. 9:10) and is devoid of the praise of God (Pss. 30:9; 115:17). In the New Testament, the resurrection of Jesus introduces the expectation of hope beyond the grave (cf. Paul's argument in 1 Cor. 15:20–28, 35–58). Old Testament believers like Job, however, did not have the benefit of knowing what the New Testament was to elucidate later.

the prologue three times describes him as blameless. No doubt Job has searched his life for anything that could possibly have displeased God, but he can come up with nothing to explain the extreme suffering he has received. This calls into question the validity of the retribution principle, that God blesses the righteous and punishes the wicked. As far as Job can see, God is pleased to oppress him even though he has been righteous, and at the same time God smiles on the schemes of the wicked. Job cannot understand how this can be right.

Job's continual affliction makes him feel judged by God, even though he knows, and he is confident that God also knows, that he is not guilty. Job's experience causes him to perceive God as probing mercilessly to dig up sin in his life, even though Job is not conscious that he has sinned at all.

In one of the most emotionally wrenching passages of the book, Job contrasts the care with which God formed his body from the time of his conception through his birth with God's present hostile attitude, since God seems determined to destroy him. In other words, the God who has previously shown great tenderness and love now seems to be antagonistic toward Job. Job's pain has prompted him to view God negatively rather than to remember that God does not change in his character and plan.

Adversity can bring a person to his or her knees, either in prayer or in despair. In this candid disclosure of Job's feelings, he comes to the point that he longs for death rather than a continuance of what appears senseless suffering. Job can see no way forward, so he looks for the only way out, in death.

As we read this chapter, it is crucial to remember that there is much more to come in the book of Job. Job 10 accurately communicates how Job is feeling at this time in his adversity, but it is not the final answer for Job or for us today. To get to that answer, Job will have to endure his pain for a while longer, but at the end his faith in God will be renewed. Even though he feels hopeless at this time, he will learn that his hope in God will not be in vain. In that he serves as an example for Christians who are weighed down with adversity and questioning whether God still cares for them.

Aphrodite, the goddess of love, has control over both mortals and immortals and wields her power in what can often be read as fickle ways. She is able to cause attraction between almost any two individuals and sometimes takes delight in making a god/goddess fall in love with a human or vice versa, sometimes in troubling ways or for petty reasons. Zeus uses his powerful weapon, the thunderbolt, in equally capricious ways.

In 10:8–9, Job asks God why, after carefully molding him like clay, God would want to destroy him. The idea of shaping the life and destiny of people is illustrated by this Egyptian relief, which shows the god Khnum next to his potter's wheel and his finished creation (Khnum Temple, Esna, Egypt).

Illustrating the Text

We may question God's goodness, even while we understand that he fashioned us.

Greek Mythology: The Greek myths often depict gods and goddesses as shifting between supporting humans and working against them, just as Job feels in 10:8. For example,

Demonstration: Job's image of God's molding him like clay reflects the work of a potter. A video clip or live demonstration of a potter at work could bring this analogy to life for the audience. While this image is often used (almost overused), it is seldom shown.

Like Job, we may feel condemned by God and even wish to die.

Film: *The Green Mile.* In this great and enduringly popular film (1999) based on a Stephen King (b. 1947) novel, John Coffey is a black inmate on death row condemned unjustly to the electric chair. Knowing the beauty of Coffey's spirit, one watches agonizingly as he is mistreated. Surely, John Coffey's pain is like Job's in some measure.

News Story: Several high-stakes and very tense trials have taken place before the watching public in recent years. The acquittals of O. J. Simpson and of Casey Anthony are examples of the stark disparity that can occur between public perception of guilt and the legal decision that is handed down by the jury. Job, too, insists that he is innocent, even though his friends are convinced that he is guilty before God.

Literature: *The Trial of God*, by Elie Wiesel. *The Trial of God* is a play by Jewish-American writer, Nobel Prize winner, and Holocaust survivor Elie Wiesel. Wiesel has written many novels and works in other genres, among them *Night*, a memoir about his horrendous experience in a number of concentration camps, an account that includes the death of his father. In *The Trial of God*, Wiesel gives us an idea of the provenance of the *din torah* ("judgment according to the Torah"): "Its genesis: inside the kingdom of night, I witnessed a strange trial. Three rabbis—all erudite and pious men—decided one winter evening to indict God for allowing his children to be massacred. I remember: I was there, and I felt like crying. But nobody cried."[1] The dilemmas of this play have often been compared to the book of Job.

Nonfiction: *Tuesdays with Morrie*, by **Mitch Albom.** In this best-selling narrative, American journalist and broadcaster Mitch Albom portrays an elderly man in pain who expresses his longing for the relief that death will bring. Although Morrie's circumstances are different from Job's, his emotions illustrate well what Job is feeling in 10:20–22.

Zophar Rejects Job's Complaints

Big Idea *Zophar dismisses Job's complaints as illogical.*

Understanding the Text

The Text in Context

In their first responses to Job, Eliphaz appeals to experience and personal revelation (Job 4–5), Bildad adduces traditional teaching (Job 8), and Zophar applies strict deductive logic to evaluate Job's situation (Job 11). Zophar seems to be the most curt and insensitive of the three friends in speaking to Job. By taking the retribution principle to its logical conclusion, Zophar insists that suffering necessarily proceeds from sin. Sounding very confident of his reasoning, as though speaking for God (11:6), Zophar observes that since Job is suffering, he necessarily must have sinned (11:1–6). He praises God's unlimited wisdom, implying Job's foolishness by comparison (11:7–12). If Job would just repent, then God would restore him to blessing

As a sign of their humility and supplication, ancient Near Eastern worshipers are often portrayed with their hands raised. Here, the Assyrian king Tukulti-Ninurta (1243–1207 BC) is shown with an upraised arm as he both stands and kneels before a representation of the god Nusku.

(11:13–20). Like Bildad, Zophar is an abstract theologian who has little pastoral instinct. He misconstrues Job's problem, so he makes an erroneous prescription to him.

Historical and Cultural Background

In 11:13 Zophar encourages Job to stretch out his hands to God. In ancient Near Eastern art, praying worshipers are often portrayed raising their hands as a sign of their humility and supplication. This action is found elsewhere in the Old Testament (Ezra 9:5; Pss. 28:2; 143:6; Jer. 4:31), and Paul also exhorts it in the New Testament (1 Tim. 2:8).

Interpretive Insights

11:2 *Are all these words to go unanswered?* Zophar perceives that Eliphaz and Bildad have not adequately answered Job, so he determines to take up the challenge. In fact, he regards it as his moral duty to uphold God's justice by silencing Job's arguments. Zophar impatiently dismisses Job's lengthy speeches as "all these words," implying that the quantity of one's words does not measure the quality of one's insight. In wisdom literature, speaking many words is often connected with folly rather than with wisdom (Prov. 10:19; 17:27; Eccles. 5:2). Thus, by his rhetorical question in verse 2 Zophar implies that he regards Job as a fool who talks too much.

11:3 *Will your idle talk reduce others to silence?* Zophar rejects Job's words as so much empty rhetoric rather than substantive argument. In his view, what Job says is mere babbling as Job tries to keep talking until the others concede to him by their silence. Zophar, then, attempts to shame Job into accepting what the friends have alleged about him. Ironically, in the third cycle of speeches, it is Zophar who is reduced to silence and who does not participate in the final round in chapter 27.

11:4 *You say to God, ". . . I am pure in your sight."* As Zophar purports to quote Job's words to God, he adds to what Job said in 9:20–21 and 10:7, and he ascribes negative motives to him. Job has said that he is *tam*, blameless, but Zophar substitutes the term *bar*, which refers to sinlessness (NIV: "pure"). By exaggerating Job's claim, Zophar renders a portrayal of him that is inaccurate, careless, and even cruel.

11:5–6 *God has even forgotten some of your sin.* Zophar speaks as though he can read God's thoughts. He predicts that if God were to speak as Job desired, then he would say that Job actually deserves far more punishment than he has received

(see the sidebar). Zophar's implication, then, is that instead of complaining, Job should be grateful for God's leniency toward him. Zophar evaluates the situation in solely theological terms, and he seems devoid of any personal compassion. He appears to have little sensitivity to Job's profound pain.

11:7–8 *Can you fathom the mysteries of God? . . . What can you know?* In 10:13 Job suggested that he knows God's thoughts that lie behind his actions toward him. Zophar, however, exaggerates what Job said into a claim that Job thinks that he knows all that God knows. Zophar's questions in verses 7–8, then, are an aggressive rhetorical attack against Job rather than genuine questions for Job to answer. By posing these questions as he does, Zophar intends to belittle Job rather than to help him. Later, in chapters 38–41, when Yahweh asks Job many questions, his purpose is to educate Job, not to humiliate him as Zophar does.

11:12 *the witless can no more become wise.* In this verse, Zophar likely uses an ancient proverb to drive home his point that it is impossible for a stubborn person like Job to become wise, just as a wild donkey cannot give birth to a human. By this cheap rhetorical shot, Zophar as much as calls Job an incorrigible idiot who cannot attain wisdom. He implies that Job functions at below the human level.

If Only God Would Speak!

In 9:16 and 10:2, Job expressed his desire that God would speak to him. This desire continues to grow in the book, until in his final confession in 31:35 Job calls on God to answer both his complaint and the indictment that has been lodged against him. In 11:5, Zophar expresses his own wish that God would speak, because he is confident that God would prove correct Zophar's assessment of Job. Little does Zophar realize that when Yahweh eventually gives his assessment of the case in 42:7–8, he will find Zophar and the other friends inaccurate in what they have alleged about Job.

11:13–14 *if you devote your heart to him.* Zophar here turns from accusing Job to exhorting him with the tone of a prophet. Following the examples of Eliphaz and Bildad, Zophar pleads with Job to repent of his sin. This counsel implies that Job's heart is not directed toward God. Using strict cause-and-effect logic, Zophar says that if Job would repent (11:13–14), then God would restore blessing to him (11:15–19). This repentance would need to include both Job's private life (heart) and his public life (hands).

11:15 *then, free of fault, you will lift up your face.* According to Zophar, it is Job's sin that has caused him to lose his standing before God. For Zophar, the answer to this problem is simple: Job needs to repent of his sin. Job's repentance will enable him to stand up in God's presence (in contrast with Job's complaint in 10:15–16). The term "fault" indicates a blemish or a disfigurement. This likely refers primarily to Job's purported moral shame before the holy God, but secondarily it could also relate to Job's hideous physical disfigurement

(2:7–8; 7:5), which is one of the aspects of his adversity.

11:17 *Life will be brighter than noonday.* At the end of his previous speech, Job reflected on his prospect of a dark and gloomy death (10:21–22). By contrast, Zophar declares that Job's repentance will result in a life of brilliant light. In the Near East, the noonday sun is especially intense and bright.

11:20 *their hope will become a dying gasp.* In contrast to the hopeful conclusions by Eliphaz (5:25–26) and Bildad (8:20–22), Zophar's first speech closes on a decidedly negative note as he describes the fate of the wicked and implicitly warns Job about his impending doom. Job said in 7:6 that his

Zophar encourages Job to stretch out his hands to God and repent (11:13). In this Egyptian painting, the priest Renpetmaa raises his arms as he prays to the god Ra-Horakhty (Twenty-Second Dynasty, tenth century BC).

days are speeding by without hope, and Zophar has spoken in 11:18 about the hope of the repentant person, but here he indicates that there is no hope for people like Job who refuse to repent. By speaking in the third person rather than directly to Job, Zophar betrays his impersonal approach to Job and his pain. To Zophar, Job is more a predictable case study than a person in anguish.

Theological Insights

Like the other speakers in the book, Zophar extols the transcendence of God. For Zophar, God's exalted status means that Job cannot know his ways, in contrast to Psalm 8, in which the psalmist draws strength and comfort from the fact that the God of creation knows and cares for humans. Zophar's counsel to Job to direct his heart to God and to put away sin in his life (11:13–14) compares well to the wisdom exhortation in Proverbs 3:7 (cf. also Pss. 34:14; 37:27; Eccles. 12:13) to fear the Lord and turn from evil. Zophar's theology is in many points orthodox, but he does not apply it appropriately to Job's specific situation.

Teaching the Text

Job's three friends are increasingly insensitive in what they say to Job. As the third speaker, Zophar takes the retribution principle to its logical conclusion, and he uses it to dismiss Job's complaints as invalid. Instead of truly feeling Job's pain and understanding his thinking, Zophar responds to him with impersonal, abstract reasoning. As a result, he proves to be of little comfort to his friend. Zophar, then, is an example of how *not* to minister to a friend in great need.

Although Zophar heard what Job said in his earlier speeches, he did not listen carefully enough to grasp Job's true meaning. Consequently, he has distorted what Job said to God, making Job sound as though he thinks he is perfect before God. Apparently Zophar is so intent on correcting Job that he twists what Job has said into a caricature that can be brushed aside. By this, Zophar demonstrates that good counsel requires careful listening rather than jumping to conclusions that are not supported by the facts.

By emphasizing the transcendence of God, Zophar comes to the logical conclusion that God's wisdom is so exalted above humans that God has actually given to Job only part of the punishment that his sin truly deserves. Zophar gives no evidence from Job's life to support this audacious claim; rather, he derives it as a logical corollary of his view of God. In actual fact, Yahweh himself has disclosed in the prologue how highly he values Job's integrity, but Zophar's tidy logical system does not lead to this conclusion. In other words, Zophar is more committed to the logic of his theological system than to the accuracy of the conclusion that it has produced. In his assessment of Job, Zophar is in fact wrong, despite what his logic maintains.

In keeping with his logic, Zophar points Job in the direction of repentance. The retribution principle holds that bad things happen to sinful people and that only a change of heart can lead someone away from folly and its destination of death to wisdom and its destination of life. Through the lens of his theology, Zophar sees this as a clear-cut case. However, he misses the special circumstances of Job's situation, so his counsel to repent is both off the mark and painful to the friend whom he has set out to help.

Zophar is accurate in his contrast between the hope of the righteous and the hopelessness of the wicked. Throughout the Bible the two ways that lead to life and death are often set before humans, who are challenged to choose life. Zophar's logic, however, has blinded him to the fact that Job has chosen the path of wisdom that leads to life, even though by all appearances he has somehow ended up at the destination to which folly leads. Zophar's counsel to repent is precisely what many people in adversity need to heed, but it does not fit Job's special case.

Illustrating the Text

God's wisdom properly weighs the circumstances of a person's suffering, even when human critics do not.

Literature: *Les Misérables*, by Victor Hugo. In this beloved work, one of the unforgettable characters is Inspector Javert, who throughout the novel relentlessly hunts down the poignant central character Jean Valjean. In Javert's obsession with duty at the expense of compassion, he becomes a maniacal, avenging force. Like Zophar, he does not

This sign at the entrance to Auschwitz, the notorious German concentration camp, proclaims, "*Arbeit macht frei*" ("Work makes [one] free"). These words, like Zophar's, completely dismiss complaints by applying impersonal, abstract reasoning.

take into account the circumstances of the person he hunts. In the musical based on Hugo's novel, Javert's fierceness and rigidity are especially exemplified by his song "Stars."

Contrasting Concept: Take time to point out that the converse of the above statement is also true: God weighs the circumstances of a person's apparent blessing and success properly, even when human admirers do not. One only has to look to the daily news to find examples of people once idolized by millions in whom corruption is subsequently exposed and whose success comes to nothing, even in this world. Point out that God is not mocked, and both the doggedly pursued innocent and the allegedly charmed charlatan are fully known to him and will both be fully loved and disciplined with infallible wisdom.

Biblical wisdom is slow to diagnose the cause behind adversity and open to the possibility of righteous suffering.

Bible: Take a moment to sketch out a few profiles of Bible characters who suffered for being righteous or obedient (Abel, Jeremiah, Stephen, Mary, etc.). In each case you cite, describe first how society perceived that person at the time, and then what the Bible reveals to us about God's diagnosis of that character's righteousness and the redemptive value of the suffering. End by pointing out the fallacy of the retribution principle by stating that if all sufferers are being punished for their own sin, then Jesus should never have hung on a cross.

Stories: Consider sharing a story about someone you know whose suffering was largely misunderstood. Try to stay away from celebrities or notorious persons about whom your listeners may already have an opinion. The main point of this story should be transformation you actually experienced in your understanding of that person and how an initial mistrust or sense of judgment you felt based on his or her suffering gave way to respect and compassion once you learned the truth about his or her situation.

Gospel Highlight: This is a great time to point out the way in which God made him who knew no sin to be sin for our sake. Consider reading the passage from Isaiah 53 about the Suffering Servant, and ask listeners to consider how others to whom they minister may actually be "filling up what is lacking in Christ's afflictions" (Col. 1:24) or sharing "abundantly in Christ's sufferings, so through Christ we share abundantly in comfort, too" (2 Cor. 1:5).

Job Presents Evidence against the Retribution Principle

Big Idea *Job points to evidence in life where God's wisdom and power work contrary to the retribution principle.*

Understanding the Text

The Text in Context

As the discussion comes to the end of the first cycle (Job 3–14), Job is not persuaded by the arguments of Eliphaz, Bildad, and Zophar. All three of the friends agree that Job must repent of his sin and then God will restore him to the blessing he enjoyed previously. In the first part of this long speech of seventy-five verses, Job speaks to his friends (12:1–13:12). After a transitional section (13:13–19), in which Job decides to turn away from his friends, he addresses God (13:20–14:22). Job sees that his only hope is to argue his case before God, because he cannot convince his friends that he is innocent. In chapter 12, Job presents evidence from his observation of life that indicates God often acts in ways that do not fit the retribution principle, which the friends have insisted on using as their measure for evaluating Job's situation.

> Job extols God as sovereign over the nations of the world and their leaders (12:23–24). The book of Esther alludes to God's control of events during the reign of the mighty king Xerxes (486–465 BC), shown here with his attendants in a relief at the remains of his palace at Persepolis, Iran.

Historical and Cultural Background

Job's hymn extolling God in 12:13–25 can be compared in some ways to the Egyptian Hymn to the Sun by Akhenaten, but numerous closer examples can be found in the biblical psalms of descriptive praise (e.g., Ps.

104). Both ancient Near Eastern literature and history contain examples of leaders such as those Job describes in 12:24—leaders who set out on ill-fated quests (e.g., the legendary Sumerian hero Gilgamesh, who searched for immortality, and Xerxes, the Persian emperor who spent many years in his vain attempt to conquer Greece).

Interpretive Insights

12:2 *Doubtless you are the only people who matter.* Using the plural personal pronoun, Job speaks sarcastically to his three friends. Job feels disgusted with them, so he uses the same dismissive tone that they used with him previously (8:2; 11:3). He implies that they regard themselves as the intellectual elite who alone possess wisdom and that they falsely suppose that when they die, wisdom will die with them. Job's caustic words and disgusted tone suggest that the friends are wise in their own eyes alone (cf. Prov. 3:7) and not in reality.

12:3 *Who does not know all these things?* Rejecting Zophar's insult in 11:12, Job insists that he is not inferior to them in his understanding, despite what they think. He describes what they have said as mere platitudes rather than genuine insight. Because Job is confident of his own grasp of wisdom, he does not yield to their arguments. Instead, he maintains his stand and does not back down under their verbal barrage. Nevertheless, Job will at last come to realize that he also does not understand as much as he has supposed (42:1–6).

12:4 *I have become a laughingstock to my friends.* Job feels that his honor has been assaulted, as his friends treat him as a mere joke. Even though he is righteous and blameless (see Yahweh's assessment of

Job in 1:8; 2:3), others have derided him. What makes this especially humiliating is that his friends are the chief offenders (cf. Ps. 55:12–15). Instead of taking Job's claim seriously, they have scoffed at his cries to God (cf. Ps. 22:6–8). Clearly, this betrayal by his friends is painful and traumatic for Job.

12:6 *those who provoke God are secure.* In 11:15–20 Zophar declared that only those who are right with God can enjoy security. Job counters, however, that sometimes evildoers, those who provoke God, are secure, in contrast to what the retribution formula predicts (see the sidebar). By presenting this evidence, Job endeavors to call into question the validity of the conclusions that the friends have drawn from his adversity. As Job views it, the friends have not really considered all of the observable evidence. Thus, they are flawed as teachers of wisdom.

12:7–8 *But ask the animals, and they will teach you.* Alluding to wisdom sayings such as Proverbs 6:6, Job uses the observational approach of traditional wisdom to counter the conclusions of his friends. Job says that if the animals could talk, they could tell how God works in his world. That is, the animals know better than the friends do. By these words, Job parodies Zophar's claim in 11:7–12 that God's wisdom is too mysterious for humans to grasp. In reality,

Why Do Good Things Happen to Bad People?

The Bible often addresses the problem of evil, why bad things happen to good people. But passages like Psalms 49 and 73, as well as Job 12, look at the converse and ask why good things happen to bad people in God's world. Both of these are exceptions to the retribution principle that can be observed readily in life.

> For I envied the arrogant
>> when I saw the prosperity of the wicked.
> They have no struggles;
>> their bodies are healthy and strong.
> They are free from common human burdens;
>> they are not plagued by human ills. . . .
> This is what the wicked are like—
>> always free of care, they go on amassing
>> wealth.
> Surely in vain I have kept my heart pure
>> and have washed my hands in innocence.
>> (Ps. 73:3–5, 12–13)

Job indicates, the animals get it, even if Zophar does not! Ironically, at the end of the book (Job 38–41), Yahweh will use the same kind of evidence in the natural world to bring Job himself to understand and acknowledge the limits of his knowledge of how Yahweh governs his world. Employing the same term in 40:15–24 as is used here for "animals" (*behemot*), Yahweh will point to Behemoth to teach Job how little he comprehends the ways of God.

12:9 *the hand of the* LORD *has done this.* This verse contains the only use of the personal name Yahweh (translated as "the LORD") in Job outside of the prologue, epilogue, and the speeches by Yahweh in chapters 38–41. Job affirms that everything in the created order, including his own adversity, ultimately goes back to the activity of Yahweh. Job is not willing to diminish Yahweh's sovereignty over all in order to explain his adversity by some other means. He proceeds to expand on this point in verses

13–25 in a hymn that extols Yahweh's control over all of life.

12:12 *Is not wisdom found among the aged?* Both Job and the three friends work within the parameters of traditional wisdom, and there is much on which they agree. For example, they all hold that humans can derive wisdom through the process of observation and that long life should enable a person to acquire extensive wisdom. Job's point in this question is to indicate to the friends that they have not used the sources of reliable knowledge that are available to them. If they had truly observed life themselves and taken to heart what others before them had seen (compare Bildad's appeal to tradition in 8:8–10), they would have recognized that there are many situations in life that call into question the validity of the retribution principle. Though it is a useful general principle, retribution does not account for every specific case in life.

12:13 *To God belong wisdom and power.* These words begin a psalm of descriptive praise[1] to God that focuses on his wisdom and power in governing the world. It is evident that Job believes that God is not thwarted in his plan and that he does not make mistakes in his rule. In his sovereign control, however, God does not always work according to the retribution formula, punishing those who are evil and blessing those who are righteous. Three of the four qualities attributed to God in this verse (wisdom, counsel, understanding) are also applied to the Messiah in Isaiah 11:2, who is empowered by the Spirit of Yahweh.

12:17–21 *He leads rulers away stripped.* There is no sphere of life outside the range of God's control and no person too exalted to be exempt from God's rule. In 12:17–21,

God is described as controlling the activities and outcomes of all humans, even the greatest of them. Under God's control are rulers and judges (v. 17), kings (v. 18), priests (v. 19), elders (v. 20), and nobles (v. 21). By humbling rulers and leading them away stripped into captivity (cf. Isa. 20:2–4; Mic. 1:8), God manifests his superiority to the supposed wisdom of humans, just as he did at the Tower of Babel (Gen. 11:1–9). Within the context of the book of Job, the implication is that even Job, "the greatest man among all the people of the East" (1:3), falls under the control of God.

12:23 *He makes nations great, and destroys them.* This description affirms that no human institution is exempt from the sovereign control of God. Just as God rules over powerful individuals (vv. 17–21), so he rules over the nations that they lead (vv. 22–23). In Daniel 2, this principle is spelled out in detail in the dream that Daniel interprets for King Nebuchadnezzar. No group of humans, however powerful they may be, can successfully thwart the purpose of Almighty God.

12:24 *He deprives the leaders of the earth of their reason.* Just as God demonstrates his transcendent power (v. 13) over humans and nations in verses 17–23, so he manifests his superior wisdom (v. 13) over the leaders of the earth in verses 24–25. As in Daniel 4, where God reduces proud Nebuchadnezzar to insanity, God can transform human wisdom into mere gibberish. When God withdraws reason from leaders, they are consigned to wander and grope with no light. As a result, they go off the path into a wasteland (*tohu,* translated "formless" in Gen. 1:2).

12:25 *They grope in darkness with no light.* Job in this hymn is realistic about human limitations in God's world. Despite all of their power and wisdom, humans are inept and in the dark before God. God will accomplish his plan, regardless of the best efforts and resources that humans can marshal.

Theological Insights

In this chapter, Job offers a rebuttal to the absolute application of the retribution principle. Like his friends, Job accepts retribution as a general pattern of how life functions in God's ordered world, but he differs with them in arguing that there is also a lot of evidence that retribution does not apply to every situation. By applying the wisdom approach of careful observation (cf. Prov. 6:6), Job concludes that precise scrutiny of life demonstrates that the connection between how a person acts and the consequences a person receives is not always maintained. Some of the wisdom sayings in Proverbs (e.g., Prov. 20:24) hint at this qualification of retribution, but Job now develops such hints into a more extensive reevaluation of retribution theology.

Teaching the Text

Job and his friends have learned well the retribution principle of traditional wisdom, but Job's experience of adversity despite living a righteous and blameless life prompts him to think more carefully about how God works in human affairs. In this chapter, Job cites specific lines of evidence that demonstrate that the retribution principle needs to be qualified. Although it is correct in general, it cannot be pressed to fit every single case. By doing this, Job opens the door to a more precise and nuanced understanding of how God rules over his world. It is not as simple and clear-cut as retribution theology teaches.

Even though his friends have criticized him severely, alleging that he is a sinner who needs to repent before God, Job does not surrender his integrity when he replies to them. He insists on examining the facts rather than merely extrapolating from abstract theology, as they have done. Job is confident that his wisdom is not inferior to what they have declared. By looking carefully at life and by considering the unchanging character of God, Job tries to make sense of what he is experiencing.

When Job looks at life, he cannot overlook situations that call into question the retribution principle that he has been taught and that he has no doubt taught to others. As he considers examples of sinful people who enjoy secure and prosperous lives, he realizes that according to the retribution formula, they should be experiencing adversity from God. Thus, their situation is a mirror image of Job's own. Job recognizes from this that his theological system will have to be amended to account for how God actually works with people in his world. We are often tempted to reduce how God typically works into a simple formula and then to apply it generally to insist on how God must act in other situations. The book of Job cautions us that God's ways may differ from what our expectations demand.

As he observes life with its unexpected complexities, Job also is careful to retain a clear vision of God's character and control. In his psalm extolling the transcendent

In 12:13–25, Job praises God for his sovereignty. Other cultures in the ancient Near East also wrote hymns to their gods. One example is Akhenaten's Hymn to the Sun, where he praises Aten for creative power and activity in the world. This Egyptian relief shows Akhenaten (Amenophis IV, ca. 1364–1347 BC), Nefertiti, and their daughter Meritaton worshiping Aten, the disk of the sun (royal palace at Tell El-Amarna, Egypt, Eighteenth Dynasty).

wisdom and sovereign power of God, Job defines the starting point for evaluating life. In the Old Testament, the fear of Yahweh is consistently presented as the foundation principle for wisdom (Prov. 1:7; 9:10; cf. Job 28:28; Eccles. 12:13). By focusing on God, Job returns to the necessary initial point for understanding life in God's world. Our adversities may cause us to lose sight of God, but what we most need during our times of pain is a clear picture of what God is truly like, as he has revealed himself in the Bible.

When Job considers how God rules his world with wisdom and power, he sees numerous examples of God's control over individual humans and over nations. Even the most powerful people come under God's sovereign rule, and no nation can thwart his plan. If God directs the course of history in such a comprehensive way as this, then Job can be confident that God's rule extends over his life as well. Even when our circumstances seem most out of control, they are firmly under God's control.

Illustrating the Text

The wicked, indeed, may prosper, and the righteous suffer.

Memoir: *These Strange Ashes*, **by Elisabeth Elliot.** In this less well-known account by the wife of martyr Jim Elliot (1927–56), Elisabeth Elliot wrestles with the question of loss and what she is tempted to see as waste. Called to the Colorado Indians of Ecuador when single, she spent almost a year reducing the language of the Indians to an alphabet in order for Bible translation to occur. Not only were her living conditions hard, but while staying among the Indians, she also saw those she loved die, her

guide murdered, and finally, the completed manuscript—her year's work, carried in a suitcase—lost off the top of a bus. The trial is almost beyond her tolerance. She writes, following her losses, of her temptation "to foreshorten the promises [of God], to look for some prompt fulfillment of the loss-gain principle."[2] The suitcase was never found. The story is unforgettable in its honest telling of one woman's battle with trusting God in adversity.

Film: God's ways stand in great contrast to many revenge movies, in which good characters decide to exact revenge on those who have wronged them, who have robbed them or murdered those they love. These "heroes" enact the retribution principle. Some examples are the *Godfather* movies, *Dirty Harry* (1971), and more recently, *Gran Torino* (2008).

The same God who directs the course of history rules over our personal lives.

Mythology: In contrast to the God of Scripture, in the Greek myths (specific stories from *Bulfinch's Mythology* could be used) the numerous gods and goddesses influence the affairs of humans and nations. However, they often work at cross-purposes, leading to confusing consequences. In the Bible, Yahweh is the only God, and he alone directs the course of history to his determined end.

Film: *Star Wars.* In the *Star Wars* movies, Yoda, the venerable Jedi master, lives to be nine hundred years old before he dies. Obviously, he is a God-like character. He is renowned for his great wisdom as a Grand Master Jedi, and he uses this insight to train Luke Skywalker, teaching him what he knows about the force and in doing so putting Luke on the path to knowing himself.

Job Turns to Speak to God

Big Idea *Dismissing the insights of his friends, Job takes his case directly to God.*

Understanding the Text

The Text in Context

Job 13 is a continuation of Job's long speech that began in 12:1 and continues through 14:22. In chapter 13, Job begins by speaking to his friends (13:1–12), as he did in the previous chapter. He concludes his reply to them by describing their words as mere "proverbs of ashes" (13:12). In 13:13–19, Job contemplates whether to turn away from his friends in order to address God. Beginning in 13:20, Job speaks directly to God.

Historical and Cultural Background

In 13:4 Job dismisses his friends as "worthless physicians." In the ancient world, medicine was not the respected scientific profession that it has become in modern times. Ancient physicians typically used a variety of herbs and drugs to treat illness (cf. 1 Tim. 5:23), but sometimes they borrowed techniques from magicians and used incantations when treating their patients.

In the ancient world, a cheap substitute for ink could be made by mixing ashes and water. This chalk-like substance was water soluble, and thus easily erased or washed away, so it was used only for informal writing rather than for legal contracts or other formal statements.[1] When Job speaks of the friends' proverbs of ashes (13:12), his image suggests that what they have said is not to be taken seriously.

Interpretive Insights

13:3 *I desire to speak to the Almighty.* Job has lost all confidence in his friends,

Job calls his friends "worthless physicians" because they cannot diagnose or treat his affliction (13:4). In the ancient world, medical treatment included the use of natural remedies and protective amulets, as well as incantations to the gods, like the one recorded on this cuneiform tablet from Mesopotamia (fifth century BC). Here Gula, the goddess of healing, is asked to grant well-being.

the human "experts," so he expresses his fervent desire for God to hear his case, just as in the New Testament Paul appeals from the provincial governor Festus to the emperor Caesar (Acts 25:11). Job is convinced enough of the legitimacy of his case to take it to God, so that he might sort things out properly. Job believes that God will respond to him differently from how the friends have. He proposes to argue his case before God, so that God can determine what is right, in contrast to what the friends have falsely alleged against Job.

13:4–5 *If only you would be altogether silent!* Job is frustrated by hearing the friends talk when they do not truly understand his situation. They started out well, sitting with Job in silence (2:13), but as they began to speak, their unjustified charges ruined the positive impact they had previously made. They are like quacks posing as physicians (13:4), making an inaccurate diagnosis and prescribing a treatment that does not apply to Job's ailment. Compared to their empty words, silence would sound like wisdom, because "even fools are thought wise if they keep silent" (Prov. 17:28).

13:6 *Hear now my argument.* Here, as in verses 13 and 17, Job wants his friends to stop talking and to start listening carefully to him. They have heard his words, and even quoted some of them in their speeches, but they have not really grasped Job's argument. Instead of truly listening, they just wait until their turn to talk, not seriously considering what Job has said. The second and third cycles of speeches do not show much evidence that the friends have heeded Job's appeal to them in this verse.

13:7–10 *Will you speak wickedly on God's behalf?* Although the friends

doubtless presume that they are defending God's cause, Job charges that they are telling lies in a vain attempt to cover up for God. As Job views it, they are committing perjury by giving false testimony against him (cf. Deut. 19:16–19), twisting the facts in order to make their points. Job accuses them of condemning him in order to protect God's reputation (13:8). He goes on to warn them that God will hold them accountable for their false testimony (13:9–10), as God indeed does in 42:7–8.

13:12 *Your maxims are proverbs of ashes.* With these words, Job strikes directly at the competence of these three wisdom teachers. They have not heard Job clearly. They do not know God correctly. Their criticisms of Job are unfounded. What they said has no substance but is as ephemeral as ashes. Job may well have accompanied these words with object lessons, picking up some of the ashes and pieces of pottery where he was sitting, to illustrate how their words will be burned up and their defenses will be broken like clay pots.

13:15 *Though he slay me, yet will I hope in him.* See the sidebar "Hope or No Hope in God?"

13:18 *I know I will be vindicated.* Job speaks like a lawyer who is fully confident of the case he has prepared. In his mind, he is convinced that when he argues his case, God will declare him innocent, thus

Hope or No Hope in God?

Job 13:15 contains a difficult and highly debated textual problem. The scribes known as the Masoretes studied the early biblical documents and established the Hebrew text that has become the standard base for modern translations. Occasionally, as in this verse, they could not decide between two alternative readings. So they put in the Hebrew text the consonants of one variant with the vowels of the other alternative. The consonantal Hebrew text (the *Kethib* reading) yields the rendering of the NJPS, "He may well slay me; I may have no hope." The Hebrew verb *yahal* ("hope") could have the nuance of "wait in silence," as it does in 32:11, 16 of Elihu's deference to his elders. If that is the case, then Job here is insisting that even if God should slay him, he would not wait in silence but would continue to bring his legal case before God (13:3, 18). This verse, then, contrasts with verse 19, in which Job says that if anyone can bring charges against him, then he will be silent and die.

On the other hand, the NIV and the KJV have adopted a translation based on the variant represented by the vowels in the Hebrew text (the *Qere* reading), which says the opposite of the written text; this reading presents Job's indomitable trust in God (cf. James 5:11). Although commentators have long disagreed on how this verse should be read, Job's attitude in this section is not hopeful toward God, and in the second line of verse 15 he resolves to defend himself to God's face. It could well be that the reading suggested by the vowels and that has become accepted by many later translations was in fact a pious interpretation that significantly altered what Job actually says at this point in his experience.[a]

---

[a] Critical commentaries on the book of Job provide detailed discussion of the textual problem in Job 13:15. An excellent succinct treatment of the issue is in Balentine, *Job*, 212.

---

admitting that he has treated Job unfairly, and that the friends will be shown to be in the wrong. At the end of the book, Yahweh does vindicate Job (42:7–8), but Job also learns how much he does not know about God and his ways (42:3). Although Job is right about the final verdict, he does not anticipate correctly the path Yahweh will take to get to that conclusion.

13:20–21 *Only grant me these two things, God.* In verse 21, Job begins the direct address to God he has anticipated in verses 3 and 15. Job believes that he cannot argue his case if God exerts undue pressure on him that subverts a fair trial. He therefore asks for two pretrial conditions, which he spells out in verse 21: God must withdraw from Job his heavy hand of affliction, and God must remove the overwhelming dread that makes Job feel intimidated.

13:22 *Then summon me and I will answer, or let me speak, and you reply to me.* What Job values most is communication with God in place of the divine silence he has experienced since his adversity began. Job is willing to take the role of the defendant to answer God's questions, or to assume the role of the plaintiff addressing his complaint against God. Either way, Job and God will both speak, and the awful silence between them will be broken. This does not occur, however, until Yahweh finally speaks in chapter 38.

13:24 *Why do you hide your face and consider me your enemy?* Like the psalmists in Psalms 13:1 and 27:9, Job feels as though God has intentionally turned his face away from him. Job cannot understand God's hiddenness, so he feels abandoned and neglected by God (cf. Deut. 31:17; Ps. 30:7). Because this kind of withdrawal by God is often prompted by divine wrath against sin (Isa. 59:2; Jer. 33:5; Mic. 3:4), Job thinks that God is treating him as a guilty enemy. In addition to hiding from Job, God seems to attack him as well (cf. Job 7:12; 10:16).

13:26 *For you write down bitter things against me and make me reap the sins of my youth.* Job acknowledges that he committed sins in his youthful years (cf. Ps. 25:7), but as a blameless man he has doubtless confessed them long before this time. He now wonders if his adversity can possibly be a long-delayed punishment for his sins as a young man, which God has recorded and remembered. Later on, in 31:35, Job will use the same metaphor of writing, as he writes and signs his confession of innocence and places his case in God's hands.

Theological Insights

In 13:21 Job calls on God to withdraw his hand from him. Throughout the Bible, the hand of God is an image that speaks of his powerful activity. God can use his hand to bring blessing, or God's hand can be the agency of his judgment and punishment. In the prologue of the book of Job, the adversary challenges Yahweh to put forth his hand to touch Job's possessions (1:11) and his body (2:5). In 6:9; 10:7; and 19:21 Job feels the hand of God's affliction in his life. In the same sense, in 13:21 Job asks God to remove his affliction from him. In Psalm 32:4 the psalmist recalls how the hand of divine conviction was heavy on him. Similarly, in the New Testament the writer of Hebrews warns that it is terrifying to fall into the hands of the living God, who punishes sin severely (Heb. 10:31). In a positive sense, in Psalm 139:5 the hand of God is regarded as the psalmist's continual protection.

Teaching the Text

Although friends can often help us to understand issues in our lives when we are blind to our own faults, all human insight has its limits. Just as Proverbs 3:5 warns us not to lean on our own understanding, so we need to be careful not to lean too much on what others think they understand about our lives. Ultimately, only God knows totally what we are experiencing, so he alone has the final answer to our questions. In Job 13, Job comes to realize that his friends cannot provide the insight he needs, so he decides to turn from them and take his cause directly to God.

In 13:27, Job accuses God of fastening his feet in shackles. This Assyrian relief depicts Nubian prisoners being led away with shackles on their feet (palace at Nineveh, 645–635 BC).

It is evident that the three friends mean well, but their evaluation of Job's situation is distorted by their overly narrow retribution theology. They have turned the general pattern of retribution in the wisdom tradition into a fixed formula that cannot truly explain Job's specific experience. Nevertheless, they insist on squeezing Job's situation into the formula, like Cinderella's sisters vainly trying to fit their own feet into her glass slipper. As a result, Job concludes that what they have said to him is as worthless as the prescriptions of a quack doctor and as empty as ashes, because they have not spoken the truth to him. Simplistic answers may fit many situations, but they may not answer the complexity of the individual cases of adversity that occur in life.

Instead of going around and around with his friends, Job determines to take his case directly to God. As he approaches God, he cannot anticipate how God will answer him, even though Job is confident that he is innocent. His experience has turned upside down the theological assumptions he had before. Job, however, also knows that only God understands him correctly, and if he is to get accurate answers to his questions, then they will have to come from God, not from his friends.

Job is most upset by God's silence. To Job, it seems as if God has turned away from him, treating him as an enemy rather than as a friend. Above all, Job wants God to speak to him, not just to answer his questions but to reassure Job that their relationship is intact. Like many people in pain today, Job feels distanced from God, for he cannot hear God's voice speaking to him, and God does not seem to respond to Job's cries. It is when God seems absent that we are most prone to slip into despair, as we lose sight of his provision and protection.

Throughout this chapter and much of the book, Job tries to understand *why* God seems to have abandoned him. The feeling of abandonment is hard enough to bear, but even more difficult is not knowing any motive that could possibly cause God to neglect one who has been faithful to him. In this, Job anticipates the cries of many Christians today who endure the dark night of the soul, when God seems far away from them and their needs.

Illustrating the Text

Human insight, even well intended, fails.

History: As George Washington neared the end of his life, his doctor used leeches in an attempt to remove the diseased blood, a common treatment of the time. Instead of having a positive effect, the procedure weakened the leader and hastened his death. In a way similar to Job's friends, the physician meant well but was ineffective in treating a man in great need.

Television: Ever since the televised series *Perry Mason*, programs have featured lawyers preparing and presenting cases in which they have great confidence. That confidence, we are sometimes reminded, does not always translate into a successful verdict.

We may go through times when we feel that God is silent.

Book: *Disappointment with God*, by Philip Yancey. This helpful book contains numerous accounts of people, including Job, who have asked if God is silent. In fact, the three central questions the book poses are Is God unfair? Is God hidden? Is God silent? In one example, Yancey relates the story of Richard, who had suffered a broken home, sickness, a failed relationship, and the loss of his job leading not to a loss of faith but a feeling of betrayal. While none of these constituted a great tragedy, Yancey began to realize that the three questions noted were ones "lodged somewhere inside all of us."[2]

Drama: *Waiting for Godot*, by Samuel Beckett. In this powerful play in the absurdist tradition, the two protagonists, Vladimir and Estragon, wait futilely hour after hour, day after day, for someone they call Godot to arrive. This and other facets of the work have elicited a number of interpretations since the play's first performance. The play is seen as one of the most important dramas of the twentieth century. Certainly one of the interpretations is that the two are waiting for God, who never appears. Biblical allusions appear throughout.

When we go through a dark night of the soul, we must persevere.

Literature: *The Odyssey*, by Homer. In the *Odyssey* (ca. 800 BC), Penelope waits for twenty years for her husband Odysseus to return from the Trojan War. Many people try to convince her that he has died. In fact, she is pursued relentlessly by suitors during these years. She finally devises a clever scheme in which she begins weaving a burial shroud, announcing that when it is done, she will choose a suitor. Every night, however, she unweaves some of her work, still believing in Odysseus's return. Penelope's faith perseveres through the years of silence until she and Odysseus indeed are finally reunited.

Film: *Clueless*. In this movie (1995) about high-school life, Cher (Alicia Silverstone) is asked, "What's a Monet?" She responds: "It's like a painting, see? From far away, it's OK, but up close, it's a big old mess." What an apt description of the nature of the impressionist painting—when one stands too close, all is visual detail in the rough. Viewed from a distance, everything is harmonious and evocative. Our perspective in the dark night of the soul is too close for us to see the full picture.

Job remains faithful to God despite his feelings that God has abandoned him and is far away. We find another illustration of perseverance in the ancient Greek epic poem *The Odyssey*. Penelope believes Odysseus has not died in the Trojan War and waits patiently for his return, despite pressure from many men who would take his place. This terracotta relief shows Odysseus, disguised as a beggar, standing before Penelope, where he learns that she has remained faithful (Melos, Greece, 450 BC).

Job Tries to Hope, but Ends Up in Despair

Big Idea *Despite his best efforts to find hope, Job can only despair in his adversity.*

Understanding the Text

The Text in Context

In chapter 14, Job continues the direct address to God that he began in 13:20. He now broadens the scope of his lament to reflect on the human condition in general, rather than just considering his own individual experience (14:1–6). Using the observational technique of traditional wisdom, Job looks at nature to discern if there is hope to which humans can cling during their adversities. He observes that a tree can grow again after it has been cut down, but humans cannot (14:7–10). Humans, like dried up seas or riverbeds, have no hope for renewal (14:11–12). Although Job tries, through his imagination, to glimpse hope for the future after death (14:13–17), he finishes on a despondent note (14:18–22). At the end of the first cycle of speeches, Job finds himself in despair because of the boundaries that God has placed on all humans.

Historical and Cultural Background

Other ancient Near Eastern cultures had various notions of an afterlife, but they did not develop the idea of human resurrection after death. For example, in the Mesopotamian Epic of Gilgamesh, the hero is given a plant by Utnapishtim, but a serpent takes it from him before Gilgamesh can eat it and receive the gift of renewed youth. A few Old Testament texts contain intimations of immortality for humans (Gen. 5:24; 2 Kings 2:11; Pss. 49:15; 73:24; Ezek. 37:1–14; Dan. 12:1–3; see the sidebar "Sheol and the Afterlife," in the discussion of Job 3 above). However, only after the resurrection of Jesus in the New Testament was the doctrine of the resurrection of humans developed explicitly. We need to be careful not to read the later New Testament revelation back into the text of Job and thus view Job as though he understood and believed what was only revealed by God much later.

Interpretive Insights

14:1–2 *Mortals, born of woman, are of few days and full of trouble.* In contrast to the final verse of the book, which describes Job as being full of days and blessing (42:17), here in chapter 14 Job concludes that humans are consigned to brief and troubled lives. Job speaks generally, referring not to himself alone but to every human, including both the righteous and the wicked. Bildad said in 8:13 that the wicked will perish, but here Job insists that all humans face a life that is full of trouble. That is, trouble is not merely a minor irritation, but for humans it is the dominant feature of life. To compound the problem, human life is also brief (14:2), like a flower that withers (cf. Pss. 37:2; 90:5–6) and a fleeting shadow (cf. Pss. 102:11; 144:4).

14:3 *Do you fix your eye on them?* Job's rhetorical question implies a positive answer, that God does indeed scrutinize humans during their brief and troubled lives. Job said previously (10:20–22) that he has been under God's constant surveillance and that God just will not get off his case. In contrast to the psalmist's delight in God's constant watching over him (Ps. 8:4), Job perceives God as looking for every opportunity to find fault with humans (Job 7:17–21).

14:5 *A person's days are determined.* In contrast to the eternality of God, humans live on earth for mere days (cf. Pss. 39:4; 103:15). The psalmist of Psalm 31:15 is confident that his times are in Yahweh's hands, but Job regards humans as powerless to transcend the divine limits that constrain their lives. They must instead live within the narrow boundaries that God has placed around them.

14:6 *till he has put in his time like a hired laborer.* Before his great adversity, Job felt delight as the friendship of God hovered over his tent (29:4). At this time, by contrast, Job senses a great social and emotional distance from God. Consequently, he

Key Themes of Job 14

- Job laments that all humans experience trouble in their fleeting lives.
- Job views humans not like renewable trees but like riverbeds that cannot be revived.
- Job cannot transcend the limitations of his knowledge.
- Job feels hopeless in the face of the adversity that God has allowed to come into his life.

pictures humans as hired laborers who are compelled to put in their time for a harsh taskmaster. In this scenario, life becomes mere tedium driven by obligation and fear, not joyful service for a loving and caring master.

14:7–10 *But a man dies and is laid low.* Unlike a tree, which can revive after it has been cut down (14:7–9; cf. Isa. 11:1), once a human dies, hope is ended. There is no hope of renewal to life after death. As Job says also in 10:21 and 16:22, the grave is a place of no return. Job does not have the doctrine of resurrection to appeal to, for he is limited in his understanding to what God has revealed at this time in history. Because of his limited knowledge, his only hope is for God to intervene for

In 14:5, Job declares that God has determined the length of everyone's life. In the Gilgamesh Epic, Gilgamesh seeks eternal life but finds that the gods have destined humankind for death. He tries to leave his legacy in other ways, such as slaying the monster/god Huwawa. This plaque may show Gilgamesh standing on the head of Huwawa.

him before he dies (cf. Ps. 27:13). After that, it will be too late.

14:13 *If only you would hide me in the grave.* This hypothetical and imaginative desire expressed by Job contrasts with his revulsion of the grave elsewhere in his speeches (7:9; 17:16). To Job, the afterlife is not a joyful anticipation but rather the unpleasant prospect of a joyless semi-existence. As Job grasps for any semblance of hope, he twists the image of the grave in a positive direction, hoping that perhaps in the dark recesses of Sheol he can find temporary concealment from God's anger. If only he could be hidden in the grave, maybe he could be kept safely out of the line of divine fire.

14:14 *I will wait for my renewal to come.* Job views his life as toil that must be endured (7:1–3). Although the hope of resurrection has not yet been revealed in his day, Job determines to wait for his restoration or release by God, apparently hoping that this positive turn of events will occur during his lifetime, not after death. Here, the endurance of Job about which James 5:11 speaks shows through his intense pain.

14:15 *You will call and I will answer you.* As Job attempts to find hope in his adverse situation, he anticipates that God will eventually break his silence and speak. This renewal of communication would remedy the awful silence that Job has endured so long. In the book, Job's hope is actually fulfilled in chapters 38–41. Job, however, is then not able to answer the numerous questions that Yahweh poses to him, as he here supposes he will be able to do.

14:17 *My offenses will be sealed up in a bag.* In the ancient world, important items, including documents and clay tablets, would be sealed in a bag for safekeeping. Job refers to that practice to describe how he hopes God will keep Job's sins out of sight or expunge them so that they will

In 14:19, Job says that God destroys a person's hope in the same way that torrents wash away the soil. This gully near the Dead Sea in Israel was carved by the rushing waters of spring floods.

not be adduced as incriminating evidence against him.

14:18–19 *as a mountain erodes and crumbles.* Job's daring hope in 14:13–17 cannot sustain him in the face of his great adversity. Once again using the procedure of observation, Job notes that an eroded mountain cannot be rebuilt, but only the rubble remains at its base. If a mountain cannot survive erosion, then what chance could a feeble human have in the face of God's inexorable laws? This reality destroys human hope (14:19).

14:22 *They . . . mourn only for themselves.* Despite his best efforts to imagine hope, Job ends this long speech on a despondent note, just as he did his previous speeches in the first cycle (3:20–26; 7:19–21; 10:18–22). Death, he says, will separate people from all that they love. They will then have no communication with those who are alive (14:21), so they will not know anything about the honor or humiliation of their children. This reference to children must have been heartbreaking for Job in his grief. In death, he will have only his bodily pain and profound loneliness, that is, deep physical and psychological loss, in contrast to the rich social connections he previously enjoyed (1:2–5; 29:4–5).

Theological Insights

Job's focus on the brevity of human life (14:5–6) utilizes a motif that is common in the Old Testament and especially in wisdom literature (e.g., 1 Chron. 29:15; Job 7:6; 8:9; Pss. 90:10; 103:15–16; Eccles. 6:12). At the time when the book of Job was written, God had not revealed explicitly the future resurrection of humans. Job had to function within his theological limitations, but

now the New Testament has provided for us greater understanding of what God will do for believers after their death (1 Cor. 15). In the same way, today we have limitations in what we can know (1 Cor. 13:12), so like Job we need to trust God for what we cannot understand. Ultimately, faith must be rooted in the God who knows all, not in the knowledge that we possess, because our knowledge is partial and incomplete.

Teaching the Text

As Job processes his adversity, he goes through the same variety of thoughts and feelings that any human does when faced with severe pain and disappointment. In chapter 14, Job desperately tries to find hope in his situation. Nevertheless, whether he looks at the patterns in the natural world or designs an imaginative scenario, he comes to the same place. His lines of thinking all lead to hopelessness, and that causes Job to despair in his adversity. This candid and transparent expression of Job's thoughts parallels closely what many people today think as they struggle with adversities in their lives.

Job's observation of human life can be summed up in two principles: life goes fast, and life is hard. As Job sees it, humans actually have the worst of both worlds, for their lives are like a fragile flower that withers quickly.

Wisdom observes the natural world and seeks to discern lessons for life from what it sees there in God's ordered world. As Job examines nature, he realizes that when trees are cut down, new life can spring up from the stump. Humans, however, are not like that; they resemble the pattern of a body of water that evaporates, leaving behind a parched, lifeless bed. Rather than drawing false optimism from the faulty analogy of the tree, Job accepts the reality that humans are more like the riverbed that cannot be revived.

As Job tries to come to terms with his adversity, he has to work within the limitations of the knowledge that God has revealed up to this time. Readers today might want to insert the New Testament teaching about the resurrection as an encouragement to Job not to abandon hope, but Job could not know that theology in his day. He had to live within the finite knowledge that was available to him. In the same way, there are aspects of truth that God has not yet made known to us today. Like

Job, we need to live by the truth that we do have, but also trust God for what he has not yet chosen to share with us. Our trust must be in God himself, who alone knows all things.

In concluding the first cycle of speeches, Job feels hopeless in the face of the adversity God has allowed to come into his life. Job does not understand why he is experiencing the kind of pain that wisdom has always associated with the punishment of the wicked. He cannot see any reason for hope either in his lifetime or afterward. He is not convinced by his friends that he needs to repent of his sin. So he is left with many questions and few answers. To understand more, Job will have to hear from God, but up to this point God is silent.

Job observes that once humans die they are more like parched riverbeds than like tree stumps (14:7–12). Trees sometimes generate new life even from a cutoff limb, as this olive tree's new shoot demonstrates.

Illustrating the Text

Because we have finite knowledge, we will at times feel despair during adversity.

Hymn: "It Is Well with My Soul," by Horatio Spafford. During a time of deep personal adversity, Spafford (1828–88) drew great comfort from the New Testament teaching of Christ's return and the resurrection of Christians. Spafford, a prominent Chicago lawyer, not only lost much of his real estate investment in the Great Chicago Fire but he also lost all four of his daughters when the ship on which they were traveling was hit by an iron sailing vessel and sank. He wrote this beautiful hymn in response to his tragedy. Consider the following words:

For me, be it Christ, be it Christ
　　hence to live:
If Jordan above me shall roll,
No pang shall be mine, for in death
　　as in life
Thou wilt whisper Thy peace to my
　　soul.

Quote: William Shakespeare. The words of Shakespeare (1564–1616) in *Macbeth* (1611), spoken by a despairing Macbeth, bear striking resemblance to Job's view of life in 14:1–2: "Life's but a walking shadow, a poor player, that struts and frets his hour upon the stage, and then is heard no more; it is a tale told by an idiot, full of sound and fury, signifying nothing" (act 5, scene 5).

Film: *The Truman Show.* In this movie (1998), the lead character, played by Jim Carrey, lives within a world with limits that he cannot perceive until the end. Even though he has the illusion of freedom, actually he is living in a world where events are written and directed by others. This parallels how Job feels in 14:5 about the limits imposed on his life.

Geography: The parched lake beds left behind in Death Valley in California and in the Great Salt Flats in Utah are apt examples of the dry lake or riverbed that Job observes in 14:11.

Eliphaz Turns Up His Criticism of Job

Big Idea *Eliphaz insists that Job is a sinner who deserves God's punishment.*

Understanding the Text

The Text in Context

Job 15 contains Eliphaz's second speech to Job, and it is evident that civil discussion between them has broken down considerably. In fact, in the second cycle (Job 15–21) the dialogue between Job and his friends becomes more strained, abusive, and insulting as the friends focus almost completely on the divine punishment due to wicked people like Job. In chapter 15, Eliphaz is not as courteous as when he first addressed Job in chapters 4–5. He now contends that Job is suffering what any wicked person deserves. Taking the tone of a belligerent prosecutor determined to prove his case, Eliphaz assaults Job with a barrage of humiliating questions intended to prove Job guilty (15:1–13). Expanding his scope in 15:14–16, Eliphaz describes all

humans as vile and corrupt before the holy God. In 15:17–35 Eliphaz lectures Job specifically about what he has observed in life, that sinners in the present receive the divine punishment they deserve.

Historical and Cultural Background

When Eliphaz asks Job if he is the first man ever born (15:7), he may be alluding to the Mesopotamian myth that Ea, the god of wisdom, gave Adapa as a model for humanity. Hints of this can also be found in Ezekiel 28, when the king of Tyre is

In 15:7, Eliphaz may allude to Adapa, who in Mesopotamian myth was one of the seven sages sent by the god Ea to teach wisdom to humankind. These sages were depicted on Assyrian reliefs as men wearing fish cloaks, like the one shown here from the temple of Ninurta at Nimrud (865–860 BC).

condemned because of his aspirations to divine authority and wisdom. By using this mythological allusion, Eliphaz likely hints that Job in his pride has tried to elevate himself to a status rivaling that of God.[1]

The rocky soil of the Mediterranean world causes olive trees to grow profusely in that region. Olives and grapes are two of the major food items grown in the Near East, so when these crops fail, life becomes desperate. An olive tree that has shed its blossoms and a vine stripped of unripe grapes (15:33) reflect staples of life that have fallen far short of their potential.

Interpretive Insights

15:2 *Would a wise person answer with empty notions?* In 12:2 Job dismissed the friends by saying that they think that with their words wisdom will reach its final end. Now Eliphaz uses the same sarcastic tone toward Job, saying in effect that Job is just full of hot air. According to Eliphaz, Job's words are like the scorching and destructive "hot east wind" that blows off the Arabian desert. In Hosea 12:1 the same image is used to speak of Israel's deceit and lies. Apparently, Eliphaz thinks that genuine wisdom should be cool, analytical, and objective, in contrast to Job's passionate intensity.

15:4 *But you even undermine piety and hinder devotion to God.* Concerned by the potential negative effect that Job's words could have on others, Eliphaz accuses Job of contradicting the fundamental wisdom principle of the fear of the Lord (cf. Prov. 1:7; 9:10; the Hebrew term for "fear" is translated in Job 15:4 as "piety") and thereby undermining faith in God. Eliphaz here directly attacks Job's piety, which Yahweh himself has praised in the

prologue (1:8; 2:3). Eliphaz does not realize that his rigid thinking has brought him to a conclusion that rejects Yahweh's assessment of Job's character. Ironically, James 5:11 will later point to Job as a positive example of perseverance in the face of suffering, not the negative example that Eliphaz decries.

15:5–6 *Your sin prompts your mouth; you adopt the tongue of the crafty.* Distorting Job's words in 9:20, Eliphaz accuses Job of being driven by his sin into dangerous words. As Eliphaz sees it, Job's sin is what prompts his speech, so Job is condemned by the testimony of his own mouth. Eliphaz even charges Job with adopting the tongue of the "crafty," using the same Hebrew term that is employed in Genesis 3:1 to describe the serpent that tempts Adam and Eve into sin.

15:7 *Are you the first man ever born?* Wisdom is often regarded as belonging to the aged (cf. Ps. 119:100), who can call upon a long lifetime of observations as the basis for their insight and instruction. Wisdom itself has been possessed by Yahweh from everlasting (Prov. 8:22–31). Perhaps alluding to ancient Near Eastern stories of the first human as one who was especially endowed by God with wisdom, Eliphaz rhetorically asks Job if he is the epitome of wisdom. Obviously, Eliphaz is convinced that such is not the case.

15:9 *What do you know that we do not know?* In 13:2 Job insisted that he is not inferior to his friends in his knowledge, but that he knows what they know. Eliphaz now exaggerates what Job said, as he inquires sarcastically not about Job's supposed *equal* knowledge but about his purported *superior* knowledge. Actually, all of the characters seem to pride themselves in what they know, or think they know, with none of them evidencing an excess of humility in this regard.

15:10 *The gray-haired and the aged are on our side.* Eliphaz claims that the aged wisdom teachers all agree with him against Job (see also 15:17–18). These experts are even older than Job's father, which means that they are vastly more experienced than Job in his relative youth.

15:11 *Are God's consolations not enough for you?* Eliphaz claims to be speaking for God and bringing to Job divine words of consolation. Job, however, does not hear him in this way, but rather Job has rejected what Eliphaz said to him in chapters 4–5. As Eliphaz assesses Job's response to him, he perceives that what God has said through him is not good enough for Job. This implies pride on Job's part, for he has dismissed as irrelevant to him what God said. In Eliphaz's estimation, when Job rejects his counsel, he rejects God's intended comfort for him.

15:14–16 *What are mortals, that they could be pure?* In 7:17–18, Job parodied Psalm 8 as he insisted that humans are scrutinized continually by God. In 15:14–16, Eliphaz also alludes to Psalm 8 as he portrays humans as vile and corrupt before the holy God. In fact, in Eliphaz's view humans sin as often and as casually as they drink water (15:16). Eliphaz's intense focus on retribution has distorted his conception of humans before God. In Eliphaz's thinking, since Job is a human he is necessarily a sinner, so he cannot be righteous before God. According to Eliphaz, all humans deserve only divine judgment.

15:17–18 *Listen to me and I will explain to you.* Drawing on what he himself has observed (v. 17) and what he has learned from tradition (v. 18), Eliphaz claims to be the spokesperson for wisdom. By exhorting Job to listen, Eliphaz assumes the role of the learned teacher, and he places Job in the role of the ignorant student. If Job would just stop talking, then he could listen to Eliphaz and learn from one who really understands how life works.

15:20–24 *All his days the wicked man suffers torment.* In 8:13–19, Bildad described what the wicked can expect in the future. Here in 15:20–24, Eliphaz uses startling language as he expounds on how the wicked, not just in the future but in the present, receive the torment that they deserve. Using a vivid term that speaks of writhing in childbirth (cf. Ps. 51:5), Eliphaz states that wicked people like Job will have a miserable life. They will experience the kind of dreadful calamities that have befallen Job.

15:25 *he shakes his fist at God and vaunts himself against the Almighty.* Eliphaz's straight-line logic ends up transforming blameless Job (cf. 1:8; 2:3) into the worst of godless infidels. According to Eliphaz's reasoning, at the root of wicked behavior is rebellion against God's authority. Job, then, has declared his independence from God and treated God with contempt.

15:27–30 *Though his face is covered with fat.* In a culture in which most people lived from hand to mouth, fatness was a tangible sign of prosperity. Here, as in Psalm 73:3–4, 7, is raised the issue of the prosperous wicked, those who are both unrighteous and affluent. Eliphaz seems to imply that Job's wickedness is related to his wealth, how he accumulated it, how he has trusted in it, and how it made him insensitive to others in need. Eliphaz goes on in verses 28–30 to say that God destroys the wealth of the wicked, clearly alluding to Job's losses in chapter 1.

Theological Insights

In his reference to God's council in 15:8, Eliphaz asks if Job is privy to the conversations between God and his exalted angels when God describes his secret plans. Similar allusions to the divine council are found in 1 Kings 22:19–22 and Psalm 82:1–4, as well as elsewhere in the Old Testament. The prologue in Job 1–2 also presents such a scene, as Yahweh debates with the adversary the character and motivation of Job. Thus, it is clear to the reader that Eliphaz is wrong in his condemnation of Job.

Teaching the Text

The more Eliphaz talks, the more he sounds like a conclusion in search of a cause to justify it. His retribution theology prompts him to regard adversity as the divine punishment for a person's sin. Looking through that lens, Eliphaz can see Job only as a sinner who deserves God's punishment. Even though this conclusion means that Eliphaz has to disregard what he previously observed in Job's life, he nevertheless plunges ahead in his misconceptions about his friend. As a result, he brings unnecessary pain to the person he set out to comfort.

Eliphaz's rigid thinking even causes him to perceive Job as rejecting divine wisdom and turning people against God. He does not realize that the questions Job has asked and the complaints he has uttered emerged from his pain

Eliphaz declares that the wicked, though fat and seemingly prosperous, will face God's judgment (15:27–28). Obesity was a sign of affluence; this statue of a seated scribe depicts him with rolls of fat on his upper abdomen to convey his wealth and prosperity (Saqqara, Egypt).

and his inability to understand why God is acting in a way contrary to all that Job has known. God will later instruct Job in a more advanced understanding of divine wisdom, but Eliphaz cannot see anything beyond the basic retribution formula. To him, any question raised against retribution is a renunciation of wisdom rather than a search for a more precise and nuanced statement of how God deals with humans.

Because Eliphaz is convinced that he understands how God works in his world, he takes an objective, analytical approach to life. To him, life is a calculation that yields definitive results. Job, however, senses that his past understanding of how the world functions has been turned upside down by his experience of adversity. His agitated passion reflects the turmoil in his heart and mind. Eliphaz faults Job for this intense emotion, misconstruing it as a rejection of God, when really it is a reflection of Job's internal confusion and pain. A comparison with the lament psalms demonstrates that godly people often have intense feelings of pain, which they bring to the Lord as they plead for his intervention in their lives.

Eliphaz's analysis leads him to the conclusion that all humans are inherently sinful and therefore incapable of standing before the holy God. To his thinking, Job as a human is sinful, and that explains completely why God is punishing him. What Eliphaz fails to think through, however, is that his line of argument has obliterated the possibility of any human experiencing God's blessing, which wisdom teaches is given to the righteous. If Job deserves divine judgment, then so should Eliphaz, and so should all other humans. In constructing his logical case against Job, Eliphaz manages

to destroy any possibility of fellowship between God and humans.

In his effort to convince Job that he is sinful, Eliphaz jumps to the unwarranted conclusion that Job has been deceived by his pursuit of wealth, as indeed many people are. Eliphaz does not directly state this accusation, but he clearly implies that this is the case. It is true that Job was wealthy (1:3) and that his possessions have been destroyed, but Eliphaz completely fails to take account of the important role of the adversary's involvement in Job's calamity. Without that crucial piece of information, Eliphaz connects the dots in a way that looks plausible to him but that grossly misjudges Job's values and motivations. While what Eliphaz says may be true for many people, it is not relevant to Job's case. Similarly, we must be careful lest in our attempts to counsel others we misconstrue what is happening in their lives and thus point them in the wrong direction.

Illustrating the Text

Human beings often grossly misjudge others, a reality Job must come to terms with.

History: During the American Civil War, President Lincoln was subjected to intense criticism and accusations that must have caused him sometimes to waver. However, he persisted in holding to what he was convinced was right, just as Job does in the face of the speeches made by his friends. In fact, Lincoln wrote the following words: "If I were to try to read, much less answer, all the attacks made on me, this shop might as well be closed for any other business. I do the very best I know how—the very best

I can; and I mean to keep doing so until the end. If the end brings me out all right, what's said against me won't amount to anything. If the end brings me out wrong, ten angels swearing I was right would make no difference."[2]

Philosophy: *Pensées*, by Blaise Pascal. Pascal (1623–62), in his famous, much-quoted work *Pensées* (posthumously published in 1669), admonishes those giving advice like Eliphaz to "correct with advantage . . . notic[ing] from what side he views the matter," and further comments that "no one" should be "offended at not seeing everything," words that would have kept Eliphaz from the gross misjudgment mentioned in this principle.[3]

Drama: In this passage and all the advice sections of Job, it could be very useful to have a group act out the scene so that the audience might see the dynamics of faulty spiritual and theological counsel.

Literature: *The Pilgrim's Progress*, by John Bunyan. Early in this timeless English allegory, when the main character, Christian, decides to begin his journey out of the City of Destruction to find relief from his burden of guilt, he is derided and mocked by his friends. They make all sorts of false accusations against him, just as Job's friends do to him in his adversity. This is contrasted with the very good advice early on of Evangelist, who rescues Christian from the Slough of Despond and points him in the right direction. Evangelist is tough yet tender.

Sculpture of Blaise Pascal (1623–62) by Augustin Pajou. Pages of his manuscript *Pensées* lie at his right foot.

Job Feels under Attack by God

Big Idea *Job feels exhausted under God's attack, but he still dares to hope for God's justice.*

Understanding the Text

The Text in Context

In his rebuttal to Eliphaz in Job 16–17, Job begins by countering many of the charges made previously by his friends. He vigorously rejects their claims to possess knowledge that is superior to his, and he dismisses their arguments as irrelevant to his specific case. Job's strong language indicates that he is indignant and disgusted with them (16:1–6). Job then addresses God directly, expressing his feelings that God is oppressing his life as an attacking warrior (16:7–17). In 16:18–22, Job expresses his longing for a witness to advocate for his innocence before God.

Historical and Cultural Background

In ancient pagan cultures, it was not unusual for the gods to act out of anger and even cruelty. For example, the Greek epics the *Iliad* and the *Odyssey* are full of deities fighting for and against various humans, often with devastating consequences. By contrast, in the Old Testament Yahweh is portrayed as just and righteous (e.g., Exod. 34:6–7) and as a warrior who comes to the defense of his oppressed people (e.g., Exod.

15:2–7). Job's adversity, however, has caused him to view God as assaulting him in anger (16:9), in terms that are more reminiscent of how the pagans often described the gods they worshiped than how the Bible presents the true God.

Interpretive Insights

16:2–3 *Will your long-winded speeches never end?* As an indication of the increasing strain between Job and his friends, Job throws Eliphaz's insult in 15:2 right back at him. Job insists that Eliphaz is the true windbag in this controversy. The friends initially intended to bring Job comfort (2:11), but instead these "comforters" (16:2) have managed to bring only trouble to Job. The last thing that Job needs to hear from them is an indictment of false guilt that only adds to his already deep pain.

16:4–5 *I also could speak like you, if you were in my place.* Job says that their talk is cheap, because it is easy to criticize someone else who has the problem. The friends know how to talk, but they do not truly understand what they are talking about. Job goes on to say in verse 5 that if their roles were reversed, Job would do better for them than they have for him. Job contends that he would provide them words to solace them in their pain, not accusations that rub salt in the wounds, as they have done to him.

16:6 *Yet if I speak . . . and if I refrain.* Job feels that no matter what he tries, he cannot find relief from his pain. When he speaks about his adversity, it does not relieve the pain he feels, but it only brings on him criticisms from his friends. When he suffers in silence, his pain continues unabated. He feels as if he is trapped, with no favorable alternatives. He is hurt deeply either way.

16:8 *You have shriveled me up—and it has become a witness.* Starting in verse 7, Job turns away from his friends to speak directly to God. He complains that God has so touched his body that, according to the retribution principle, it is exhibit A of his guilt (cf. the question by Jesus's disciples in John 9:2). His gaunt body looks like a ghost rising up as a witness against Job. People who observe Job cannot look past his hideous appearance to see anything other than what they wrongly suppose is incontrovertible evidence of divine condemnation.

16:9–12 *God assails me and tears me in his anger.* Instead of coming to Job's defense, God seems to be fighting as a warrior against him. The vivid language Job uses describes God as assailing him, that is, hating or bearing a grudge against him (cf.

> ### Key Themes of Job 16
>
> - Job dismisses the speeches of his friends as unhelpful.
> - Job perceives that God as a warrior is attacking him rather than defending him.
> - Job feels as if he is as good as dead.
> - Job dares to keep hoping for God's justice.

Gen. 27:41). Also, God seems to stalk him as a fierce animal preparing to maul him with a lethal blow. With these descriptions Job echoes the intense language of the imprecatory psalms as the psalmists cry out to God to protect them from the attacks by their vicious enemies (e.g., Ps. 57:4, 6).

16:14 *he rushes at me like a warrior.* Throughout the Old Testament, Yahweh is portrayed as a warrior who comes to the defense of his people in need (Exod. 15:1–21; Deut. 33; Judg. 5; Ps. 46; Hab. 3). Similarly, the book of Revelation pictures the return of Jesus Christ to earth as the conquering King of kings (Rev. 19:11–16). Here, by contrast, Job describes God as a warrior who attacks him (cf. the many parallels to the language of Lam. 3), which seems to contradict God's just character. Job insists consistently that he is innocent and therefore undeserving of God's punishment. He cannot understand how God could be involved in what appears to be a great injustice.

In 16:9, Job describes God as attacking him as a lion might do, with gnashing teeth tearing his flesh, much like the scene on this ivory plaque (Nimrud, 800–750 BC).

Sackcloth and Mourning

16:15–17 *my prayer is pure.* Job consistently rejects as inaccurate the allegations by his friends (Bildad in 8:5–6 and Eliphaz in 15:4–5) that he is a sinner who needs to repent. Instead, Job insists that he is innocent and his heart is pure (see the sidebar), thus fulfilling the standards required of those who would fellowship with Yahweh (Ps. 24:4). Also, it is evident that Job has not given up on God, because he continues to pray to him.

16:18 *Earth, do not cover my blood.* Throughout this speech, Job oscillates between discouragement and hope, reflecting his feelings, which are on an emotional roller coaster. Like Abel (Gen. 4:10), he is innocent and his blood cries out to God for justice. Job, therefore, appeals to the earth to serve as an objective witness to his innocence. He wants the evidence justifying him to be preserved, so that he will eventually receive the justice he deserves. If his blood were covered, the crime against him would be concealed, and Job does not want his case to be obscured and forgotten.

16:19 *Even now my witness is in heaven; my advocate is on high.* Job wants a witness to advocate for his innocence (cf. 9:33; 19:25), as Abraham appeals to Yahweh for his nephew Lot in Genesis 18. Even though he has no idea that Yahweh has already spoken on his behalf against the adversary in the prologue, Job clings to the hope that he will have an advocate to testify for him in heaven. Later Christian interpretation reads the mediatorial work of Christ into this statement as well as into Job 19:25–27, but Job does not have the advantage of knowing that subsequent revelation.

In the ancient Near East, wearing sackcloth was the conventional sign of mourning. This end panel from the sarcophagus of King Ahiram shows grieving women wearing sackcloth (tenth century BC).

16:20 *my eyes pour out tears to God.* Job's friends have failed to minister compassionately to him (cf. 6:14), so Job directs his tear-filled eyes to look at God. Although Job perceives that God is assailing him as an enemy (16:9–14), he nevertheless turns toward God in his need.

16:22 *Only a few years will pass before I take the path of no return.* Job has the profound sense that time is running out for God to come to his help, so once again (cf. 3:25–26; 7:21; 10:21–22) he expresses his longing for a quick resolution to his situation before he dies. Job does not have God's later revelation about the afterlife or the future resurrection, so his limited understanding makes his predicament harder to bear. He has to live and think within the constraints of what God has made known at this time in history.

Theological Insights

The polytheism that characterized ancient pagan thought could conceive of evil as the conflict between rival deities. Job, however, believes in one God, who is sovereign over all of life. Thus, when faced with severe adversity, Job is compelled to trace his problems back to their ultimate cause in God himself. The classical formulation of the problem of evil asks this question: if God is all-powerful and all-good, then why do bad things happen to good people in God's world? (Compare the interchange between Habakkuk and Yahweh in Hab. 1:2–2:3.) Job is not willing to diminish either God's power or his goodness, nor will Job admit to sins that he has not committed. This conundrum is at the heart of Job's consternation as he views his personal experience within the theological context of

God's character and rule, and it leads him to appeal to God to exercise justice on his behalf (cf. the lament psalms, esp. Ps. 44).

Teaching the Text

As Job reels under the continual blows of his adversity, he feels weaker and weaker. By Job 16, he is exhausted under the relentless attack that has affected him physically, psychologically, socially, and spiritually. It would not be surprising to the reader if Job decides at this point to give up on life and on God, but he does not. Rather, even in his great pain Job persists in looking to God for help. In what appear to be hopeless circumstances, Job keeps hoping in God's justice. Job will learn and grow much in his faith in God over the course of the rest of the book, so what he says in chapter 16 is sometimes startling to read. Nevertheless, his fervent anticipation of God's justice is a good pattern for us to follow.

Job begins his response to Eliphaz by dismissing the speeches of the friends as unhelpful. Instead of encouraging him, as Job would have done were he in their place, the friends utter long speeches that bring only trouble and pain to Job. They began with the good intention of being a comfort to Job, but they actually have exacerbated his problem. As a result, Job feels isolated from the very people whom he needs to draw close to him in his time of trouble.

What is even more excruciating to Job is his perception that God as a warrior is attacking him rather than defending him. Using vivid language, Job describes how God seems like a vicious enemy who keeps pommeling

Even though Job insists that his hands are not guilty of violence and his prayer is pure, under the divine assault he feels as good as dead. He goes into mourning because of his dire predicament, and his face is stained by his incessant weeping. He has no visible reason to hope, for as far as he can see all is lost.

Nevertheless, Job dares to keep hoping for God's justice. He calls on the earth to preserve the evidence of his innocence and of the unjust punishment he has received. Looking toward heaven, Job places his hope in an advocate whom he wishes would plead his cause before God, as Abraham earlier pleaded for the deliverance of Lot from the divine judgment directed at Sodom. Job has no clear revelation as to who this advocate will be or when he might arise, but Job hopes for divine justice all the same. His hope is in God, even though he has no idea how his hope might be fulfilled.

Job describes God as a warrior who attacks him. Shown here is a bronze figurine representing the god Baal wearing a sword, carrying a shield, and poised to strike with his battle ax.

him again and again. Under this barrage, Job buckles in pain. Instead of coming as a champion to defend him, God appears to take the offensive against Job, and Job cannot understand why that should be. As so many Christians experience, pain and adversity prompt deep and troubling theological questions that are not easily dismissed or answered.

Illustrating the Text

Job becomes exhausted in the face of his friends' verbal attacks.

Film: *My Fair Lady*. The musical *My Fair Lady*, as well as the film of the same name starring Rex Harrison and Audrey Hepburn (1964), is based on George Bernard Shaw's play *Pygmalion*. In the musical and the film version, in a song called "Show Me," Eliza Doolittle complains about how Professor Higgins is all talk and no action, a parallel to Job's description of the long-winded speeches of his friends.

Job perceives that God is a warrior attacking him relentlessly.

Film: *Schindler's List.* In this 1993 movie directed by Steven Spielberg, British actor Ralph Fiennes plays the role of a German commandant of a concentration camp who takes sadistic joy in targeting and assaulting the prisoners relentlessly. It is not, perhaps, far-fetched to suggest that Job feels this kind of assault from God.

Though Job sees no visible reason for hope, he dares to hope for God's justice.

Quote: *Disappointment with God*, by Philip Yancey.

> Despite the fact that all but a few pages of Job deal with the problem of pain, I am coming to the conclusion that Job is not really about the problem of pain. Suffering contributes the ingredients of the story, not the central theme. Just as a cake is not about eggs, flour, milk, and shortening, but uses those ingredients in the process of creating a cake, Job is not 'about' suffering; it merely uses such ingredients in its larger story. . . . The more important battle, as shown in Job, takes place inside us. Job teaches that at the moment when faith is hardest and least likely, then faith is most needed.[1]

Film: *Conviction.* This film (2010) contains the inspirational true story of a sister's unwavering devotion to her brother. When Betty Anne Waters (played by Hilary Swank) finds that her older brother Kenny (Sam Rockwell) is arrested for murder and sentenced to life in prison in 1983, Betty Anne, a Massachusetts wife and mother of two, dedicates her life to overturning the murder conviction, something she succeeds in doing after grueling years of persistence.

Job Finds No Hope in Life or in Death

Big Idea *Wherever he looks, Job can see no hope.*

Understanding the Text

The Text in Context

In chapter 17, Job continues the speech that he began in chapter 16. In the previous chapter, Job primarily complained about God's treatment of him. In chapter 17, although he still speaks of God, his emphasis has shifted to how his friends have mistreated him in his time of great need. Job's language is strong and bitter as he describes how the friends have mocked him (17:1–10). He ends his speech by saying that he cannot see hope in either life or death (17:11–16).

Historical and Cultural Background

In 17:3, Job uses the language of ancient commercial law when he calls upon God to accept a pledge for him against his friends' charges that he is guilty of sinning. He supposed that the friends would stand as character references to defend him, but instead they have witnessed for the prosecution against him. Job, then, pictures himself as a debtor who offers security for a loan that he cannot presently repay (cf. Gen. 38:17–18; Exod. 21:2–6; Deut. 24:10–15). His words reflect the custom that a piece of property could be given by a debtor to a creditor as a pledge until the debtor could pay off his obligation (cf. Job 24:9). Job here calls upon God to trust him until his innocence can be proved.

The legal language Job uses to talk about a pledge and putting up security (17:3) is also found in ancient Near Eastern contracts. This cuneiform tablet (right), along with its envelope (left), is a contract dealing with the loan of silver and the pledge of repayment at harvesttime (Kültepe, Turkey, ca. 1850 BC).

Interpretive Insights

17:2 *Surely mockers surround me.* In chapter 17, Job shifts his focus from the useless words of the friends (16:3) to the hurtful attitude they have displayed toward him. Although they purport to be his friends and they came originally to comfort him (2:11), Job now hears them as scoffers who speak with hostility against him. Job feels disgraced by them, as the psalmists are by people who mock them (e.g., Pss. 22:7, 13; 119:51).

17:3 *Who else will put up security for me?* Because Job regards the three friends as mockers (17:2), he cannot turn to them for help. Although he feels under attack by God (16:9–14), Job still believes that God knows that he is innocent. With no human to testify on his behalf, Job in effect calls on God to be a cosigner for him, to provide security until Job's innocence can be proved. Job's only recourse is in God, even though God seems to have failed him (17:6) by making him an object of ridicule.

17:5 *If anyone denounces their friends for reward.* Perhaps employing a familiar proverb of his day, the precise meaning of which is now difficult to understand, Job uses harsh language to criticize his friends. Apparently, Job perceives that they are trying to impress God by upholding the retribution formula as they condemn Job. For his part, Job regards their allegations against him as perjury, and he says that if they have wrongly denounced him as foolish, then their children will have to bear the consequences of their false and damaging testimony against him.

17:8 *The upright are appalled at this.* Job insists that because his situation is a troubling aberration of the retribution principle, righteous people should be appalled at the adversity that he is experiencing. According to the retribution formula, those who are righteous are blessed by God, but those who are wicked receive adversity from God. Job says that if a righteous person like him could suffer as he does, then others who are righteous could suffer as well. By saying this, Job implicitly calls into question the supposed righteous character of his friends, because they have defended their theological dogma at the price of defaming Job's innocence.

17:10 *I will not find a wise man among you.* Far from conceding to the friends' negative assessment of him as guilty, Job discounts them all as foolish. They purport to be wise teachers, but they are in fact fools (cf. Rom. 1:22), so Job has lost all confidence in their counsel. He dares them to bring on their best arguments, but he is convinced that nothing they could say would be wise. Job categorically rejects them and all that they have said as foolish.

17:11 *My days have passed, my plans are shattered.* Before his extreme adversity, Job assumed that he would live out his days in prosperity and peace (29:18–20), but what has actually transpired is the opposite of his optimistic expectations. As he surveys his life, he sees it passing away quickly without his dreams coming to fruition. Rather, all that he has planned is now destroyed and in pieces. Unable to find hope in his life, Job turned hopefully to his friends, but they have provided no help for him.

Key Themes of Job 17

- Job regards his friends as hostile and unhelpful mockers.
- Job feels that God has made him an object of ridicule.
- Job senses that his life is passing by without his hopes being fulfilled.
- Job can foresee no hope in death.

17:12 *turn night into day.* Job insists that his friends have totally misconstrued his situation. In Isaiah 5:20, Isaiah pronounces an oracle of divine judgment against people of his day who substitute ethical darkness for light and light for darkness. Using the same language, Job says that what is bad the friends call good, and what is good they reject as bad. As they desperately try to hold on to the retribution principle (cf. Bildad's words in 8:5–7), despite Job's adversity that calls it into question as an absolute formula, they have managed to conclude that Job must be guilty, when in fact that is not the case. They have gotten it exactly wrong.

17:14 *if I say . . . to the worm, "My mother" or "My sister."* Throughout the book of Job, the worm is used as a metaphor for decay. In 7:5, Job's flesh is clothed with worms. Worms eat decaying corpses in 21:26. Worms eat the wicked in 24:20. Bildad's final assessment of humans is that they are mere maggots and worms before the transcendent God (25:6). Here, Job asks about the implication of being closely related to the worm, that is, being a human who will suffer decay in death. If that is all there is for him to anticipate, then what kind of hope is that?

17:15 *where then is my hope?* Earlier in the book, Job considered death as a welcome escape from his intense pain (3:11–13). By now,

however, he has come to realize that death is in reality corruption, and that it is not a source of genuine hope. Job is therefore left with no hopeful prospect in life for the present, or in death in the future. If he has no hope either in life or in death, then he must either yield to despair or find hope in some other source. By asking "Where then is my hope?" Job frames the right question, but he does not as yet know the right answer. That answer will come to Job only when Yahweh finally speaks to him in chapters 38–41.

17:16 *Will we descend together into the dust?* Job is feeling the keen sting of grief from the loss of his family, and he realizes that death cannot give his children back to him. As in 3:17–19 and 7:9 (cf. Ps.

In 17:16, Job talks about going down to the gates of death. In this scene from the Book of the Dead of the scribe Nebqed, a doorway is shown leading down the tomb shaft, into which the dead man's soul, pictured as a bird, descends (Egypt, Eighteenth Dynasty, fourteenth century BC).

6:5), death is viewed as a shadowy and joyless semi-existence in which the dead are trapped. Job's hope will not come in his death, for the grave cannot restore to him a sense of family.

Theological Insights

Job feels that he has been treated so poorly by others that people even spit in his face (17:6), which was the ultimate expression of contempt in his culture, as in many cultures since then. Rather than receiving the respect that his noble behavior deserves (Job 29), Job instead is the object of despicable insults that he does not deserve (Job 30). What Job describes in likely exaggerated language is what Jesus actually endured as he was treated shamefully during his trial. Specifically, Jesus was spat on by members of the Jewish council (Matt. 26:67) and by the Roman soldiers (Matt. 27:30), as he humbled himself by becoming obedient even to death on the cross (Phil. 2:8).

Teaching the Text

As Job continues to struggle with the adversity that has afflicted him, he tries to find hope to sustain him. In his speeches, Job looks in various directions to see if he can discern a reason to be optimistic. His mind pursues one direction after another, but each time he comes to the sobering realization that he cannot anticipate any relief from the pain he is experiencing. Wherever he looks, Job can envision no hope. Readers of the book of Job who feel trapped by a severe medical condition, financial hardship, deep grief, or profound loneliness can relate to the feelings of hopelessness that Job expresses in this chapter.

Job's three friends arrived with the good intention of bringing comfort to him. However, the more they talk, the less insight they seem to communicate. As Job listens to them, he becomes increasingly upset with them. By this point in the book, Job regards his friends as hostile mockers who only make his problems worse by what they say. He finds no hope in them. When even his friends have failed him, Job more and more has to turn to God.

Job, however, also feels that God has not helped him in his time of need. Rather, God's actions toward him have only made Job an object of ridicule. Job's piety seems like a waste, and his trust in God appears ill founded, because Job's adversity continues unabated. Those who view Job through the lens of retribution theology can only conclude that Job is sinful and self-deceived. Thus, at this stage in the book Job finds no hope in God.

As Job considers his life, he senses that it is slipping away quickly without his hopes being fulfilled. Even though Job's understanding of wisdom prompts him to look for hope in this life, all he finds is disappointment. As much as he wants to enjoy the desires of his heart during his life on earth (cf. Pss. 27:13; 37:3–5), he has to concede that he can find no hope in life.

Earlier in the book, Job expressed his hope that death would provide relief from the adversity he is experiencing. Nevertheless, as he ponders that idea Job comes to the realization that death means decay and the grave is not a place of life, joy, or praise. Therefore, Job concludes that if he is to have hope, it cannot be found in death.

Job feels that instead of bringing comfort, his friends have mistreated him in his time of great need. Gustave Doré interprets the scene of Job speaking to his friends in this illustration from Doré's English Bible (1866).

This chapter is sad, because it describes Job's problem without disclosing the solution to his problem. Job has a clear understanding of where hope cannot be found, but as yet he cannot see where his hope lies. Only as the book continues to unfold will Job come to discover where he can find the hope he needs to sustain him. As readers, we must not press the pause button at this point, but we must move forward with Job to learn the final answer, which is found in God alone at the end of the book.

Illustrating the Text

It is possible to know where hope cannot be found yet to be unable to see where hope lies.

Poetry: "A Man Said to the Universe," by Stephen Crane. The American novelist, short story writer, and poet Stephen Crane (1871–1900) was an influential writer who died before he was thirty. Crane was considered a realist and a naturalist, naturalism being generally defined by the belief that the natural world is the whole of reality. Many of his short stories, poems, and other works show what could be interpreted as bitterness and anger or, sadder yet, a kind of resignation to the idea that God is absent. The following brief poem indicates such a philosophy.

A man said to the universe:
"Sir, I exist!"
"However," replied the universe,
"The fact has not created in me
A sense of obligation."

One can imagine that Job might have been tempted to feel this way.

Literature: *The Scarlet Letter*, by Nathaniel Hawthorne. Across most cultures, one of the worst insults a person can receive is to be spat upon by others. Both Job and Jesus suffered such insult. The book *The Scarlet Letter* (1850) by Hawthorne (1804–64) depicts the drama of Hester Prynne, a young Puritan woman living in New England who is condemned to forever wear on her clothing the label of adulteress, in retribution for transgressing the bonds of her loveless marriage with Roger Chillingworth. Hester Prynne commits the act with an initially unknown man in the story, the Reverend Arthur Dimmesdale. While, unlike Job and Jesus, Hester is certainly guilty of breaking a law, she becomes a figure who is spat upon, openly mocked, and hated even when she has accepted full responsibility and lives with dignity.

Biography: *John McCain: An Essay in Military and Political History,* by **John Karaagac.** In this book, Karaagac cites John McCain's words describing his solitary confinement after being shot down on his first mission over Hanoi. He had already completed twenty-three solo missions over Vietnam. Karaagac quotes McCain as saying, "It's an awful thing, solitary. It crushes your spirit and weakens your resistance more than any other form of mistreatment. . . . The first few weeks are the hardest. The onset of despair is immediate, and it's a formidable foe."[1] Job must have felt that he was in solitary confinement. Job's infected, diseased body likely confined him to live alone, a sharp contrast to the vigorous health and lifestyle he had previously enjoyed. In addition, even though his friends were physically present and speaking to him, their inability to comprehend and sympathize with his plight made Job feel emotionally isolated.

Bildad Again Beats the Retribution Drum

Big Idea *Bildad's theological system leaves no room for a righteous person to suffer as Job has.*

Understanding the Text

The Text in Context

Bildad's second response to Job, in this chapter, echoes many of the points made by Eliphaz in his second speech, in Job 15. As a theoretical thinker, Bildad views Job's situation as a generic case study of retribution, not as the unique, personal tragedy that it is. Bildad's rigid thinking, therefore, leaves him little room to encourage Job. Bildad begins with a strong retort against Job (18:1–4), rejecting as nonsense what Job has said. The major portion of Bildad's speech (18:5–21) is a lecture; he contends that the world functions as a machine in which wickedness is always judged by God. In this speech, Bildad considers only the negative side of the retribution principle, that bad things happen to bad people. Doubtless he believes that the positive side of the equation, that God blesses those who are righteous, is irrelevant to Job's situation. In the third cycle, Bildad will speak only briefly (25:2–6), so chapter 18 constitutes the major statement of his position.

Historical and Cultural Background

In 18:13–14, Bildad twice uses descriptions that are reminiscent of the Canaanite god Mot. As he alludes to Job's debilitating skin disease, Bildad speaks of death's firstborn devouring the limbs of the wicked person (18:13). In the Canaanite literature, Mot is the god of the underworld, who has a voracious appetite for humans. In the context of Job 18, the term "firstborn" could refer to disease, but more likely it speaks of Mot's exalted status as the god of death (contrast Christ, who is described as "the firstborn over all creation" in Col. 1:15). Mot is also depicted as the king of the demons who brings pain to the living (cf. 18:14).[1]

Interpretive Insights

18:2 *When will you end these speeches?* Job ended his previous speech, in chapter 17, with a list of rhetorical questions, and Bildad opens his second speech in the same fashion. Once again, too, the speaker starts with a verbal barrage of insults (cf. Eliphaz in 15:2–3 and Job in 16:2–3). Bildad charges that Job (or perhaps the other friends, because "you" is plural) has been playing clever word games rather than entering into serious debate. By urging Job to be sensible, Bildad implies that Job's words are nonsense and that therefore there are no reasonable grounds for conversing with him. It is evident that by this time all of the speakers are frustrated, curt, and ineffective with one another.

18:4 *is the earth to be abandoned for your sake?* Now using the singular pronouns and distorting Job's previous words in 14:18 and 16:9, Bildad wrongly portrays Job as insisting that God's moral order must be overturned just for him. According to Bildad, Job holds that everybody else is wrong, and only he is right, making him sound like a petulant child who

In Job 18, Bildad uses descriptions reminiscent of the Canaanite god Mot. The Baal Epic, on the tablet shown here, tells the story of Baal's death and his victory over Mot.

Key Themes of Job 18

- Bildad dismisses Job as speaking nonsense.
- Bildad insists that the wicked are always just a step away from calamity.
- Bildad provides no hope for Job in the past or in the future.
- Bildad's viewpoint marginalizes God's activity in his world.

demands his own way. He sees Job as consumed by his angry emotions rather than thinking through the issue reasonably.

18:5 *The lamp of a wicked man is snuffed out.* In Bildad's system of thought there is no room for ambiguity or for exceptions. Rather, life is thoroughly predictable, because wickedness is always punished without fail (cf. Ps. 1:6; Prov. 12:21). The fact that God is not mentioned at all until verse 21, and then only in passing, suggests that Bildad views the retribution formula as an inflexible natural law, much like the law of gravity. From Bildad's perspective, God set into motion the moral universe, and now it proceeds by the retribution principle, almost like a machine without divine intervention.

18:6 *The light in his tent becomes dark.* Bildad uses the image of life as a tent in 8:22, and he will refer to it again in 18:14, 15. Because Bildad continues to use the same metaphor, the reader wonders if he has indeed heard anything that Job has said in the interval, or if Bildad has instead just waited impatiently and inattentively until it was his turn to speak again. In the book of Job, light often refers to life and darkness to death (3:5; 10:21; 17:13). The wicked will be driven from light into darkness, that is, from life into death (18:18). This is the only possibility in Bildad's tidy world, which is driven by the retribution formula.

Fire and Brimstone

Bildad's graphic language is reminiscent of the description of God's destruction of the wicked cities of Sodom and Gomorrah in Genesis 19:24, 28, as well as predictions of the eschatological judgments in Ezekiel 38:22 and Revelation 9:17–18; 14:10. Burning sulfur, or brimstone, produced total, catastrophic devastation that left long-term barrenness on the land. For this reason, at times it was used by ancient armies to destroy a vanquished city's ability to rebuild. Therefore, fire and brimstone became a cliché for an agent of total destruction.

18:8–10 *His feet thrust him into a net.* Bildad continues to emphasize that there is no way for the wicked to avoid just retribution for sin. In verses 8–10, six different terms for trap are used. This concentration of similar language indicates that wherever the wicked go, they are just a step away from being caught and ensnared in a trap that they cannot foresee. There is no way that they can avoid the judgment that their sin deserves. To Bildad, judgment for the sinful is thoroughly predictable.

18:14 *He is torn from the security of his tent.* Picking up his reference to the tent of the wicked in verse 6, Bildad goes on in verse 14 to say that the wicked person is snatched from the supposed safety of that person's dwelling. Throughout this extended poem in 18:5–21, Bildad repeatedly alludes to the details of Job's calamity, and he connects them with the destructive consequences that come to the wicked. Bildad clearly hints that Job's sin has set into motion the calamities that he has experienced. To Bildad's thinking, Job is receiving only what his sin deserves.

18:15 *burning sulfur is scattered over his dwelling.* See the sidebar, "Fire and Brimstone."

18:17–19 *The memory of him perishes from the earth.* Bildad says that the wicked will both die and be forgotten. They have no physical descendants (18:19), offspring who could provide a biological future for them. In the Old Testament, barrenness or death without surviving descendants was regarded as a deep grief (cf. the anguished cries of Rachel in Gen. 30:1 and Hannah in 1 Sam. 1:11–16). Those who had no physical posterity to carry on their name resorted to other means to gain some form of social immortality. For example, Absalom builds a monument by which he can be remembered (2 Sam. 18:18). In Psalm 49:11 the rich call their lands after their own names. Bildad in this passage concludes that the wicked are left without any future, because no one remembers them (18:17) and they have no offspring to survive them (18:19).

18:21 *such is the place of one who does not know God.* Bildad's only reference to God in this speech comes in his very last word. This mere passing nod to God suggests that Bildad has constructed a deistic system that works mechanically, and in which God does not actively intervene to alter the retribution formula. In Bildad's thoroughly predictable world, justice requires the punishment of the wicked, and adversity is proof positive that a person is sinful. Bildad's system of thinking is so rigidly dogmatic that no exceptions are considered, so the prospect of a righteous man suffering what Job has endured is ruled out by definition. Instead of seeing Job's situation for what it actually is, the case of a righteous man suffering a terrible calamity, Bildad insists on viewing Job in stereotypical terms that fit his retribution formula.

Theological Insights

In Job 18, Bildad pictures in vivid terms the triumph of death over the wickedness of humans. In the larger context of the Bible, however, death does not give the final answer, because both the Old Testament (Isa. 25:8) and the New Testament (1 Cor. 15:50–57; Rev. 21:4) promise that death itself will be defeated by the Lord. Death, which entered into the human experience due to the disobedience of Adam and Eve (Gen. 3), will eventually be conquered by virtue of the substitutionary death and resurrection of the Son of God. As Bildad speaks confidently to Job in this chapter, he fails to understand how what Job is experiencing fits into God's larger narrative of redemption.

Teaching the Text

As Bildad presents his second speech, it is evident that his theological system leaves no room for a righteous

> Bildad uses the imagery of various trapping devices to describe the fate of the wicked. This Assyrian relief shows deer being trapped with a net. On the right side, by the Assyrian hunter, one deer has become ensnared in its mesh (palace at Nineveh, 645–635 BC).

person to suffer as Job has. Bildad thinks in clearly defined, black-and-white categories. To his way of thinking, the retribution principle is a fixed formula that always applies in every situation. Thus, wicked people always receive adversity, and adversity only comes upon wicked people. To Bildad, Job is simply another case that can easily be categorized.

Bildad uses poetic language to draw a picture of a wicked person who is always just a step away from calamity in a world governed by retribution. Using a variety of terms describing different kinds of traps, Bildad indicates that for the wicked it is only a matter of time until their sin is punished as they deserve. The question is not *if* they will receive punishment, but only *when* it will overtake them. Obviously, Bildad thinks that Job has already been entrapped because of his sin.

Bildad offers to Job no hope for the present or for the future. Cruelly alluding to the destruction of Job's children, Bildad insists that the wicked have no future, either biologically or socially. Job will not have the

joy of children to survive him, and neither will others remember him after his death. Job, then, is left with no hope to which he can cling. The first rule in comforting others is to give them the grounds for hope. Bildad is a vivid example of how *not* to provide comfort to a person in pain.

Throughout his speech, Bildad does not speak of God until he finally mentions him in his very last word. This verbal pattern in Bildad's speech parallels the way in which Bildad marginalizes God's activity in the world. Bildad confidently describes how the world works according to a rigid retribution formula that continues to function almost like a machine. To Bildad's thinking, God started a system that proceeds to work like a clock without any intervention by God. What Bildad presents as though it were an unchangeable law is a far cry from what the prologue indicates about Yahweh's active governance of his world. For godly people in pain, the providential care of the Lord is the ground for confident hope even when all seems hopeless. God's continual super-intendence of the world is a far cry from Bildad's position that relegates God to the corners of life, when in fact he works all things according to his plan, although that plan is often inscrutable to humans.

Illustrating the Text

Christians are not spared from suffering; to argue otherwise is unbiblical.

Film: *Indiana Jones and the Last Crusade.* Bildad's picture of the traps that threaten the wicked person can be illustrated by *Indiana Jones and the Last Crusade* (1989), in which Indiana Jones (played by Harrison Ford) has to make perfect decisions about where to step as he approaches the Holy Grail. Even the slightest misstep will

Shown here is the site known as Bab edh Drha, one possible location of ancient Sodom.

bring his immediate death. Such depictions are not comforting to a friend suffering adversity.

God is a personal God involved in our lives, unlike Bildad's portrait of God.

Literature: *Tess of the D'Urbervilles*, **by Thomas Hardy.** Hardy presents an unrelenting deistic and naturalistic view in all his novels, a fully developed version of what Bildad pictures. In this literary work, Tess is doomed by an impersonal notion of justice that fails to consider any mitigating factors in her experience (her youth, her rape). Fate seems to move her relentlessly and cruelly toward her end. She says at one point, "You, and those like you, take your fill of pleasure on earth by making the life of such as me bitter and black with sorrow; and then it is a fine thing, when you have had enough of that, to think of securing your pleasure in heaven by becoming converted!"[2]

Poetry: "Affliction (IV)," by George Herbert. In a wonderful poem called "Affliction (IV)," the British metaphysical poet and beloved pastor George Herbert (1593–1633) wrote the following lines indicating his trust in God's involvement with even the deepest suffering. These are the last two verses of the poem:

> Oh help, my God! let not their plot
> Kill them and me,
> And also thee,
> Who art my life: dissolve the knot,
> As the sunne scatters by his light
> All the rebellions of the night.

> Then shall those powers, which
> work for grief,
> Enter thy pay,
> And day by day
> Labour thy praise, and my relief;
> With care and courage building
> me,
> Till I reach heav'n, and much
> more, thee.[3]

Geography: Verse 15 could be illustrated by way of a photograph or descripton. The traditional site of Sodom and Gomorrah along the shore of the Dead Sea is to this day uninhabitable, as pictures of the region clearly demonstrate.

Job's Hope against Hope

Big Idea *In a situation that seems hopeless, Job maintains a ray of hope in God.*

Understanding the Text

The Text in Context

In chapter 19, Job responds to Bildad's second speech. Job uses a mixture of lament and legal language to express how abandoned he feels by his friends (19:1–6), by God (19:7–12), and by the full range of people in his community (19:13–19). In the final verses of the chapter, Job pleads with his friends for compassion (19:20–22), he articulates his hope for a redeemer to take up his cause (19:23–27), and he warns his friends that they will have to face God's judgment (19:28–29). Job does express some faint hope in God, even though his predominant emotion at this time is hopelessness. Only after Yahweh speaks to him in chapters 38–41 will Job's hope find its fulfillment.

Historical and Cultural Background

In Job 19:25 "redeemer" is a translation of the Hebrew word *go'el*. This term was used in Old Testament legal literature to refer to a near relative who was called on to perform several important roles. If a family member was forced into slavery due to debt, the *go'el* was responsible to pay the debt and

release him (Lev. 25:47–48). The *go'el* also was required to remove a mortgage from a relative's property (Lev. 25:25), to marry a childless widow and produce an heir for the deceased (Ruth 4:3–5), and to avenge the death of a relative who had been killed wrongfully (Num. 35:12). In addition, the *go'el* likely served as a legal advocate for his relative. The term came to be applied figuratively to Yahweh as he liberated the people of Israel from bondage in Egypt (Exod. 6:6) and later from their Babylonian captivity (Isa. 49:7–9).

Interpretive Insights

19:2–3 *How long will you torment me?* With these words, Job echoes Bildad's opening questions in 8:2 and 18:2. Job, however, uses the plural form of "you" to indicate that he is complaining against all of the friends. Using the round number "ten" to refer to an indefinite but large number (19:3; cf. Gen. 31:7), Job accuses them of repeatedly hurting and humiliating him by what they have said and how they have spoken. Job has already been broken by his calamity, and now he also feels crushed by their shameless words. He has no patience left for these disappointing friends.

19:4 *my error remains my concern alone.* Job suggests that the friends speak as though he has offended them. Using hypothetical language rather than admitting to any sin, Job insists that if he has committed a minor, inadvertent error (cf. Lev. 5:18; Num. 15:28), not the kind of heinous, intentional crime that they have accused him of committing, then it would be a matter between God and him alone. The friends have no legal standing for prosecuting him as they have. Nevertheless, they are intruding where they do not belong. Job as much as tells them to mind their own business and leave him alone.

19:6–7 *then know that God has wronged me.* In this chapter, Job feels wronged both by his friends (19:3) and by God (19:6). Rejecting Bildad's earlier implication that God does not pervert justice (8:3), Job perceives God as breaking his own righteous rules in how he treats Job. Despite Job's scream of outrage (19:7), God seems to dodge acquitting Job, and he keeps Job hanging for a resolution to his case. In short, in Job's eyes God has failed to give him a fair trial.

19:8–12 *He has blocked my way so I cannot pass.* In picturesque and vivid language, Job complains that God has treated him as though he were an enemy (19:11). Rather than vindicating Job, God has worked against him in a multitude of ways. God will not let him escape, but

instead he hinders Job's flight (19:8). This is the opposite of the divine protective hedge around Job that the adversary complained about in 1:10. God also has removed Job's honor (19:9), in contrast to the exalted

Job feels as though God is treating him as an enemy, sending troops and building siege ramps (19:12). In this portion of the Assyrian relief showing the attack on the Israelite city of Lachish, Assyrian soldiers are advancing up a siege ramp (Sennacherib's palace, 700–692 BC).

place of humans in Psalm 8:5. All in all, Job feels as though he is under a frontal assault by God's massed armies, which threaten him so much that he has no hope for survival (19:12).

19:13–19 *He has alienated my family from me.* In 19:13–19, Job reflects the deep and pervasive social isolation that he is feeling. By citing twelve individuals or groups of people, Job indicates that his sense of community has been totally broken as his social world has collapsed. His relatives and friends have abandoned him (19:13–14). Rather than treating Job with respect and eager obedience (cf. Ps. 123:2), his servants ignore him (19:15–16). His immediate family regards him as repulsive (19:17). Even the little boys in his society ridicule him (19:18), and his closest friends detest him (19:19). Job feels that all those on whom he thought he could depend have turned against him.

Consequently, he is left all alone as a social pariah to face his great adversity.

19:21–22 *Have pity on me, my friends, have pity.* With these pathetic words, Job calls on his friends to act as true comrades by being compassionate to him. Despite all they have said and done to him, Job still looks to them with hope. He asks them why they have joined God in hounding him (19:22). Job sees himself as struck by the hand of God, so he needs his friends to side with him, not against him.

19:23–24 *Oh, that my words were recorded!* Job insists that he is innocent, but he has no expectation that anyone else will stand up with him in his defense (19:13–22). Sensing that he could well lose this legal dispute because the deck seems to be stacked against him, Job longs for a permanent record to be made that could witness forever to his character. He does not want justice to die with him; rather, he wants his claim to keep speaking even after his death.

19:25 *I know that my redeemer lives.* See the sidebar.

19:26–27 *yet in my flesh I will see God.* Job's hope, however, is not just for the future. Here Job may well be thinking, or at least desire, that after his severe suffering God will intervene on his behalf to restore him within his lifetime on earth (cf. Ps. 27:13). Indeed, in 42:5 Job does at last get to see Yahweh and he does receive the restoration for which he has longed, including God's legal pronouncement of his innocence (42:7–8). Because Job's language speaks about seeing God after his skin has been destroyed, many have taken this verse as an Old Testament anticipation of the personal resurrection of the Christian, but that is likely adding much to what Job himself means to say.

Theological Insights

Job 19:25 may be the best-known verse in the book of Job, but often it has been read through the lens of the New Testament doctrine of resurrection, most famously in Handel's aria in his oratorio *Messiah*. The content of the book of Job makes it highly unlikely that Job is here thinking of resurrection at the end times, because that would be revealed by God only much later in history. Similarly, only in the New Testament would the concept of redemption be developed to speak of what Christ has accomplished for humans as the divine provision for the justification of sinners (Rom. 5:8–9); as the ultimate redeemer for sinful humans, Christ is able to plead successfully for them on the merits of his own perfect substitutionary atonement for sin.

Teaching the Text

The book of Job will eventually end on an optimistic note as Yahweh speaks to Job in chapters 38–41 and then restores him to a place of blessing in chapter 42. At this point in the story, however, Job is nearly consumed by a feeling of hopelessness. Wherever he looks, he finds ample reasons for giving up. Most people in this kind of traumatic situation would abandon all hope, but even when all seems hopeless Job maintains a ray of hope that sustains him. Although a careful analysis of Job 19 in its context does not support reading it as a reference to Christ's resurrection and final judgment, nevertheless Job with the limited revelation available to him is able to keep hoping that he

Job wishes his words could be recorded on a scroll or engraved in rock, where they would remain forever (19:23). The Behistun Inscription, shown here, was an attempt by King Darius the Great to have his victories remembered forever. After the relief and inscription were carved, the cliff face was sheared off (Bisitun, Iran, 520–519 BC).

will see God, that is, that he will be restored to favor with God.

The misguided attempts by Job's friends to explain why Job is suffering are both inaccurate and insensitive. As a result, Job does not feel comfort from them but rather he feels humiliation. Their words crush Job as the friends become harsher and more shrill in their accusations. By speaking beyond what they truly understand, the friends only add to the deep pain Job is feeling. He complains that they are stepping in where they do not belong and speaking in ways that do not help him.

Even more troubling to Job is his sense that God is treating him wrongfully. Job cannot comprehend why God would bring adversity into his life and then refuse to answer his complaints. Job calls out for God's justice, but all he has received from God is silence. From Job's perspective, it seems as though God has sent his armies to besiege him as an enemy. All of this is beyond what Job can understand. It does not fit the theological system of retribution that Job previously held as true. It makes no sense to him that God would treat him as though he were wicked, when Job knows in his heart that he is innocent before God.

As Job describes his treatment by various people in his community, the full range of his social isolation comes into focus. He is estranged from his relatives, forgotten by his friends, ignored by his servants, offensive to his wife and brothers, and ridiculed even by the town boys. Physically and emotionally, Job is reduced to skin and bones, and he desperately needs human compassion. Despite the apparent hopelessness of his situation, Job is able to imagine a desirable future for which he can hope, if only dimly. He states that he knows that someone will stand up as his *go'el* to be his legal defender. He cannot identify who that defender will be, but he is confident that after the deep adversity that has destroyed his life, he will at last see God and be restored to favor with the Lord, who has seemed to forsake him. This is Job's hope against hope that sustains him in the deepest days of his adversity. In the meantime, Job will have to wait, placing himself and his cause in God's hands. In this, he serves as an example to us today as we must wait on the Lord while enduring our adversities (cf. Ps. 27:14; Isa. 40:31).

Illustrating the Text

Like Job, we may feel wronged by God when we go through adversity.

Hymn: "How Tedious and Tasteless the Hours," by John Newton. This hymn was written by Newton (1725–1807), who is perhaps best known for his hymn "Amazing Grace." What follows are the first and last verses of the song. Frank Boggs, a traditional musician, made a wonderful recording of this song.

> How tedious and tasteless the
> hours,
> When Jesus I no longer see;
> Sweet prospects, sweet birds and
> sweet flowers,
> Have all lost their sweetness to me;
> The midsummer sun shines but dim,
> The fields strive in vain to look gay.
> But when I am happy in Him,
> December's as pleasant as May.
>
> Dear Lord, if indeed I am Thine,
> If Thou art my sun and my song,
> Say, why do I languish and pine?

And why are my winters so long?
O drive these dark clouds from the
    sky,
Thy soul cheering presence restore;
Or take me to Thee up on high,
Where winter and clouds are no
    more.

We must look beyond the present to a hopeful future, based on our knowledge of God.

Autobiography: *The Hiding Place*, **by Corrie ten Boom.** Ten Boom (1892–1983) tells the story of how her sister Betsie was able to maintain hope in God while suffering unimaginable deprivation in a German concentration camp during World War II. Betsie, never strong in health, grew steadily weaker and died in the camp on December 16, 1944. Some of her last words to Corrie looked to the future: "We must tell them what we have learned here. We must tell them that there is no pit so deep that He is not deeper still. They will listen to us, Corrie, because we have been here."[1]

Film: *The Fugitive.* This suspenseful movie (1993), starring Harrison Ford and Tommy Lee Jones, is based on the much earlier television series by the same name. In this story, a prominent physician has been wrongfully accused and convicted of murdering his wife. Escaping his captors, he is pursued relentlessly. He maintains a sense of hope and endurance that helps him to stay alive, elude his accusers, and finally bring about justice. This hope is based on the solid foundations of his innocence and on the profound belief that he will be able to prove that innocence to his pursuers, a feat he does accomplish. This hope keeps him calm and focused.

History: Statue of Liberty National Monument. Job's desire for his words to be inscribed permanently can be illustrated by Emma Lazarus's memorable poem inscribed on a tablet at the base of the Statue of Liberty on Ellis Island. Some of the famous words from that inscription read, "Give me your tired, your poor, / Your huddled masses yearning to breathe free." Just as Job's words "I know that my Redeemer lives" become the rallying cry of his life, a cry based on what he knew about God, so too Emma Lazarus's words, based on a nation's stated goals, have given hope to millions of immigrants.

Zophar's Final Words for Job

Big Idea *Zophar insists that God always punishes the wicked.*

Understanding the Text

The Text in Context

In Job 20, Zophar speaks to Job for his second and final time, because in the third cycle Zophar chooses not to answer him. So this chapter constitutes Zophar's final answer to his friend. Numerous times he alludes to details in Job's previous speeches, often trying to turn Job's words against him, but in particular Zophar responds indignantly to Job's reproof in 19:28–29. However, he dismisses what Job says rather than really interacting seriously with the points he has raised. For Zophar, there is no room for an exception to the retribution formula, as Job claims he is. Zophar insists that the pride of the wicked will be humbled (20:1–11), the appetite of the wicked will destroy them (20:12–23), and the destruction of the wicked is certain (20:24–29). Considering only the negative side of the retribution principle (cf. Eliphaz in 15:17–35 and Bildad in 18:5–21), Zophar contends that it is a fixed law by which God always decrees judgment on wicked humans.

Historical and Cultural Background

When Zophar describes God's judgment as a "bronze-tipped arrow" (20:24), he alludes to one of the primary weapons of the ancient warrior. For hand-to-hand combat, the sword and dagger were used, and at the medium range the spear was the first choice. But to make a long-range impact, the warrior would employ a bow and

In 20:24, Zophar describes God's judgment as a "bronze-tipped arrow." In ancient Israel, arrowheads were made from flint, bone, or metal. Shown here are bronze arrowheads found during the excavations of the city of David in Jerusalem (ninth to eighth century BC).

arrows (see Ps. 127:4–5 for a metaphorical use of this image to speak of the effect a father can have through his children).[1] A weapon made of bronze would be especially lethal. Although Zophar speaks specifically of a bronze bow, that would be unwieldy and too rigid to launch arrows with potent force, so many translations paraphrase the expression to make it refer to an arrow that has been fitted with a bronze head.

Interpretive Insights

20:3 *I hear a rebuke that dishonors me.* When the first few verses of each speech in the book of Job are examined, it appears that all the speakers have a thin skin. They find it easy enough to dish out insults, but they complain about being dishonored when someone says the same kind of things to them. Their elevated sense of honor and shame does not allow them to accept a rebuke silently or graciously. As a result, as the book progresses the tone of the conversation rapidly degenerates into meanness and ridicule. In this passage, Zophar seems much more concerned about his own wounded ego than about Job's grievous pain and humiliation.

20:4–5 *the mirth of the wicked is brief.* Zophar cannot tolerate even the flickering ray of hope that Job expresses in chapter 19. Seeking to quench what he considers unwarranted optimism, Zophar insists that any happiness that the wicked do enjoy is at best temporary. In Zophar's view, the wicked always die young, not full of days (but contrast Job's long life in 42:17). Zophar assumes that the retribution formula is well established by tradition (20:4), but in verse 5 he unwittingly undercuts his own argument. If the

wicked enjoy even temporary joy, then the retribution formula is not as absolute as Zophar presumes. In effect, he is agreeing in principle with Job, even though not to the same degree; Job argues that his adversity, despite his blamelessness, demonstrates that there is not a perfect correlation between how a person behaves and the consequences received.

20:6–11 *Though the pride of the godless person reaches to the heavens.* In 20:6–11, Zophar develops the principle that the higher a wicked person rises, the harder he or she will fall, likely subtly alluding to Job's former lofty status as "the greatest man among all the people of the East" (1:3). Using vivid language, Zophar pictures the proud wicked perishing like dung (20:7). Insensitive to Job's recent loss of his family, Zophar goes on to say that the children of the wicked will have to compensate the poor, no doubt for what their father has extracted wrongfully from them (20:10). Although Zophar's principle can be seen at work in God's judgment on the hubris of various people (e.g., Gen. 11:1–9; Isa. 14:12–20; Ezek. 28:1–19), and it echoes the wisdom saying that pride goes before destruction (Prov. 16:18), he is off the mark when he implies that this is what is happening in Job's experience.

20:12–19 *his food will turn sour in his stomach*. In 20:12–19, Zophar describes how God uses the sins of the wicked to bring about their destruction. The prominent imagery in this passage is eating, as Zophar says that what they eat will eat at them. By this means, Zophar vividly applies the maxim of Proverbs 26:27, which notes that people get what they deserve, because evil acts contain within them the seed of their own punishment. Thus, the very food that is ingested by the wicked will become the source of poison within them.

20:20–22 *In the midst of his plenty, distress will overtake him*. In 20:20–22, Zophar asserts confidently that the wicked, despite their brief prosperity, will inevitably suffer a tragic reversal. Their greed will lead to cravings that cannot be satisfied (20:20), their treasure will not endure (20:21), and their plenty will be overtaken by misery (20:22). Later, in chapter 30, Job will lament how his past blessings have deteriorated into his present adversity. As Zophar describes the divine judgment on the wicked, his point is evident: what Job has suffered is due to his personal sin, and it is not an anomaly at all, as Job has wrongly maintained.

20:24–25 *a bronze-tipped arrow pierces him*. Similar to the image in Job's earlier complaint in 6:4, God is pictured here as an archer who attacks the wicked. The arrow speaks of a weapon that can make a long-range impact, and a bronze tip on the arrow would give it especially lethal force. This image, therefore, pictures the sudden and unexpected judgment by God on sinners, and it echoes similar language

According to Zophar, the wicked will not be able to flee from God's anger. God's judgment, like well-aimed arrows, will find its intended target. This Assyrian battle scene shows both the king and his god with bows drawn and an enemy fallen with two arrows in his back (palace at Nimrud, 865–860 BC).

in the Psalms (18:14; 21:12; 64:7; 77:17). Zophar's implication is that the wicked may run, but they cannot escape God's judgment (cf. Amos 5:18–19).

20:26 *A fire unfanned will consume him.* With these words, Zophar either intentionally or insensitively alludes to the fire of God that destroyed Job's sheep and servants in 1:16. It seems that Zophar is so caught up in his argument that his rhetoric runs roughshod over Job's feelings as he grieves his profound losses. As a result, Zophar makes his own point by kicking Job when he is down.

20:27 *The heavens will expose his guilt; the earth will rise up against him.* In ancient Near Eastern treaties, the heavens and the earth were the traditional witnesses to the covenant agreement, and this same language is used in the Bible (Deut. 32:1; Isa. 1:2). When Job maintained his innocence in 16:18–19, he appealed to the heavens and the earth as witnesses that could corroborate his claims. Zophar now insists that all of creation will testify to the guilt of the wicked person. Because of that, there is no place for the wicked to hide from God's justice.

20:29 *Such is the fate God allots the wicked.* Zophar does not directly condemn Job in this chapter, but all of his allusions to Job's experience make it evident that he is not just talking about abstract theology but is implying its relevance to Job's situation. Zophar considers Job so hopeless that he does not even appeal to him to repent, as he did in his first speech (11:13–19). In Zophar's opinion, Job is too far gone, and he can only anticipate total destruction from God, because God invariably destroys the wicked. God's rigid moral order guarantees the fate of Job, because Zophar's tight system leaves no place for an exceptional case

or for divine grace to the sinner. Because Zophar has now spoken his final word, he remains silent when it is his time to reply to Job in the third cycle of speeches.

Theological Insights

Zophar's description of the wicked losing the riches that they have accumulated (20:15) connects with a familiar theme in the Bible. The problem of evil asks why bad things happen to good people in God's world, but passages like Psalms 49 and 73 ask why good things happen to bad people (see the sidebar "Why Do Good Things Happen to Bad People?" in the discussion of Job 12 above). Similarly, in Luke 16:19–31 Jesus tells the story of the wicked rich man and the beggar Lazarus, in which the roles of the two individuals are reversed after death. Both Hannah (1 Sam. 2:1–10) and Mary (Luke 1:46–55) celebrate how God elevates the righteous poor above the wicked rich. In all these cases, God evens the scales so that justice is done, sometimes during earthly life and other times after death.

Teaching the Text

Job 20 contains the final speech by Zophar, and it is apparent that he is resolutely fixed in his position. Zophar views life in black-and-white terms as he presents an extreme form of retribution theology. Looking only at the negative side of the equation, Zophar insists that God always destroys the wicked. Zophar cannot conceive of a special case, as Job claims to be, in which a righteous person could suffer adversity in God's ordered world. For Zophar, all one has to do to determine the inner character of a person is to observe what that person experiences in life. If a person receives the kinds of affliction that have come upon Job, then that person is indeed wicked, because God always repays sinners with affliction. In times of adversity, it is tempting to seek clear, definite answers. However, the book of Job teaches us that God does not always explain what he is doing, and his plans may deviate from the general patterns that we observe in life. Some things we must leave in God's hands, for they are mysterious from our limited perspective.

Despite his inflexible conclusion, Zophar has to recognize that the wicked do enjoy some happiness at times. Nevertheless, he states that sinners can at best experience only temporary joy (20:4–5). Zophar does not seem to realize that this concession flies in the face of the certainty that he insists on later in the chapter. He fails to notice that a careful observation of life actually supports Job's claim that the retribution principle has exceptions. Zophar turns a blind eye to this evidence that should have prompted him to revise the absolute categories in his system of thinking. As we evaluate life and as we counsel others, we must be careful to consider all the facts, not just those that agree with the conclusion we want to maintain.

Zophar focuses his attention on how the proud wicked are humbled (20:6–11). Those who are elevated in their status, as Job has been esteemed as the greatest man in the East, will have to suffer a downfall that fits their great sin. Those who at one time viewed them with respect will come to scorn them. What they have extorted from the poor, their children will have to repay. Zophar pictures a reversal, in which those who were formerly rich and powerful will have to go cap in hand to those whom they previously oppressed.

Zophar's vivid illustrations in 20:12–23 develop the point that sinful acts carry within them the seed of the destruction of those who perpetrate them. Thus, the punishment of sinners is not arbitrary or erratic but is a consistent and necessary consequence of doing what is evil. The cravings that drive people to do what is wrong will cause them to eat what will eventually destroy them, just as a fish in consuming the bait also swallows the hook that brings its demise.

By the end of Zophar's speech, he leaves no room for Job to expect anything but God's judgment. In Zophar's mind, Job stands guilty and condemned, without any other possible result. Zophar does not plead with Job to repent, as the other friends have done, but rather he paints a picture of certain and total destruction. As far as Zophar is concerned, Job's adversity is proof positive that he is wicked, and his wickedness requires that he must necessarily be punished by God. Nothing that Job has said could alter the firm conclusion to which Zophar has come. In arguing that the wages of sin is death, Zophar is on solid biblical ground. But we must also remember that Romans 6:23 goes on to say that the gift of God is eternal life. Along with his judgment, God also extends his grace to sinners.

Illustrating the Text

Punishment is a result of wrongdoing; surrender to evil will destroy the sinner.

Film: *The Days of Wine and Roses.* In this beautifully acted and compelling old movie (1962) starring Jack Lemmon and Lee Remick (remade as *When a Man Loves a*

Woman in 1994), we see the consequences of addiction, a condition that is probably one of the most powerful examples of the destruction of sin. In the film Lemmon, an alcoholic, introduces an innocent girl to drinking; she eventually capitulates to his pressure. At the end, he has been rehabilitated but must live with the knowledge that she may never make it out of addiction.

Sports: Many athletes in the doping scandals of recent years consumed performance enhancement drugs, but the very drugs that enabled them to achieve athletic success not only damaged them physically but also stripped them of their honors, ruining the reputation they had worked to achieve.

News Story: In recent history, two governors of Illinois (representing both political parties) have been tried for some kind of political manipulation (George Ryan and Rod Blagojevich). George Ryan was sent to jail, even having to stay there while his wife was dying of cancer. Rod Blagojevich also went to jail. A number of senators and members of Congress have had their reputations ruined for perverse and undignified sexual activities. The brazenness of the behavior in so many cases indicates that they must have thought they would get away with it.

Film: *The Principal* (1987). In this unsentimental treatment of an inner-city, crime-ridden high school, a new principal, played by James Belushi, arrives. Having nothing to lose because of past failure in his personal life, he sets about challenging the brutal students who have taken over the power base. "No more" becomes his theme. It is a hard battle, fraught with danger, but Belushi (with the help of a security guard, played by Louis Gossett Jr.) is unrelenting. Evil choices render evil, but they can be defeated through good choices.

God will bring justice, either during earthly life or after death.

Literature: *Shane*, **by Jack Schaefer.** In the old Western movies, the standard plotline was that the good guys (usually wearing white hats) always succeeded in the end, and the bad guys were killed or brought to justice. Everything was resolved in tidy categories, just as in Zophar's system in the book of Job. Unlike Zophar's system, however, God's is not tidy or predictable. His is more like the classic Western novel *Shane* (1949) by Jack Schaefer, thought to be the best-written Western of all time. While the good guy wins in ways that are not stereotypical, the battle is complex and shows great restraint.

Job Destroys the Friends' Major Argument

Big Idea *Job demonstrates that the observable evidence argues against the absolute application of the retribution principle.*

Understanding the Text

The Text in Context

Up to this point in the book, Job has been on the defensive as his friends argue that the retribution principle is an absolute pattern for life. In particular, the friends have insisted that Job must be a sinner, because the wicked are always judged by God with adversity. In his speech in chapter 21, Job unhooks the necessary connection between a person's acts and the experiences that follow. Job repeatedly states points that have been made by the friends, and then he refutes the points by citing specific observable examples that clearly contradict their major argument. Again and again, Job shows that in fact the wicked often prosper, in stark contrast to what the retribution principle teaches. By the end of the chapter, Job rejects the friends' answers as empty. With these dismissive words, Job brings the second cycle of speeches to a close.

Historical and Cultural Background

As Job describes the idyllic life he has observed being enjoyed by many wicked people, he pictures the family of the wicked singing to the music of the tambourine, the harp, and the flute (21:12; NIV: timbrel, lyre, and pipe). In the ancient Near Eastern world, these three common instruments represented the percussion, string, and wind families. More significantly, in a cultural context in which most people had to work long hours just to subsist, making music represented a rare life of privileged affluence. The wicked about whom Job speaks are able to enjoy the good life, as did Job's family in the prologue (1:4), a stark contrast to Job's miserable situation after his adversity has set in.

Interpretive Insights

21:3 *Bear with me while I speak.* As Job reflects on what his friends have said, he senses that they have given up on him. They do not seem to be interested in listening *to* Job but only in talking *at* him. No doubt his words are punctuated by frustration as he urges them to be silent and to listen carefully to what he is trying to say to them.

After that, they can continue to deride him. Just as the friends have dismissed Job as arrogant and blasphemous (cf. Eliphaz's charges in 15:2–13), so he writes them off as mockers who only want to ridicule him.

21:4 *Is my complaint directed to a human being?* Job realizes that if his dispute were with the friends or with any other human, then there would be established legal procedures for handling the case. Job's complaint, however, is with God, so he cannot figure out how to get the matter resolved. As the rest of the chapter will reveal, the prosperity of the wicked, along with the adversity that Job, although righteous, has endured raises profound theological problems for him. He hoped that the friends would stand as allies with him in his affliction, but they have in fact added to his trauma by blaming him (21:5–6).

21:7–15 *Why do the wicked live on?* The friends' unwavering commitment to retribution theology has caused them to accuse Job of wickedness. By this time in the story, Job has taken enough of their rhetorical punches, so in chapter 21 he launches a counteroffensive against their position. By pointing to numerous examples in life, Job demonstrates that the friends are blind to what actually occurs in human experience. In fact, Job's description of the prosperity of the wicked (21:7–15) closely parallels Eliphaz's portrayal of the righteous person in 5:17–27, and it directly contradicts Zophar's assertion in 20:5–11 that the joy of the wicked is only fleeting. Job points out that the wicked often live to old age and prosper (21:7), they have happy families

and secure possessions (21:8–9), their cattle bear profusely (21:10), they enjoy family tranquility (21:11–12), they do not suffer debilitating disease but die painlessly (21:13), and they enjoy all of this even as they reject God (21:14–15). The observable facts, then, do not support the claims by Job's friends that sinful acts and painful consequences are invariably linked together.

21:16 *I stand aloof from the plans of the wicked.* Echoing the language of Psalm 1:1, Job emphatically rejects the charges by the friends that his adversity proves that he

Job observes that the wicked sing and make merry to musical instruments and spend their years in prosperity (21:12–13). In this modern cast of an ancient plaque from Mesopotamia, the upper register shows banqueters enjoying the music of a harpist.

is wicked. On the contrary, Job does not stand in the way of sinners, but is righteous, rejecting the wicked and disavowing all they stand for.

21:17–21 *Yet how often is the lamp of the wicked snuffed out?* In 18:5–6, Bildad asserted that the light of the wicked goes out. By asking this question, Job now inquires rhetorically if Bildad's claim is well founded on evidence. Job goes on to use observation, the typical means for acquiring knowledge in traditional wisdom (cf. Prov. 6:6–8), to counter what Bildad has said. Similarly, Zophar in 20:23 contended that God sends his anger against the wicked, so Job asks how often divine calamity actually comes upon sinners. Also, in 5:4 Eliphaz stated that God punishes the children of the wicked, but Job counters by saying that that is not really judgment on the wicked themselves (21:19–21; cf. Ezek. 18:1–4, which insists that the one who sins is the one who will be punished). Job's conclusion is that when actual experience is evaluated, the retribution principle does not hold consistently.

21:22 *Can anyone teach knowledge to God?* Job's rhetorical question clearly anticipates a negative answer, because the data that Job has discussed demonstrate that God's exercise of justice transcends what humans can comprehend. The point that Job draws from this is that the retribution formula assumed by his friends is not adequate to explain how God always works. Consequently, their insistence on applying the retribution formula to Job's situation is not valid. Later on, Job himself will have to admit that neither does he understand the ways of God (42:2–3).

21:23–26 *Side by side they lie in the dust.* Retribution theology tries to evaluate a person's acts and consequences as black and white, but Job demonstrates from actual examples in life that such a rigid distinction does not hold up under careful scrutiny. In 21:23–26 Job insists that there is not a strict correlation between one's morality and the prosperity or adversity that comes to one's life. Two people living very differently can come to the same apparent end (cf. Eccles. 9:1–3). Therefore, within the bounds of observable life, the retribution principle does not always hold true.

21:29 *Have you never questioned those who travel?* Job challenges the friends to expand their range of observation to ask people who have been around what they have seen elsewhere. His implication is that the perspective from the friends' theological ivory tower is too narrow for them to see fully what life can teach them. Their commitment to retribution theology has blinded them to some of the relevant data, so they have neglected evidence that contradicts the conclusion they have drawn.

21:32 *They are carried to the grave.* Job continues to press his point that the friends' formula does not fit all the facts. Far from being consistently punished, the wicked are often honored, even with grand funerals. Despite what the friends have contended, when life is considered in its entirety, evil people do often avoid punishment during their lifetimes. They seem at times to avoid their moment of truth before the divine Judge.

21:34 *Nothing is left of your answers but falsehood!* Job is not comforted or convinced by what the friends have said. In fact, the more he evaluates the issue, the more problems he has with the legitimacy of the retribution formula, because it does not fit his personal situation, and it does not explain many other cases he has observed. Job, therefore, rejects their answers as nonsense (*hebel*, perhaps better translated "enigmatic," as its sense often is in Ecclesiastes) and falsehood, a betrayal of true friendship.

Theological Insights

This chapter brings into high relief the contrast between, on the one hand, the retribution principle found frequently in Proverbs and maintained absolutely by the friends and, on the other hand, Job's position that the retribution principle must be significantly amended. Just as Job has argued that his adversity does not mean that he is wicked, so now he demonstrates from observation that the wicked often enjoy the full range of blessings that retribution would reserve for those who are righteous before God. As Job points to the prosperity of the wicked, he echoes other Old Testament passages, such as Psalms 49 and 73 and Jeremiah 12:1–4. All of these passages complain that the wicked sometimes prosper and the righteous sometimes suffer adversity in God's world. Even though they raise deep and troubling questions, in their larger contexts they all point in the direction of God's sovereign, but at times inscrutable, will. The classic example of this disconnect between one's personal character and how one is treated is the death of Christ, in which the sinless Son of God suffered crucifixion at the hands of evil men, all within the predetermined plan of God (Acts 2:22–24).

Teaching the Text

In this chapter, Job uses observable evidence to demonstrate that the facts argue against the absolute application of the retribution principle that the friends have vigorously applied to his situation. They have insisted that Job's adversity proves that he is a sinner, because bad things invariably happen to bad people. Job turns their teaching on its head by scrutinizing what actually happens to wicked people. What he has observed time and again is that wicked people actually often prosper in life. If that is the case, then the necessary link between a person's acts and the

Job points out that even in death the wicked may still receive honor rather than punishment, with funeral processions and guarded tombs (21:32). In Egypt, elaborate funeral processions were common, such as the one shown on this reproduction from the Book of the Dead (Papyrus of Ani, thirteenth century BC).

consequences that that person receives from God is broken. By this means, Job endeavors to show that the friends' condemnations of him are not valid. Although retribution is a general pattern in life, we must not press it into a rigid formula. There may well be additional factors at work in God's sovereign plan, as Jesus notes in John 9:1–3.

As Job observes wicked people, he sees that they often live long and well. They prosper across the full range of life, including their families, their possessions, and their personal happiness. This is not an anomaly; it is a frequent occurrence that seriously calls into question the retribution principle. Traditional observation-based wisdom taught that retribution is the pattern that God uses as he governs his world. Job takes that same approach, but he looks more carefully at life, and what he sees with more precise observation drives him to a different conclusion. Theology often tries to give clear and definitive answers, but at the same time it must be open and flexible enough to include all of what God is doing in his world.

With this evidence in mind, Job argues that God does not always judge the ungodly during their lifetimes. Even those who have no interest in the things of God at times enjoy undiluted prosperity, and sometimes they even make it to the grave unscathed by divine judgment. How God actually deals with humans, then, cannot be explained by the tidy formula of retribution, because that does not fit all the observable evidence that Job has adduced.

Because of this, Job reasons that humans are not in the position to teach God how he should deal with humans. What God does transcends the knowledge available to humans. Both righteous people and wicked people may come to the same apparent end—that cannot be explained by the human mind. Humans must therefore concede that the ways of God are inscrutable rather than try to shoehorn God's ways into categories that satisfy what finite humans can comprehend. As Job will come to learn at the end of the book, humans need to accept that what God does may transcend what they can understand. Because God is trustworthy, we must leave in his hands those things that surpass our understanding, confident that our wise and good Lord knows and controls all the factors that elude our comprehension.

As Job evaluates what the friends have said in the light of the evidence he has observed, he concludes that they speak to him in an enigmatic and unfulfilling way. Here at the end of the second cycle of speeches Job rejects their total line of argument and dismisses their answers to him. His frontal assault on the position that the friends have so confidently asserted marks the approaching deep impasse between Job and the friends. Job's argument has devastated the retribution formula as the sole explanation for his adversity. However, Job does not yet have another compelling alternative to put in its place. He, like us, will have to trust God for what he does not yet comprehend, rather than lean on his own faulty understanding (cf. Prov. 3:5).

Illustrating the Text

The retribution principle is, as Job has discovered, false.

News Story: One can cite many contemporary examples of prominent world leaders,

actors, musicians, sports heroes, and politicians who are thoroughly ungodly in their lifestyle yet still seem to prosper in their lives. Idi Amin (1925–2003), military leader and president of Uganda, is an example. Amin's rule was characterized by human-rights abuse, political repression, ethnic persecution, extrajudicial killings, nepotism, corruption, and gross economic mismanagement. The number of people killed as a result of his regime is estimated by international observers and human-rights groups to range from one hundred thousand to five hundred thousand. He died in exile, but he was not really brought to justice. The same goes for countless other despotic leaders.

Astronomy: In ancient times, observations by astronomers and astrologers of the heavens led to the Ptolemaic view of the solar system, in which the earth was the center. However, more careful observations by Copernicus in the sixteenth century caused people to view the solar system as revolving around the sun, a different and finally accurate perspective. Job similarly argues that better observation counters the retribution principle, in contrast to what less rigorous observation previously suggested.

God's inscrutable ways sometimes transcend the knowledge available to humans.

Classic Poetry: Emily Dickinson. This great American poet (1830–86) wrote more than a thousand poems but had only a handful published in her lifetime. Throughout her work, she carried on significant, often troubled, conversations with God. In a number of her short poems, such as #1551, she labors over the hiddenness of God:

> Those—dying then,
> Knew where they went—
> They went to God's Right Hand—
> That Hand is amputated now
> And God cannot be found—

In lines from another, #1601, she expresses the problem of not even knowing what she has done wrong:

> Of God we ask one favor,
> That we may be forgiven—
> For what, he is presumed to
> know—[1]

Eliphaz Condemns and Counsels Job

Big Idea *Eliphaz accuses Job of sins he has not committed and gives Job advice that does not apply to him.*

Understanding the Text

The Text in Context

Job 22 begins the third and final cycle of speeches, and it is evident that Job and his friends are rapidly reaching an impasse. In the third round, the speeches are much shorter than before, and eventually the dialogue disintegrates completely when Zophar's turn comes but he does not speak (after chapter 26). In addition, the speakers are increasingly frustrated and caustic with one another. In Job 22, Eliphaz takes a hostile tone of condemnation as he seeks to maintain his own theological dogma by attacking Job's integrity. He begins by stating that Job's situation is of little concern to Almighty God (22:1–5). He goes on to charge that Job is ethically wrong in his behavior (22:6–11) and theologically wrong in his beliefs (22:12–20). Eliphaz finishes by counseling Job to submit to God so that his prosperity can be restored (22:21–30).

Historical and Cultural Background

In Job 22:14, as in Isaiah 40:22, God is pictured as reigning in the vault of heaven above the earth. Similar descriptions can be found in other ancient Near Eastern literary texts. In Mesopotamia, the sun god Shamash directs the earth from the circle of heaven, which could be construed either as a flat disk or as a dome above the earth. In Egypt, the sun god Ra or Aton exercises much the same function in terms that are reminiscent of Psalm 104. From this exalted position, God should be able to observe all human activity (Job 22:12), but Eliphaz falsely charges Job with saying that God's sight is obscured by clouds, so that God cannot see what is occurring in the human realm of life (22:14).

Interpretive Insights

22:2–3 *Can a man be of benefit to God?* This is the first of eight rapid-fire questions that Eliphaz poses to Job in 22:2–5. As in his earlier speeches (4:2, 6–7; 15:2–3), Eliphaz gives Job no time to answer his queries, but now his questions become even more aggressive and accusatory. In effect, Eliphaz uses his questions as a club to beat on Job rather than as a pedagogical strategy to bring him into greater understanding, as Yahweh later does by his queries in chapters 38–41. When he asks if a man can be of benefit to God, Eliphaz implies that the transcendent God is so distant that the good or evil that humans do is of no concern to him (22:3). Eliphaz fails to realize that if human behavior means nothing to God, then the whole retribution principle, which insists that God always rewards the righteous and always punishes the wicked, is invalidated.

22:4 *Is it for your piety that he rebukes you?* With this sarcastic question, Eliphaz demonstrates that he has totally misjudged Job's character and attitude toward God. Eliphaz intends to strike at the heart of Job's self-defense that he is innocent before God, but Eliphaz does not realize that it is Job's

piety, commended by God himself in 1:8 and 2:3, that prompted the adversary to accuse him. In reality, Job's piety stands at the root of the adversity he has endured, but not at all in the sense that Eliphaz wrongly supposes.

22:5–9 *Is not your wickedness great?* After posing this rhetorical question, Eliphaz goes on in 22:6–9 to accuse Job of a series of flagrant ethical offenses. Without acknowledging

Eliphaz describes God's dwelling place in terms that reflect the ancient cosmology of his day. This drawing illustrates an Israelite perspective on that cosmic geography. The earth was regarded as disk shaped and supported by pillars, with the netherworld beneath it and cosmic waters around it. Mountains at the edges held up a solid dome, which separated the sky from the heavens. God ruled from his temple and throne, which were located above the upper waters.

Preaching to the Wrong Audience

In 22:21, Eliphaz begins to preach a great sermon, but unfortunately he addresses it to the wrong audience. No doubt, Eliphaz has a sincere concern for Job's welfare, but his diagnosis of Job's situation is faulty, so his prescription to Job is off the mark as well. He presumes that what Job has experienced is rooted in his lack of piety, but in reality there are much larger forces at work, as the prologue details. Without realizing it, Eliphaz comes to much the same point as what the adversary has alleged in 1:9, that Job's apparent piety is simply a calculated ploy to maintain the prosperity that God could give to him. Eliphaz presses Job to submit to God by confessing his sins, so that he can regain his former state of divine blessing. However, Yahweh's final commendation of Job and his criticism of Eliphaz in the epilogue (42:7–8) will make it evident that Eliphaz has erred in his prescription for Job.

that he is contradicting how he previously commended Job in 4:3–4, Eliphaz invents crimes to justify from his perspective the extreme punishments that Job has received (even though the prologue states that Job shunned evil [1:1, 8; 2:3]). Giving no objective evidence to sustain his serious charges, Eliphaz accuses Job of extortion (22:6), withholding charity (22:7), abuse of power (22:8), and oppression of helpless widows and orphans (22:9). All of these alleged offenses pertain to Job's treatment of people in need, and they are all linked to financial matters in some way. In chapter 31, Job will categorically deny all these charges.

22:10 *That is why snares are all around you.* Eliphaz seems not to have heard or grasped Job's point in chapter 21 that the wicked often prosper, along with its implied corollary that the righteous may suffer adversity. Using the same imagery of traps that Bildad emphasized in 18:8–11, Eliphaz continues to insist that Job's adversity is proof positive of his grievous sins, and that God is bringing upon Job the judgment that his sins deserve.

22:13–14 *Yet you say, "What does God know?"* In this verse, Eliphaz misconstrues Job's previous complaints about God's silence. He accuses Job of saying that God is unable to know what Job is doing, so he can sin with impunity. By contrast, Job spoke in 7:17–20 about how he feels under constant scrutiny by God. Rather than hearing Job accurately, Eliphaz has actually superimposed his own extreme position about God's transcendence upon Job, when that is not at all what Job believes.

22:15–17 *They were carried off before their time.* Eliphaz rhetorically asks Job in verse 15 if he is going to proceed down the same path that evil humans have taken in the past. Then Eliphaz alludes to the generation of Noah, when virtually the whole human race was destroyed by God because of its profound wickedness (Gen. 6). They, too, presumed that God's judgment would not touch them (Job 22:17; cf. Matt. 24:37–39), but they suffered divine punishment, as Eliphaz implies will also come upon Job.

22:21–22 *Submit to God and be at peace with him; in this way prosperity will come to you.* See the sidebar "Preaching to the Wrong Audience."

22:23–25 *then the Almighty will be your gold.* With these words, Eliphaz hints that the love of wealth is the root of Job's evil (cf. 1 Tim. 6:10). Eliphaz presumes that Job's gold has become his god, turning his heart away from the Almighty. According to Eliphaz, Job needs to renounce his desire for wealth and make God first in his heart. That, Eliphaz supposes, will resolve Job's problem and remove his adversity.

22:26 *Surely then you will find delight in the Almighty.* Eliphaz completes his final speech on a rhetorical roll, as he paints for Job an idyllic picture of his spiritual renewal and restored prosperity. All that Job needs to do is confess and forsake his sin of loving wealth, and then all can be well. In the light of the epilogue of the book, what Eliphaz says is ironic, because Job does come to enjoy the divine blessings that Eliphaz describes (42:10–17), but not because he follows the route that Eliphaz maps out for him.

22:27–28 *You will pray to him, and he will hear you.* Eliphaz gives a simplistic answer to Job's complex situation. Applying the retribution formula, Eliphaz gives no consideration to the possibility that there might be any other relevant factors at work in what Job has experienced. What Eliphaz counsels would indeed fit many situations, but it does not fit all cases, and in particular it does not address the specific case of Job. Actually, Job has already prayed fervently to God, but God has not answered him. Ironically, at the end of the book Job does pray to God, not to repent of his sin, but to intercede for Eliphaz, who Yahweh says has not spoken the truth (42:7–10).

Theological Insights

In 22:14 Eliphaz portrays Job as saying that God is veiled by thick clouds so that he cannot see human behavior. Numerous times in the Old Testament, Yahweh

In 22:24, Eliphaz tells Job to discard his "gold of Ophir." This ostracon, which mentions the "gold of Ophir," was found at Tel Qasile near Tel Aviv (eighth century BC). The location of Ophir is debated, but it was known for very-high-quality gold.

is pictured as in or accompanied by storm clouds. He speaks the Ten Commandments from a terrifying storm on top of Mount Sinai (Exod. 19:18–20:18). In Psalm 29, the transcendent Yahweh is depicted as a thunderstorm that moves across the land of Israel. Yahweh surrounds himself with clouds in Psalm 97:2, and he rides upon the clouds as his chariot in Psalm 104:3. At the climactic moment in the book of Job, when Yahweh at long last breaks his silence, he speaks out of a storm (38:1). Although he is exalted far above his creation, Yahweh is the omniscient God who knows completely all that transpires in the world he has made (Ps. 139:1–6).

Teaching the Text

Eliphaz has good intentions, but he fails to provide the kind of help that Job truly needs. Eliphaz insists on viewing Job's experience solely through the lens of retribution theology, and as he does that, his focus becomes blurred and his vision distorted. He does not accurately perceive the reasons that have prompted Job's adversity, so he accuses Job of sins that he has not committed, and he gives Job advice that does not apply to him. Because of this, Eliphaz fails to give the comfort that Job has hoped to receive from him. Eliphaz evidences that simple answers may not accurately resolve the complex questions in life.

In addition to not seeing Job's situation clearly, Eliphaz also has misconceptions about God. As he tries to defend the retribution principle, his reasoning leads him to the conclusion that retribution works so consistently that even God is unaffected by the good or evil that humans do. Eliphaz wants to impress on Job that God is not arbitrary but that he acts by fixed moral laws. However, Eliphaz ends up depicting God as so exalted that what humans do is of no particular concern to him. Instead of maintaining the theological balance that holds on to all the attributes of God, Eliphaz elevates one aspect of God's character above another. This imbalance brings Eliphaz to an inadequate and skewed view of God. Similarly, we must be careful to hold together biblical truths that may seem to be contradictory. For example, the Bible teaches that God is both just and gracious, that God is sovereign and yet humans are responsible for their actions, and that salvation is by divine election but also is offered to whoever will accept it.

Earlier in the book of Job, Eliphaz commended Job for his generous treatment of needy people. Nevertheless, contradicting what he previously has known to be true, Eliphaz in this chapter charges Job with all sorts of grievous sins against others. Once again, Eliphaz lets his logical reasoning compel him to a conclusion that is not accurate. Instead of speaking about what he *knows*, Eliphaz asserts what he thinks *should be* the case. By this means, he falsely represents Job as a terrible sinner rather than as the generous benefactor whom he previously admired.

Eliphaz also misjudges Job by putting erroneous words in his mouth instead of listening to what Job has really said and meant. What Eliphaz says about Job fits his own line of reasoning, but it is not an accurate record of what Job himself

At the end of his speech, Eliphaz encourages Job to "lift up your face to God. You will pray to him, and he will hear you" (22:26–27). This stele shows an Egyptian praying to his god. Notice the ears along the top left side. These were included in the painting to assist the god in hearing the prayers (Thebes, 1200 BC).

believes. If Eliphaz were more careful to listen to Job rather than let his theological commitment to retribution determine what Job must be thinking, then he would not accuse Job as he does. Effective counsel to people who are hurting requires careful listening to what they are saying and what they truly mean.

Because Eliphaz has erred in these fundamental ways, it is not surprising that his final counsel to Job is well off the mark. Eliphaz exhorts Job to submit to God, that is, to confess his sins. If Job does that, then as the retribution principle dictates, his prosperity will be restored. This makes perfect sense within the system of retribution theology that Eliphaz assumes. However, the rest of the book will make it evident that Eliphaz does not comprehend Job's situation nearly as well as he thinks he does. As a result, Eliphaz's counsel to his friend is not helpful but hurtful.

Illustrating the Text

Eliphaz falsely concludes God is too lofty to be concerned with human activity.

Philosophy: *Beyond Good and Evil*, by Friedrich Nietzsche. In the book *Beyond Good and Evil* (1886), the German philosopher Nietzsche (1844–1900) argues that good and evil should not be measured by reference to God or Christian values. Eliphaz's words were written long before Nietzsche lived, but Eliphaz also assumes a great distance between human morality and God when he asks if a human could be of benefit to God.

Short Story: "The Open Boat," by Stephen Crane. In this dark short story by the great American author (1871–1900), four men are tossed about in a lifeboat from a sunken ship, the *Commodore*. Their fate appears to be random; there is no transcendence. One of them says, "If this old ninny-woman, Fate, cannot do better than this, she should be deprived of the management of men's fortunes." [1]

Discern whether those who counsel offer a skewed view of God or use inaccurate reasoning.

Film: *It's a Wonderful Life.* In this beloved movie (1946) directed by Frank Capra, George Bailey (played by Jimmy Stewart) is well regarded for his legendary generosity to the people of Bedford Falls. Then, he is falsely accused by Mr. Potter of embezzlement. His life unravels, and he is thrown into despair. While the story eventually resolves, the journey is a hard one since Bailey does not keep his head about him and depend on the truth he knows about himself. He not only takes too seriously the inaccurate assessment of Mr. Potter but also falls into inaccurate reasoning about himself.

Literature: *The Pilgrim's Progress*, by John Bunyan. One of the themes one sees often in this classic allegory is the importance of having discernment. No one person consistently sees through the inaccurate reasoning he or she may hear, Bunyan seems to argue, so companionship is necessary. One of the deceitful characters, who mesmerizes with his words but who is insubstantial in his beliefs and seeks to confuse, is Talkative, who talks at length with the character Faithful. Faithful, discerning Talkative's skewed view of God, finally says, "I saw you forward to talk, and because I knew not that you had aught else but notion . . . your conversation gives this your mouth profession the lie." [2]

Job Feels Both Confidence and Terror

Big Idea *God's justice draws Job toward confidence, but God's sovereignty intimidates him.*

Understanding the Text

The Text in Context

In Job 23, Job rejects what Eliphaz has just said in the previous chapter, when he counseled Job to "submit to God and be at peace with him" (22:21). This is yet another indicator that the communication between Job and his friends is breaking down. Instead of speaking directly either to his friends or to God, Job speaks in a soliloquy, as he did in chapter 3. His internal conversation reflects how solitary and lonely he feels, as he is increasingly isolated from both humans and God. In the first twelve verses, Job expresses confidence before God but also his inability to find God in order to present his case before him. In verses 13–17, however, Job discloses that he also feels terror before Almighty God.

Historical and Cultural Background

In 23:10, Job alludes to the refining of gold as he expresses what God seems to be doing in his life. In the ancient world,

In 23:10, Job says that God is refining him like gold. This Egyptian relief from the tomb of Mereruka shows metalworkers at a forge (ca. 2350–2181 BC).

gold was refined by placing it in a crucible along with lead. As great heat was applied to it, the gold melted, and when it cooled the dross would adhere to the lead, leaving the purified gold (cf. Ezek. 22:17–22). In 23:10 this process is used to picture how God employs adversity either to refine Job from his sin (as the friends insist), or, better, to reveal the sterling quality of Job's life, which will be indicated by Yahweh's reproof of the friends in 42:7–8. The same image is used in Psalm 66:10, only with adversity being compared to the refining of silver, rather than gold.

Interpretive Insights

23:3–4 *If only I knew where to find him!* Job does not follow the counsel of his friends, who urge him to repent of sins that Job knows he has not committed. Confident of his own innocence, Job has a strong desire to meet God face-to-face, so that he can present his legal arguments before him (23:4). Job is prepared to argue for his own innocence, but he cannot find the Judge. Job does not suggest that he can manipulate or deceive God into doing his bidding, but he wants a fair trial that will clear him of the false charges that the friends have raised against him.

23:5 *I would find out what he would answer me.* Because Job cannot locate God, he is unable to present the evidence for his own innocence. Worse than that, God will not speak to Job, so Job is left to speculate what God would say if he were to break his silence. When Yahweh eventually does speak, beginning in 38:1, what he says is different from what both Job and the friends have anticipated.

23:6–7 *No, he would not press charges against me.* Job here is more optimistic than

he was previously, in chapter 9, when he thought that God would pronounce him guilty, even though he is blameless. He now is confident that God will pay attention to him and treat him justly (23:7). Because Job anticipates that he will be able to establish his innocence before an impartial judge, he believes he can come before God with confidence.

23:8–9 *But if I go to the east, he is not there.* In verses 8–9, Job looks in all directions for God, but he cannot find him wherever he searches. Because God seems inaccessible, Job feels frustrated. If Job cannot locate the courtroom and the judge, then how will he be able to get his case resolved? Job will have to wait until God chooses to reveal himself, and there is no way that Job can compel him to do that.

23:10 *But he knows the way that I take.* This statement by Job has been interpreted in two different ways. The NIV interprets it to refer to the omniscient God knowing the way that Job takes, in contrast to Job's lack of knowledge of God's whereabouts (23:8–9). Literally, the Hebrew reads, "God knows [his] way with me," which means that God knows what he is doing in Job's life. This more likely reading indicates that God is sovereign in directing Job according to the path that he has ordained for his servant (cf. 23:11–12). Job here reflects his trust that God knows what he is doing, even if Job cannot discern how this all makes sense.

when he has tested me, I will come forth as gold. Job is clearly convinced that God is not punishing him for his sins, so it is not likely that he here is referring to God's process of refining impurity out of his life. Rather, what God is doing through this intense adversity will demonstrate that Job's character has been gold all along. Through this painful experience, the exemplary quality of Job's character, which has been in dispute, will be recognized. This, then, is not refining that will make Job into gold, but it is an evaluation that will reveal that Job already is gold in God's eyes.

23:11 *I have kept to his way without turning aside.* The Old Testament wisdom literature often speaks of walking in the way of the Lord. Job does not turn aside to the right or to the left (cf. Prov. 4:26–27), but he keeps on God's path. God's way means following God's word (23:12; cf. Ps. 119:105). By his commitment to God's way, Job demonstrates that Yahweh's original evaluation of his life in 1:8 and 2:3 was accurate.

23:12 *I have treasured the words of his mouth more than my daily bread.* How a person lives reflects what a person loves, because actions follow values. Job's heart is devoted to God, so his behavior is directed according to God's way. By his commitment to God's words, Job evidences that he values God's wisdom more than even his daily food (cf. Prov. 8:10–11). Job lives a godly life because he loves God and all that God says.

23:13 *He does whatever he pleases.* Job's friends have insisted that the retribution formula is a rigid and reliable description of how God always works in the world. By their reckoning, God always rewards those who are righteous, and he always punishes those who are wicked, so that when a person like Job experiences adversity, that means he must have sinned. Job argues against his friends that God as sovereign is free to work according to his own plan, and he is not bound by some external rule like retribution. Even if God typically acts consistently with the retribution principle, his actions cannot be reduced to a neat and predictable formula that dictates how he must act at all times. Job has not arrived there yet, but in his thinking he is beginning to move toward the recognition of this that he will come to at the end of the book. No one is able to manipulate or coerce God to act in a particular way, because God's actions are totally under his own control.

23:15–16 *when I think of all this, I fear him.* As Job reflects on God's transcendent knowledge and power, he confidently feels drawn to God, but he also feels intimidated by him. The term "fear" in this verse is a different word from the one used in the expression "the fear of the Lord," which is the beginning of wisdom (Job 28:28; Prov. 9:10). Job here speaks of the terror that is evoked in his heart by God's overwhelming power; in verse 16, he continues by saying, "God has made my heart faint; the Almighty has terrified me."

Theological Insights

In Psalm 139:7–12, the psalmist states that no matter what direction he may go, God will certainly be there. The omnipresence of God is a great comfort to the psalmist. By contrast, in Job 23:8–9 Job searches for God in the east, west, north, and south but is incapable of finding him. This hiddenness of God prompts Job to wonder if God is not there, or if he is there but not willing to communicate with Job. This silence of God is difficult for Job to understand or to accept, just as it is for many of the psalmists (e.g., Ps. 13:1–2).

The language of divine testing is used frequently in the Old Testament. In Genesis 22, God tests Abraham's faith by directing him to offer up his son Isaac as a sacrifice. Psalm 66:10 pictures God as testing humans, using the language of the refining of silver. Because the Bible reveals God as omniscient, knowing all things, this testing is not designed to teach God something that he does not already know. Rather, testing, as in Job 23:10, is a demonstration of what is actually in the heart of the person who experiences God's affliction.

Teaching the Text

In chapter 23, Job is torn between two strong and conflicting feelings. On the one hand, as he reflects on God's justice, Job feels confident. Unlike the pagan gods of the ancient Near East, who are morally arbitrary and capricious, Yahweh is just in his character. Because Yahweh is just, Job can be confident that Yahweh will do the right thing for him. On the other hand, as the Sovereign God, Yahweh is free to do as he pleases. Job, therefore, cannot manipulate what Yahweh does, and he finds this disconcerting and even intimidating. We can be confident that the Lord will always be true to his unchanging holy character, but we also must remember that his ways are higher than our ways (Isa. 55:9).

Job can have confidence in God's actions because God's character is just. This is in contrast to the pagan gods, who could be capricious and arbitrary, requiring religious rituals (illustrated in this Egyptian painting) to be conducted precisely in order to gain their favor. Here offerings are presented to the god Osiris by the scribe Nebqed (fourteenth century BC).

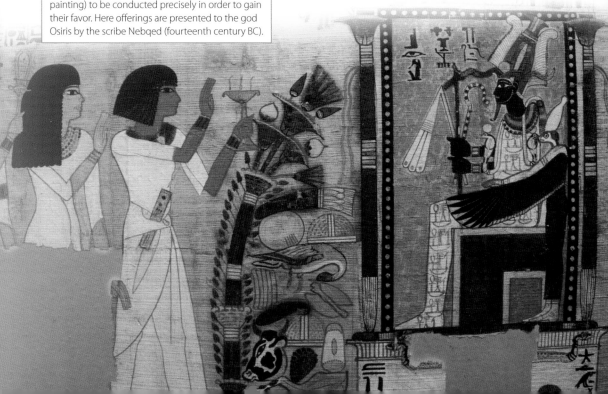

Friends can often be a useful mirror to us, because they can see aspects of our lives that we are prone to overlook. In particular, they can alert us to flaws and faults that we conveniently neglect to observe in ourselves. Job's friends think that they are helping Job by insisting that he needs to confess the sins that have brought adversity into his life, but in fact they are seeing things that are not really there. As Job searches his heart, he cannot agree with them. When he scrutinizes his actions, attitudes, and motives, Job does not detect sin but rather finds genuine righteousness. Because of this rigorous self-examination, Job is confident that he is innocent before God as he seeks to approach God with his legal defense.

Like many of the psalmists, Job complains that God seems silent and hidden. As Job prays and cries out to God, God does not answer him. No matter where he searches for God, Job cannot locate him. Job longs to regain communication with God, and he wants to stand before God to appeal his case, but God is nowhere to be found. Job's prolonged time of waiting is often echoed in the lives of Christians who have to learn through long and painful experience to trust God even when he seems silent and hidden.

Despite all his unanswered questions, Job also has some answers to share. He insists that God knew what he was doing as he ordered Job's life. Job also knows that his adversity, as painful as it is, will clearly demonstrate the quality of his life as a righteous man. He is confident that he has followed God's steps and treasured God's words. Job does not know what God is doing in his life, but he is convinced that God does know what Job is doing. By this, Job teaches us to place our trust in God himself, even when we cannot make sense of what he is doing in our lives.

Job is beginning to realize that God is both just and free. Job senses that in his sovereignty God acts in ways that may diverge from his general pattern. This unpredictable aspect of God's activity may be disconcerting, but to a person who truly

In 23:11, Job says, "My feet have closely followed his steps." While this is figurative language, we can find a visual picture at the ruins of a temple at Ain Dara, Syria. Here we see giant footprints, as if the god himself were walking into the temple. Those who served in the temple could then follow in the steps of the god.

trusts God, this divine sovereignty can be a welcome mystery. Every time we receive a surprising answer to prayer or an unexpected blessing, we experience God's sovereign freedom as his gift to us.

Illustrating the Text

At times, God seems silent and hidden to his children, as he does to Job.

Memoir: *Lament for a Son*, **by Nicholas Wolterstorff.** Wolterstorff is an American philosopher and professor emeritus of philosophical theology at Yale. In this moving and beautifully written piece, composed after the tragic death of his son in a mountain-climbing accident, Wolterstorff records the process of grieving, one similar to Job's. In a dark time Wolterstorff writes, "I am at an impasse, and you, O God, have brought me here. From my earliest days, I believed in you, I shared in the life of your people: in their prayers, in their work, in their songs. . . . For me your yoke was easy. On me your presence smiled. Noon has darkened. . . . And where are you in this darkness? I cannot find you." He concludes this passage: "The songs I learned were all of praise and thanksgiving and repentance. Or in the dark, is it best to wait in silence?"[1]

Song: "I Still Haven't Found What I'm Looking For," by U2. In one of contemporary music group U2's most famous songs, the lead singer, Bono, sings that he still hasn't found what he is looking for. He illustrates with several scenarios, returning to the lines "but I still haven't found what I'm looking for." The artist's search for meaning in life is comparable to Job's; however, Job explicitly searches for God, while Bono's search and repeated disappointments ultimately lead him to God.

Even when God is silent, we can trust in divine sovereignty as a welcome mystery.

Human Experience: Adversities as different as floods, volcanoes, earthquakes, recession, job loss, and illness all have the same effect: they reveal who people really are inside. When health and wealth are stripped away, how a person responds eventually shows either good character or poor character inside that person. Job's response to his adversity demonstrates that he is indeed every bit the righteous man that Yahweh said he was at the beginning of the book. In recent times, the various responses to the September 11 attack spoke volumes about the true values of many people. Every week one can find stories of people's responses to hardship.

Literature: *The Lion, the Witch and the Wardrobe*, **by C. S. Lewis.** In the Chronicles of Narnia, Lewis (1898–1963) pictures Aslan (who represents Christ) as a powerful lion. When the question is asked if Aslan should be feared, it is made clear that Aslan is great, but he also is good. He will not abuse his power to do what is evil, but his goodness means that he can be trusted to use his power for blessing, just as the Lord does.

Job Asks Why God Allows Sin to Continue Unpunished

Big Idea *Rampant injustice in the world prompts Job to long for God to bring justice.*

Understanding the Text

The Text in Context

Job's final point in chapter 23 was that the Sovereign God is free to act in ways that may not fit into a tidy formula of retribution. In chapter 24, Job builds on that point by demonstrating that the retribution system of his friends does not explain all of life. Observation clearly shows that people do sin, even in grievous ways, and yet they are not brought to judgment. In 24:1–12, Job points to the widespread oppression of the poor and the needy. In 24:13–17, he describes people who flagrantly rebel against God's moral standards. In 24:18–24, Job either expresses his longing for divine judgment on these evildoers or predicts that God will eventually judge them. He closes his speech with a fiery challenge to his friends, daring them to prove him false if they can (24:25). Bildad's perfunctory final speech in chapter 25 and Zophar's failure to speak in the third round indicate that the friends are not up to Job's challenge.

Historical and Cultural Background

Job's description of the brutal and heartless actions by the wicked closely parallels crimes that were widely condemned in ancient Near Eastern legal codes. These actions that defrauded the needy of their property, peace, and protection denied basic human rights and dignity to those who were powerless—the orphan, the widow, and the poor. Even though behaviors like these were condemned by virtually all cultures, Job complains that God does not step in to charge the perpetrators with wrongdoing (24:12). Consequently, God seems to apply lower moral standards than what the pagan cultures require, and Job cannot understand why that should be.

Interpretive Insights

24:1 *Why does the Almighty not set times for judgment?* By this rhetorical question, Job implies that by neglecting to bring regular and swift judgment upon evildoers, God seems not to enforce his own righteous standards. It appears that there is no impending judgment day scheduled for those who act unjustly.[1] This serves to discourage those who are righteous, who look forward in vain to their divine vindication.

24:2 *There are those who move boundary stones.* In the ancient world, as in many places today, boundary stones were used to mark property lines. By this means, societies protected the land and financial security of families. Throughout the ancient Near East it was considered a grievous crime to move a boundary stone, because that was tantamount to stealing a portion of another's property. In the Old Testament, this illegal practice is roundly condemned

Key Themes of Job 24

- Job observes that God seems to allow injustice to continue without stopping it.
- Job thinks it is not hard to find examples in life of the powerful oppressing the poor.
- Job observes that because God allows injustice to continue, the wicked act as if there is no God.
- Job longs for God to assert his judicial authority against the wicked.

(Deut. 19:14; 27:17; Prov. 22:28; 23:10). Job has observed people doing this and yet not being judged by God for their sin.

24:5 *the poor go about their labor of foraging food.* In contrast to Eliphaz's accusation of him in 22:5–7, Job clearly empathizes with the plight of those who are oppressed and in dire financial need. He has seen how the wicked have reduced the poor to abject destitution rather than using their resources to assist those in need, as he has done (cf. 29:14–16). As a result, the poor are reduced to having to forage in the wasteland for their sustenance as though they are wild animals, even though there is very little food to be found there for their hungry children.

24:9–11 *the infant of the poor is seized for a debt.* In several ancient Near Eastern cultures, children could serve as collateral for their father's loan, and thus they could be taken to settle a debt. In 2 Kings 4:1, a widow's complaint to Elisha indicates that she fears she will lose her sons because of

Throughout the ancient Near East it was a crime to move a boundary stone. This is a boundary stone of the Babylonian king Marduk-aplaiddina II (eighth century BC).

the debt of her deceased husband. Job here points to a particularly horrific example of oppression, as creditors insist on seizing a nursing infant as payment for a debt. He goes on to show how the poor suffer the loss of their family, home, clothes, and dignity (24:10–11). Nevertheless, in this extreme situation God does not intervene, not even when the suffering of the poor reaches such a terrible level.

24:12 *But God charges no one with wrongdoing.* After describing the desperate condition of the poor as they are oppressed by those who are evil, Job states in verse 12 that God does not step in to stop the wrongs they do. They seem to get away with their evil, and that is profoundly troubling to Job. Job has managed to demonstrate that the retribution formula of the friends does not hold up under scrutiny, but in doing that Job comes to an even more troubling observation, that the just God does not seem to insist on justice in his world. Too many times people do what is wrong and get away with it. Too many times those who are oppressed unjustly cry out hoping for God to intervene on their behalf, and yet he does not respond to them, in contrast to his response to the cries of the Israelites in their Egyptian bondage (Exod. 2:23–25). This is indeed a troubling state of affairs for Job, because God's inactivity against injustice seems to conflict with his holy character.

24:13–17 *For all of them, midnight is their morning.* In verses 13–17, Job describes the unimpeded wickedness of those who flout God's righteous standards. They maliciously plan to defraud others by murder, adultery, and theft. They are unrestrained by God's law, and they have no fear that they will be called to account for their criminal acts. Working under the cover of darkness (cf. John 3:19, where Jesus says that "people loved darkness instead of light because their deeds were evil"), they suppose that if no human can see them, then their wrongdoing will remain undetected. They act as if there is no God who can see through the darkness to observe their sin.

24:20–21 *the worm feasts on them; the wicked are no longer remembered.* In the book of Job, the worm is repeatedly used to picture decay (7:5), because it feeds on rotting corpses (21:26). In Psalm 22:6 and Job 25:6, "worm" is a derogatory expression for what is revolting or despised. By picturing the wicked in this way, Job desires God to bring total destruction and humiliation to them, or he anticipates that this is what God will do to them eventually.

In the ancient world, much emphasis was placed on being remembered by future generations. Typically, this was accomplished through children, and that is why to be childless is regarded as a great grief by Abraham (Gen. 15:2–3) and by Hannah (1 Sam. 1:1–20). Some try to gain a form of social immortality by building monuments to themselves (cf. Absalom in 2 Sam. 18:18, who has no son to preserve his name) or by calling their lands after their own names (Ps. 49:11). In Psalm 83:4, the enemies of Israel want to defeat them so thoroughly that their name will not be remembered. This is the degree of divine judgment that Job wants to see upon the wicked who oppress others so severely.

24:22–24 *But God drags away the mighty by his power.* Even though Job is hurting deeply, and he cannot understand why God does not exact swift judgment on evildoers, he does not become cynical against God. Job derives hope from his faith that God will act justly and powerfully to take down sinners. Job believes that in the big picture God will do as the retribution doctrine teaches. However, in the short run there are apparent anomalies in which God works in ways that escape human comprehension as he accomplishes his overall purpose, which is just and good.

24:25 *If this is not so, who can prove me false?* As Job completes his speech in chapters 23–24, he throws out a challenge to his friends. He dares them to try to disprove his argument that there is observable injustice in the world today but that God will eventually balance the scales of justice in his world. If they cannot meet Job's challenge, then their silence will tacitly acknowledge that he is right. It is significant that none of the friends takes Job up on his challenge.

Theological Insights

Throughout the Old Testament, God is repeatedly presented as caring for those who are poor and needy. As Exodus 2:23–25 demonstrates, God's compassion for the Israelites who are crying out to him in their Egyptian bondage prompts him to intervene powerfully to deliver them from their oppression. The Lord is the defender of those who are most vulnerable in society, such as the orphans and the widows (Pss. 113:5–9; 146:8–9). Set against this theological backdrop, Job's argument in this chapter takes on even greater significance. The same God who sides with the needy also at times seems to let oppression against the needy go unchallenged and uncondemned. As Job observes this frequent pattern, he asks why God remains silent as injustice runs rampant in his world. What Job is experiencing and observing seems to contradict

In 24:11, Job cites an example of how the wicked oppress those under them by letting them go thirsty in the hot sun while treading grapes. Shown here is an ancient winepress; the depression in the upper rock is where grapes were crushed, and then the juice would flow into the lower basin.

the righteous character of God, and he cannot understand why this antithesis should continue.

Teaching the Text

Job wants to demonstrate to his friends that bad things can happen to good people like him, but in making his point he opens up a bigger and more troubling problem. As Job identifies various examples in life that counter the retribution formula, he realizes that there are *many* cases in which injustice seems to triumph in life. In fact, injustice often runs rampant, and that prompts both Job and Christians today to long for God to bring justice to the world.

Job's description of the injustice in his day sounds very familiar to us, because we hear of the same kinds of things every day on the news. Like Job, we see people today who cheat others, even the most vulnerable people in our society, such as the poor, the elderly, and the homeless. While many people enjoy a good measure of prosperity, there are others who are consigned to desperate, grinding poverty. Within the same city some children profit from an excellent education while others are consigned to inferior schools in which they fall further behind each year. These deplorable and unjust conditions continue without God intervening to stop them. For Job and for us today, this raises profound theological questions. Why does God allow this state of affairs to go on? Why does God not bring to judgment those who oppress and exploit people who are vulnerable? Is God indeed in charge of the world, as the Bible claims?

In recent years the problem of bullying in schools has been increasingly highlighted by news stories. When bullies are allowed to intimidate other children, they are only emboldened to do worse and worse things, and their victims are tormented all the more. Because they have no fear of punishment, they live as a law unto themselves. Job speaks of the same pattern in murderers, adulterers, and thieves who get away with their crimes. Because God does not intervene to stop them, they suppose that he does not see them, or that if he does see them, he is powerless to prevent what they are doing. As a result, they act as if God does not exist, and they proceed to do wrong to others. When people live as if there is no divine judge to whom they must answer, then they cast off all restraint. Their criminal behavior runs roughshod over the rights of others, and all are vulnerable to their oppression.

Rather than stooping to their level by paying back evil with evil, Job places this unjust situation in God's hands. He longs for God to assert his power against the wicked and to bring justice to the world. By his example, Job points in the same direction that Jesus later does when he teaches his disciples to pray that God's kingdom come, and God's will be done, on earth as it is in heaven (Matt. 6:10). As Christians, we are obligated to do all that we can to encourage and to insist on justice being done, but we must also remember that only the Sovereign God has the power to enforce justice completely. For justice to come to earth, more than human effort is required. God alone is sufficient to counter fully the wicked schemes and actions of humans, and to bring true and lasting justice for those who are oppressed.

Illustrating the Text

In many cases, injustice seems to triumph in this world.

Literature: *Lord of the Flies*, by William Golding. In this well-known novel, British novelist, poet, and playwright Golding tells the story of a group of British schoolboys who are stranded on a desert island after what seems to be a nuclear war. Left alone and without the restraint of adult supervision, they vie for leadership, form cliques, and proceed to be corrupted by power and hurt one another terribly, the most sensible and sensitive of them dying in the process. It is a profound study in the native evil of human beings and their will to power.

We often long for justice from God and are puzzled by its absence.

Song Lyrics: The spirituals of the African American slaves frequently called upon God to bring justice and relief from the oppression that they had to endure in preabolition times. In one of them, "'Buked and Scorned," the words provide an excellent illustration of Job's longing.

We must remember that God alone can bring lasting justice.

Hymn Text: "Battle Hymn of the Republic," by Julia Ward Howe. The words of this song (1862), often sung only on patriotic occasions, have a timeless message about God's calling his people to remember the truth of God's justice.

> Mine eyes have seen the glory of the
>   coming of the Lord,
> He is trampling out the vintage where
>   the grapes of wrath are stored;
> He hath loosed the fateful lightning
>   of His terrible swift sword;
> His truth is marching on.
>
> He has sounded forth the trumpet
>   that shall never call retreat;
> He is sifting out the hearts of men
>   before His judgment seat;
> O be swift, my soul, to answer Him!
>   Be jubilant my feet,
> Our God is marching on.

Just as Job expresses his desire for the Almighty to administer justice, the spirituals composed and sung by African American slaves express their longing for God to free them from oppression. This photo shows descendants of those slaves picking cotton in Georgia.

Bildad's Final Attempt to Answer Job

Big Idea *Bildad concludes that humans have no hope before God.*

Understanding the Text

The Text in Context

Job 25 contains Bildad's third and final speech, but he has little to say to Job. Clearly running out of steam, Bildad speaks only briefly before he and the friends tail off into silence. For all practical purposes, the dialogue is over, with Job and his friends not a bit closer to each other in their positions. Bildad's firm commitment to

> Bildad affirms God's sovereignty by stating that God has established order in the heights of heaven (25:2), which implies that chaos has been defeated. This idea of vanquishing chaos to establish order is pictured on this seal impression, which shows a warrior god battling the forces of chaos depicted by the serpent/dragon figure (900–750 BC).

retribution theology leads him to conclude that before the transcendent God humans are worthless and contemptible, a conclusion that is hardly satisfying or comforting to Job. Many scholars have speculated that Bildad also spoke the words attributed to Job in 26:5–14 and that Zophar also had a third speech in 27:13–23,[1] but there is no textual evidence to support these theories. The present arrangement of the speeches in the third cycle suggests that the dialogue between Job and his friends has totally collapsed.

Historical and Cultural Background

Bildad's reference in 25:2 to God establishing order (literally, "peace") in the heights of heaven may be compared to the Babylonian and Canaanite myths of the defeat of the powers of chaos by Marduk or Baal. Unlike the ancient Near Eastern religions that held to polytheism, in the Bible Yahweh is revealed as the only true God, who is supreme over all other subordinate powers. Although the language of the defeat of chaos may be used as a literary figure in texts such as Genesis 1:2–3; Job 9:13; and 26:12–13, the Bible consistently affirms that Yahweh alone is God.

Interpretive Insights

25:2 *Dominion and awe belong to God.* Instead of responding to the evidence of injustice that Job detailed in chapter 24, Bildad just restates his previous points more emphatically. Apparently, Bildad is unwilling or unable to revise his position in the light of the clear facts Job has adduced. To Bildad's mind, God is so powerful that it is inconceivable that anyone could rebel against his rule. Bildad focuses so much on the transcendence of God that God becomes inaccessible and unfathomable, and his sovereign control prompts a sense of dreadful awe from his creatures. As a result, as Bildad sees it, there is no conflict in God's realm, because his power establishes order in the heights of heaven, and that suggests there is necessary order on earth as well. To Bildad, Job's claim that his situation is an exception to the rule of retribution is an impossibility.

25:3 *On whom does his light not rise?* By asking two rhetorical questions in verse 3, Bildad expresses the conviction that God is unlimited in his power and control over the world. Wherever the sun shines, God's rule is in effect. God's innumerable angels are his eyes and ears to detect and expose any wickedness in his world. In Bildad's theological system, no one can escape the long reach of God's justice. This position, however, fails to account for the observable evils in God's world that Job described in chapter 24. Rather than answering Job, or

attempting any explanation for the oppression to which Job has pointed, Bildad simply evades the issue as though it does not really exist. No wonder Elihu later is angry at the friends for their failure to answer Job (32:3–5, 11–16).

25:4 *How then can a mortal be righteous before God?* Once again (cf. Eliphaz in 4:15–19; 15:14–16), the comforting words of Psalm 8:4 are distorted by one of Job's friends. By measuring humans against the perfect righteousness of Almighty God, Bildad concludes that humans are helplessly corrupt. The Bible does teach that all humans are sinful and guilty before God (Ps. 14:1–3; Rom. 3:10–12), but Bildad has left out of the picture what the Bible teaches about divine grace and forgiveness, and also God's commendation of those who obey him. Bildad's theology paints in black and white, not with the full pallet of God's truth. Because Bildad is so intent on defending the validity of the retribution formula, he has to conclude that Job's adversity is due to his personal sin. And to substantiate his condemnation of Job, Bildad resorts to condemning the whole human race as inherently and incorrigibly corrupt before God. Of course, the clear implication of Bildad's point is that he himself must be hopeless before God, but he does not take his argument to that next logical stage.

of desperation that raises more questions than it resolves. According to Bildad, in the great pyramid of being, God is at the top and humans are at the very bottom. What Job is suffering at the ash heap is all that any human deserves. Bildad misconstrues God as viewing humans like Job with utter revulsion, as just maggots and worms, when in fact God created humans in his own image and gave them responsibility to rule over the earth (Gen. 1:26–27). If Bildad could have heard how Yahweh commended Job in the prologue (Job 1:8; 2:3), he would have realized that Yahweh regards Job highly, not with the disdain with which Bildad views humans.

Theological Insights

In 25:3, Bildad pictures God as the heavenly warrior whose angelic forces defeat his foes. When this imagery is used elsewhere in the Bible, the Lord triumphs over the enemies of his oppressed people. For example, in Exodus 15:3 Yahweh delivers the Israelites from their Egyptian bondage. Bildad, however, does not present humans as rescued by the compassionate Lord but rather depicts them as mere maggots and worms before the transcendent God. By overemphasizing God's transcendence, Bildad underestimates both his immanence and the value he places upon humans, whom he made in his image. By contrast, the Song of Hannah (1 Sam. 2:1–10), the Magnificat by Mary (Luke 1:46–55), and many of the Psalms emphasize that Yahweh deeply cares for humans, especially those who are oppressed. In particular, Psalm 113:5–9 links Yahweh's transcendence and his immanence in language that is a great comfort to his people:

In 25:3, Bildad reflects on the vast number of angelic forces God has at his command. This painting depicts God's heavenly militia trampling a long, twisting serpent (Ridolfo di Arpo Guariento, painting for a private chapel, AD 1357).

25:5 *and the stars are not pure in his eyes.* "Pure" here probably refers not to moral purity but to the brightness of the stars. The two lines in verse 5 are parallel, for both the moon and the stars may be obscured by clouds so that they can be seen only dimly. Similarly, humans (25:4, 6) are morally impure before the righteous God.

25:6 *a human being, who is only a worm!* With these harsh words Bildad completes his third and final speech. Bildad wants to make the point that no humans, including Job, are in a position to call God's justice into account. However, Bildad overshoots his mark, because to support his position he has to devalue profoundly the whole human race. This, then, is an argument

Who is like the LORD our God,
    the One who sits enthroned on
      high,
who stoops down to look
    on the heavens and the earth?
He raises the poor from the dust
    and lifts the needy from the ash
      heap;
he seats them with princes,
    with the princes of his people.
He settles the childless woman in
      her home
    as a happy mother of children.
Praise the LORD.

Teaching the Text

In his final speech, Bildad is short and to the point, as he concludes that humans have no hope before God. Bildad and the other friends come originally to comfort and encourage Job, but instead Bildad ends up offering the opposite. According to Bildad, no human, including Job, is able to satisfy God's righteous standard.

By speaking about the awesome dominion of God and his powerful angelic forces, Bildad emphasizes that God is great. However, Bildad focuses exclusively on the transcendence of God, so he misses other aspects of God's nature that are recorded in the Bible. Bildad's God is so exalted that he is distant and remote from humans. His God demands justice to such an extent that there is no room for his grace or forgiveness. Bildad's one-sided doctrine of God leads him to draw false conclusions about how God regards humans in general, and by implication Job in particular. One's view of God will inevitably affect how one views humans, whom God has made.

Bildad seems to want to defend his theological system of retribution at all costs. Building on the reality of God's transcendence, Bildad insists that God's rule allows for no disorder in his world. God has innumerable angels to do his bidding, and his realm extends wherever the sun shines. Therefore, it is logical to Bildad that no one could ever thwart God's will. According to Bildad, all is peaceful in God's kingdom. That makes perfect sense to him, and if it were true, then that would validate his retribution theology.

What Bildad fails to do is to consider the evidence that Job has just cited (Job 24) of the many cases in which sinful actions appear to go unpunished. Rather than answering Job, or attempting to explain the evidence that Job has presented, Bildad ignores the facts of observable injustice in God's world. By simply stating his own position more emphatically, he holds on to his inadequate belief system, even though it is contradicted by the facts.

Bildad also goes one tragic step further. Applying logic to his theological position of retribution, Bildad comes to the terrible conclusion that no human can ever be righteous before the transcendent God. Therefore, he concludes that God views all humans as repulsive maggots and worms. This assessment directly contradicts Psalm 8, in which humans are exalted by God, in accordance with his original creation of them in his image (Gen. 1:26–27). Bildad's conclusion may follow logically from his assumptions, but because his premises are incomplete, his conclusion is well off the mark. All theological systems must use logic to reason from the explicit teachings in the Bible to the questions of contemporary life that are not addressed specifically in Scripture. Logical implications, however, must not be held if they contradict other clear teachings of God's Word. Our theological conclusions must always be evaluated by and consistent with the total revelation that God has given in the Bible.

Illustrating the Text

Bildad wrongly focuses on God's transcendence to the exclusion of other attributes.

Quote: *Renewed Day by Day*, by A. W. Tozer. In the following excerpt, Tozer (1897–1963) corrects Bildad's contention based on retribution theology.

> God is uncreated, self-existent, infinite, sovereign, eternal; these attributes are His alone and by their very definition cannot be shared with another. But there are other attributes which He can impart to His creatures and in some measure share with His redeemed children.
>
> Intellect, self-consciousness, love, goodness, holiness, pity, faithfulness—these and certain other attributes are the points where likeness between God and man may be achieved. It is here that the divine-human friendship is experienced. . . . Unquestionably the greatest privilege granted to man on earth is to be admitted into the circle of the friends of God.[2]

Bildad inaccurately concludes that God views humans as maggots and worms.

Literature/Television: In many novels and stories, both in British and American literature and popular fiction, Christian and non-Christian, there is a vast chasm between the elite aristocrats and the common people, so that someone who is born a commoner is greatly discouraged from aspiring to rise into the upper class or to importance. Many years ago a popular British public television series called *Upstairs, Downstairs* concerned the goings-on of the servant class who lived downstairs and the aristocratic class who lived upstairs. There is a sharp distinction; those downstairs must retain their consciousness of station and never cross lines even if they are smarter and shrewder. Another recent British series that has gained wide popularity, *Downton Abbey*, takes place in a fictional manor house in Yorkshire, England. Once again, the distinctions are sharp between the servants and their masters: when one of the upper-class daughters falls in love with one of the servants, there is a great deal of trouble. When Bildad argues that all humans are incorrigibly corrupt before God, so they can never be acceptable to him, he creates a kind of spiritual class system that is even more extreme and dismissive than an upstairs, downstairs mentality.

History: There are many examples throughout human history in which

Bildad wrongly concludes that God views all humans as repulsive maggots and worms (25:6), like the beetle larvae shown here.

a group of people have enslaved others and treated them like property or animals. At times they have so dehumanized them that they have conducted animal-like research upon them (as in Nazi Germany, where Hitler believed in Aryan superiority) or bred them like cattle (as in slavery in nineteenth-century America). These are modern analogies to Bildad's view of humans as maggots and worms, chattel that are controlled, not beings created in God's image with dignity and responsibility.

We must check our theological conclusions against the totality of God's revelation.

Book: *Love Wins*, by Rob Bell. In 2011, Bell, then a prominent pastor of a large congregation in Grand Rapids, Michigan, published a best-selling book, *Love Wins: A Book about Heaven, Hell, and the Fate of Every Person Who Ever Lived*, that stirred fierce debate about sin, salvation, and judgment. His book is often characterized as a problematic compendium of bits of truth and error that does an injustice to the whole of God's revelation, one that seems to be aimed more at disgruntled evangelicals than at non-Christians. Among the criticisms of his book is that his theology is heterodox, his history often inaccurate, and his use of Scripture flawed. He thins out the gospel, redefines the concept of hell, and appears to paint a universalist God. Here is a human work that must be read with God's revelatory truth as the standard.

Job Hears the Whispers of God's Works

Big Idea *When Job considers God's greatness, he realizes how little he himself knows.*

Understanding the Text

The Text in Context

When Bildad says in Job 25:6 that humans are mere maggots and worms before the transcendent God, Job apparently interrupts him. Although Job agrees with much of Bildad's lofty view of God, he draws different implications from their shared theology. Bildad claims that God's greatness means nothing can thwart his justice, so life in God's world is thoroughly predictable, but Job declares that God's greatness implies that humans cannot understand all he is doing, so some aspects of life must be left in mystery. In 26:1–4 Job dismisses Bildad's ability to speak wisely, and in 26:5–14 Job describes God's activity as surpassing human comprehension. In this final section of the chapter, Job's words anticipate what Yahweh will say when he speaks at last in chapters 38–41.

Historical and Cultural Background

In the ancient world, the universe was often viewed as consisting of three

The ancient Near Eastern view of the world pictured the earth as a flat disk surrounded by water. In this tablet from the seventh century BC, the earth is drawn as a circle with Babylon in the center. The circle is surrounded by another circle, which marks the boundaries of the ancient ocean.

parts—the heavens, the earth, and the underworld. The earth was considered a flat disk that divided a large sphere into two parts. Above the earth was the half-sphere of the sky, where the gods dwelled. Beneath the earth was the half-sphere of the underworld, where the dead resided. Job's use of this familiar language does not mean that this is exactly how the world exists in God's perfect knowledge, but rather that this is how it is perceived by Job and his ancient Near Eastern contemporaries (see the sidebar).

Interpretive Insights

26:2–4 *How you have helped the powerless!* It is quite possible that as Bildad was speaking of humans as maggots and worms (25:6), Job in disgust interrupted him. Job sarcastically dismisses Bildad as giving no practical help and as expressing no wise insight (26:3), even though Job has repeatedly referred to his own weakness (6:11–13; 9:19; 12:16; 24:22). To Job's ears, Bildad's claims sound bankrupt, and his counsel seems misguided. Job wonders about the source of Bildad's words (26:4), because they do not have the ring of authenticity. Job's intense and bitter words make it evident that as the dialogue draws to an uneasy close, no one is attempting to be polite to the others anymore.

26:7 *He spreads out the northern skies over empty space.* As Job describes God's greatness in the natural world, he uses some of the language found in the Canaanite mythological literature. The Canaanites considered the north, the site of Mount Zaphon, as the location of the assembly of the gods, similar to the Greek Mount Olympus. This is reflected in Psalm 48:2 when Mount Zion, the city of Yahweh the

Key Themes of Job 26

- Job rejects Bildad as unhelpful and without insight.
- Job recognizes the infinite knowledge of God.
- Job recognizes the overwhelming power of God.
- Job realizes that humans can understand only a portion of God's ways.

King, is compared to the heights of Zaphon. In Isaiah 14:13–15, the king of Babylon is taunted for his vain effort to be enthroned on Zaphon. The God of the Bible towers over all that is in his created world, even Zaphon.

26:8 *He wraps up the waters in his clouds.* As Job describes various aspects of God's control over his world, Job's speech reflects a tone of amazement. In contrast to his friends, who suppose that they can define exactly how God works in his world, Job comes to realize, through his observation, that God transcends human description and explanation. Our modern scientific knowledge of the water cycle comprehends more than Job can, but when God collects the water vapor and suspends it in the clouds, we humans must ask in wonder, "How does he do that?" How can clouds that float across the sky contain all the heavy water vapor that condenses into rain that can flood the earth with devastating effect? These are questions that continue to puzzle humans today.

26:10 *He marks out the horizon on the face of the waters.* The creation account in Genesis 1 pictures the earth floating upon the waters, until Yahweh marks out the horizon of the earth upon the face of the deep (cf. Prov. 8:27–29), thus establishing a boundary between the land and the sea.

26:11 *The pillars of the heavens quake, aghast at his rebuke.* In describing God's rule over the natural world, Job employs

God's Creation of the World

Job's description of God's activity in the creation of the world in 26:12–13 uses poetic imagery drawn from ancient Near Eastern mythological literature. As in chapters 9, 38, and 41 (see also Pss. 74:13–14; 89:9–10; 104:5–9, 25–26; Prov. 8:29; Isa. 51:9–10), Job in this passage pictures God as subduing the sea and the monster or dragon that lives in it. Both of these images represent chaos that has been brought under the control of the Sovereign God. God is consistently portrayed in the Bible as the sovereign over all potential or supposed rivals, whether they be the forces of nature or the false gods of the surrounding nations.

colorful language that reflects ancient conceptions of the cosmos. He pictures the world as a house or temple, with the heavens like a vast roof supported by pillars. When God created the world, his voice rebuked the water of chaos that covered the land (Gen. 1:2; Ps. 104:5–9), and all of creation shook in response. As Psalm 46:6 indicates, the divine voice that created the world is the same voice that now controls even the powerful nations and kingdoms of the earth. The Creator God is also the Sovereign Lord.

26:12–13 *By his wisdom he cut Rahab to pieces.* The Hebrew

term *rahab* (not to be confused with the name Rahab in Joshua 2, which is spelled differently in Hebrew) means "pride," but it is also used as a proper noun several times in the Old Testament. Sometimes "Rahab" is a metaphorical reference to Egypt (Ps. 87:4; Isa. 30:7), likely because of the arrogant attitude of that nation. Here, however, the parallel to the sea indicates that the term is used to refer to the mythological sea monster that is a picture of chaos subdued by God (cf. Job 9:13; Ps. 89:9–10; Isa. 51:9–10). Rahab is closely connected with Leviathan, which is featured in Yahweh's speeches in Job 38:8–11 and 41:1–34. In all these passages, God is firmly in control of these symbols of chaos.

26:14 *Who then can understand the thunder of his power?* As Job concludes this speech, he acknowledges that how God works in the natural world only points to his greatness, which cannot be described fully by finite humans. What Job can see and comprehend only hints at the full measure of God's greatness. As Isaiah 55:8–9 states, God's ways lie beyond the frontier of human understanding, so there is much that must be left in the realm of mystery. Job has come to realize that he and his friends are not experts after all, and that they must take their humble place as students in the school of God, the Master Teacher. This statement, then, is a foreshadowing of Job 38–41, in which Yahweh's numerous unanswerable questions will compel Job to admit that he

---

As Job extols the power of God, he talks about God making the pillars of the earth tremble and subduing chaos, which is represented by the sea and its monsters, such as Leviathan. This reflects the belief in the ancient Near East that the earth rested on pillars. These pillars can be seen standing vertically near the edges of this small stone stela from Mesopotamia known as a *kudurru*. Also seen here is a cosmic sea creature under the control of Marduk (twelfth century BC).

does not truly understand how Yahweh rules his world (42:2–3). Job is now beginning to recognize the limits of human knowledge.

In contrast to Bildad, for whom God's greatness leads to viewing humans as worthless (25:6), Job has a sense of wonder at the greatness of God. Job is beginning to move away from the question "why?" which dominated his speeches up to this point, and now he is shifting his focus to God himself. Job realizes that God is great, so humans are overwhelmed by his thunderous power, but Job also senses that there is much more to God's rule than what humans have perceived, because they can hear only a faint whisper of his ways.

Theological Insights

The Old Testament teaches that Yahweh is omniscient, possessing complete knowledge of all that is in the world that he created and over which he rules. In Psalm 139:7–12, the knowledge of Yahweh is connected with his presence everywhere all the time. This divine knowledge extends even into Sheol, or the grave (Ps. 139:8), because "the realm of the dead is naked before God" (Job 26:6). God's perfect knowledge is a great comfort to his people who depend on his care, because they know that they are never out of God's sight. By contrast, however, those who are wicked long to be hidden from the sight of the holy God (Rev. 6:15–17), because they fear his judgment on their sins.

Teaching the Text

By this time in the book, Job has lost patience with irrelevant and simplistic answers to his problem. So when Bildad's exclusive

focus on God's transcendence leads him to regard humans as mere maggots and worms before God, Job has heard quite enough. He jumps in, rejecting Bildad as unhelpful and without insight. No doubt, Bildad means well, but his dogmatic commitment to his one-dimensional theological system causes him to draw conclusions that contradict what Job knows to be true. Job's exasperation is evident in his strong, sarcastic words to his friend.

As Job shifts his attention to God, he extols God for his infinite knowledge. The realm of the dead lies beyond human observation, but it is completely open to God. God is not limited in his knowledge, as humans are; his knowledge extends far beyond what humans are able to comprehend. Whatever need we experience, God knows all about it. Whatever question we have, God has the answer. Whatever fear lurks in our heart, God sees it completely.

Job particularly emphasizes the overwhelming power of God. Both in his original creation, when God overcame the power of chaos, and in his ongoing governance of the world, God's might is immeasurable. Job will not diminish the greatness of God just to resolve his own situation. He will not say that though God is good, he is not powerful enough to protect Job from adversity. In his popular book titled *When Bad Things Happen to Good People*,[1] Harold Kushner concludes that God should apologize to humans because he is not able to prevent the adversities that they experience. In maintaining that evil is real and that God is good, Kushner rejects that God is all-powerful and in charge of the world. Like Job and unlike Kushner, we must resist the impulse to view God through the lens

In Job 26, God's activity in the ancient world is described in terms similar to those used in other ancient Near Eastern literature. In this reproduction of a drawing from Egypt, the cosmos is pictured with the air god Shu kneeling on the earth god Geb. Shu's upraised arms support the sky goddess Nut, who has stars across her body. Nut is stretched out over the earth, and the sun god Ra travels in his solar barque through the upper waters, which she holds back.

of our experience, but must instead view our experience through the lens of God's greatness and goodness.

As Job considers the implications of God's infinite knowledge and overwhelming power, he concludes that humans are limited in what they are able to know. Humans can know in part, but they cannot know fully, as the omniscient God knows. Similarly, humans can act, but they cannot accomplish what God does, because their power is limited. Job is beginning to realize that he and all humans have to take a humble position before God, recognizing that there is much that God does and knows that lies outside the range of our limited ability and knowledge. Instead of finding fault with God, Job recognizes that much of what God does has to be left in the realm of mystery, because humans can understand only a portion of God's ways. Humans cannot always comprehend what is happening, or why it is happening, but they can trust in God, who is always in charge. For Job and for us, it all comes back to faith in the God who knows all and who controls all in his world.

Illustrating the Text

Assess the counsel of even those who seem wise and theologically sophisticated.

News Story: Stories have abounded through the years, and continue to do so, of prominent political and religious leaders who have started well, seemed sound, and then led their nations or congregations astray. The followers, trusting what they had originally been promised or what they had heard, became passive and undiscerning, leading to their disillusionment with Christianity or even their eventual destruction.

Reflecting on God's greatness and power can bring us back to who God truly is.

Magazine: *National Geographic.* This beautiful magazine often contains articles about the marvels of the natural world. Articles and pictures about the earth in space and about clouds can illustrate Job's description of God's activity in 26:7–9.

Mythology: Most cultures contain myths about the origin of the world. It would be interesting to compare stories of the creation from ancient cultures such as Greece, Rome, Egypt, Canaan, and Mesopotamia with Job's description in 26:12–13. In addition, nations such as China and India and cultures such as the Aztecs and the Mayans could provide parallels.

Film: *Powers of Ten.* This much-praised short documentary film (1968) was written and directed by Americans Charles Eames and his wife, Ray, adapted from Kees Boeke's book *Cosmic View* (1957). The film presents the universe on a relative scale in units of ten. This video is a dramatic portrayal of how little humans can really see, or how rarely the significant scope of the world is appreciated. Like Job 26:14, the film demonstrates how humans can see only the outer fringe of God's works.

Job Speaks in Place of Zophar

Big Idea *Job longs for God to bring justice to him and to the wicked.*

Understanding the Text

The Text in Context

Job 27 brings the dialogue section of the book to a ragged conclusion. It is clear that Job and the friends have become completely polarized in their perspectives. Despite all their talk, they have failed to convince one another; instead, their communication breaks off as they come to an impasse. The friends do not budge from their commitment to the retribution principle and its apparent condemnation of Job, whom they regard as suffering because of his sin. Job, on the other hand, tenaciously insists on his integrity, so he refuses to confess to fabricated sins just to have his previous blessing restored by Yahweh. Contrary to what the adversary suggested in the prologue (1:9–11), Job's righteousness is indeed genuine, and not merely calculated to secure divine blessings, as the adversary suggested in the prologue (1:9–11).

The introductory statement in 27:1 is unusual when compared to other chapters

Job compares the fate of a wicked person's house to a watchman's hut. This watchtower has a raised platform on which a temporary shelter could be built.

in the book, as it portrays Job continuing his discourse. This suggests that Job has waited for Zophar to speak, but when the friend remains silent, then Job resumes talking. As he speaks, Job first insists again on his innocence (27:2–6). Then, in strong language Job condemns his critics (27:7–12). The final section of the chapter (27:13–23) could well be a quotation of the "meaningless talk" to which Job refers in verse 12. In citing what his friends say about the fate of the wicked, Job declares what he thinks Zophar would say if he were to speak again.

Historical and Cultural Background

When Job describes how precarious the life of the wicked is, he says that the houses they build are like moths' cocoons and like huts made by watchmen (27:18). In ancient times, during the harvest the laborers would erect temporary shelters as lodging out in the fields. These were not intended to be substantial, permanent structures adequate for long-term needs; rather, they were flimsy shacks that were sufficient only to provide minimal protection from the elements. Jonah makes this kind of hut to provide shade from the sun in Jonah 4:5. Yahweh prophesies in Isaiah 1:8 that when he comes in judgment, then the people of Judah will be like a hut in a cucumber field, not at all able to withstand his punishment. Job indicates that though the wicked may suppose they have secure protection, their shelter will crumble before God's judgment.

Interpretive Insights

27:1 *And Job continued his discourse.* After completing his speech in the previous chapter (26:14), Job apparently waits

for Zophar to make his third speech. Because Zophar does not speak, Job resumes talking. His speech at this point is described as a "discourse." The Hebrew term used here, *mashal*, in this context suggests a formal pronouncement before a court, as it introduces Job's formal oath in verses 2–6. With this strong language, Job indicates his intention to hand his case over for God to adjudicate. After an interlude in chapter 28, in 29:1 Job continues his *mashal*, which is not completed until 31:40, but the verdict will have to wait until 42:7, when at last Yahweh publicly exonerates Job.

27:2–5 *As surely as God lives.* By using the name of God, Job expresses the most solemn and binding oath possible. If Job were swearing falsely, then this oath in God's name would call down upon him divine calamity (cf. 1 Sam. 28:10). Job reinforces this positive oath with a negative oath in verse 5 (cf. 1 Sam. 12:23; 26:11, which use the same Hebrew expression). With this intense language, Job appeals to God to declare him in the right against all those who have accused him, and also against what God himself seems to indicate by all the adversity that Job has endured. In effect, Job insists that he is innocent, and he places his case into the hands of the very one who up to this point has denied him the justice that he believes he deserves. Job dares God to do what is just toward him.

27:6 *I will maintain my innocence and never let go of it.* Although Job's friends have repeatedly urged him to confess that he has sinned against God, Job refuses to own up to contrived sins that he has in fact not committed. He will not mouth inauthentic words of contrition just to get God's blessing back into his life. In contrast to the adversary's cynical charge in 1:9–10 that Job craves his prosperity above everything, and that he was just using Yahweh to get the blessings he could gain from him, Job insists that he will never abandon his conviction that he is innocent, no matter what it might cost him. Job is certain that he has not sinned against God, so he adamantly refuses to yield his claim of innocence. He will not sin against his conscience, regardless of the pressure that his friends bring to bear on him or how grievously his adversity weighs upon him.

27:7 *May my enemy be like the wicked!* Just as Job is convinced of his own innocence, he is also certain that those who have accused him are wrong. Upset by their false accusations that he is guilty of sin, Job utters a powerful imprecation, or curse, against them. Job wants God to treat them as wicked men deserving divine judgment. All three of the friends have called Job wicked, so now he turns the tables on them and says that they are the ones who are wicked. He calls upon God to punish them for their sin against him.

27:8–10 *For what hope have the godless when they are cut off, when God takes away their life?* Even though Job has pointed out many observable examples from life in which the retribution principle does not hold (chap. 24), he does not abandon his belief that God rules over the world in justice. For the friends, everything is black or white, but Job realizes that some factors in life, such as his own situation, are not so clear-cut and predictable. Instead of totally discarding retribution, Job qualifies it. Job affirms that God does inevitably punish wickedness (cf. Pss. 1:4–6; 73:3, 16–20; Prov. 24:20), but also that in the short run there might be apparent anomalies, such as what he is experiencing.

27:13–23 *It hurls itself against him without mercy.* The view of retribution presented in 27:13–23 pictures God's judgment as a powerful wind (27:21) that carries the wicked off to destruction, just like the great wind that destroyed Job's children in 1:18–19. What is particularly significant is that this judgment was without mercy. The friends rightly understand that the righteous God judges

In 27:16–17, Job says that though the wicked heap up silver like dust, their fate will be that the innocent will divide their silver. Shown here is a hoard of silver ingots from En Gedi (eighth to seventh century BC).

sin, but they have no room in their tidy system for divine mercy. Neither can they account for cases when adversity envelopes a righteous man like Job. See the sidebar for a further discussion of these verses.

Theological Insights

The Old Testament several times teaches that those who accumulate wealth by their wicked actions will lose it, and ironically they will lose it to those who have lived righteously (27:16–17). This principle is taught in the traditional wisdom sayings in Proverbs 13:22 and 28:8. It also occurs in Ecclesiastes 2:26, which notes that God has given to the sinner the task of gathering and collecting so that the one who pleases God may be the beneficiary. In the short run, the wicked may appear to prosper, but in the long run God sees to it that justice is done.

Teaching the Text

As Job draws the dialogue section of the book to a close in chapter 27, he longs for God to bring justice both to him and to the wicked. Even though Job has pointed to many observable cases in which people commit evil and yet are not immediately punished, he still believes that God is just. Because of this confidence, Job wants God to do for him what is right and for those who have sinned against him what is just. Job does not believe that God is morally arbitrary, and he does not want to live in a world in which justice is abandoned. He desires for the righteous God to bring

Who Speaks in Job 27:13–23?

Job 27:13–23 sounds a lot like what Zophar said previously in chapter 20, and Zophar's concluding words in 20:29 are repeated almost exactly by Job in 27:13. Many scholars looking at the data suggest that this is actually Zophar's third speech, but there is no textual evidence to demonstrate that. Others point to Job's reference to meaningless talk in verse 12 and conclude that Job is now mocking Zophar by parroting sarcastically Zophar's earlier vapid words. However, it must be noted that Job agrees with the friends on the legitimacy of the general retribution framework, and that is why Job is so confused and upset by the adversity he has experienced. Job takes the long view of retribution, that God will eventually reward the righteous and punish the wicked. The friends want to insist that retribution is a fixed formula that applies to every specific incident in life, but Job's experience of adversity, despite his innocence, has caused him to resist taking retribution to that extent. Job agrees that the general doctrine of retribution is sound, but he believes that specifically applying it to cases like his is pressing retribution too far.

justice to all. In this, Job is an example to us to keep holding to the justice of God even when life seems terribly unjust (cf. the righteous martyrs who plead for the Lord's justice in Rev. 6:9–11).

Job's integrity has come under withering attack by his friends, but he knows in his heart that he is innocent. He will not utter an insincere confession for sins that he has not in fact committed. He insists that he is right, no matter what the friends say or how long his adversity persists. As much as he wants to be relieved of his pain, he will not compromise his integrity just to get relief. By his example, Job challenges us to be honest before God, remembering that God searches our hearts and knows our thoughts (Ps. 139:23–24).

Just as Job wants God to exonerate him from false accusations, he wants those who have falsely accused him to be judged by God. By misconstruing his actions and motives, they have lied against Job, so Job

This colored engraving depicts Joseph Cinque (ca. 1814–79), the leader of the mutiny aboard the *Amistad* who was wrongly imprisoned after his arrival in the United States.

far the retribution principle can be extended into specific cases in life. Unlike the friends, who say that retribution applies universally, Job has already demonstrated that wicked people do not always suffer immediately for their sins. This suggests that some righteous people, like him, may suffer adversity despite their godly lives. We need to remember that the retribution principle is only a general pattern for how God works but that other complicating factors can also affect individual cases (e.g., John 9:1–3).

For the most part, Job agrees with Zophar's general point that God will punish the wicked. Zophar, however, has left no room for divine mercy in his view of God's retribution. Job implies that within the larger retribution framework, God also shows grace to sinners and at times allows adversity in the lives of the righteous. As we counsel people in pain, or as we evaluate our own adversities, we need to draw upon all that God reveals in the Bible about his nature and plan.

calls on God to punish them as the wicked people they have proved to be. Although his language is very intense, echoing the imprecatory psalms, Job places his adversaries into God's just hands rather than exacting his own vengeance upon them, thus taking the very approach commanded in Romans 12:17–21.

The friends have tried to instruct Job about how God works in his world, but Job resolves now to teach them about the ways of the Almighty. Job does not understand all of the intricacies of God's governance of the world, but he is confident that in general terms the righteous God will judge those who are wicked. Where Job parts company with his friends is on the question of how

Illustrating the Text

There are those who, like Job, will not compromise in the face of false accusation.

News Story: In the news, one can often find reports of accused criminals who refuse to accept a plea bargain because they insist on their innocence. Even though that means they are sent to jail, they will not admit to crimes they maintain that they did not commit. Some of these are later exonerated when new evidence emerges; others spend years, even decades in jail, wrongfully imprisoned. Ninety-five of these cases are reported and described on a website, "The Falsely Accused and the Wrongly Imprisoned." Some remain in prison; others were set free, in some cases after two or three decades.[1] One well-known case is that of Nelson Mandella, a South African politician and antiapartheid activist, who spent twenty-seven years in prison on trumped-up charges.

History: Job's call to God to bring justice on his false accusers can be compared to the fate of victims of racial discrimination in the United States in the 1960s and 1970s, individuals who appealed to the courts for equal application of the law. They wanted justice for themselves, but they also wanted those who had mistreated them to be brought to justice for their wrongdoing. Mamie Till-Mobley, the mother of Emmett Till (1941–55), fought for the cause of her unjustly and brutally murdered son until she died, a fight that was rewarded much later with an acknowledgment of the wrongdoing against her son, though no one was ever jailed. The case is still a catalyst in racial relations.

Film: *Amistad.* In this film (1997) based on historical events, *Amistad* is a ship carrying slaves between Cuba and the United States in 1839. During the crossing, one of the Africans named Cinque, a former tribal leader, incites those with him to mutiny, and they take charge of the ship. They sail it onward to what they hope will be a place where they will be accepted. However, upon landing in the United States, they are taken to prison as runaway slaves, without much hope of a future, since they cannot speak English. Then a lawyer who is an abolitionist comes to their rescue and puts forth a case in which he claims they are not slaves because they have been free citizens in another land. Finally, the Supreme Court is given the case, and John Quincy Adams pleads with powerful language and passion for their freedom.

We can be confident that God is righteous, even in the midst of our suffering.

Hymn: "Moment by Moment," by Daniel W. Whittle. This old hymn (1893) expresses the core of the principle that one is kept by God's love no matter what the circumstance. Following are stanzas 2 and 3:

> Never a trial that He is not there,
> Never a burden that He doth not
>   bear,
> Never a sorrow that He doth not
>   share,
> Moment by moment I'm under his
>   care.
>
> Never a heartache and never a
>   groan,
> Never a tear-drop and never a
>   moan;
> Never a danger, but there on the
>   throne,
> Moment by moment, He thinks of
>   His own.

But Where Can Wisdom Be Found?

Big Idea *Despite the best efforts of humans, only God understands wisdom.*

Understanding the Text

The Text in Context

Job 28 does not have a specified speaker, so scholars have viewed it in a variety of ways. Some commentators regard Job as the speaker from chapter 26 through chapter 31, including this chapter. However, the tone of Job 28 is calm, in contrast to the turgid emotions of Job's speeches both in chapter 27 and in chapters 29–31, and its content is quite distinctive as well. It may well be, then, that Job 28 is an interlude spoken by the narrator. If so, it serves as a transition from the three rounds of dialogue (Job 3–27) to the three extended monologues by Job (chaps. 29–31), Elihu (chaps. 32–37), and Yahweh (chaps. 38–41). The soliloquy in this interlude pauses and muses on where wisdom can be found, implying that Job and his friends have not yet found wisdom, and it points ahead to the need for Yahweh to speak, because wisdom is a mystery that only God understands fully. The chapter is divided into three sections: human searching cannot find wisdom (28:1–12), human wealth cannot purchase wisdom (28:13–22), and God alone understands the way to wisdom (28:23–28).

Historical and Cultural Background

Job 28:1–11 presents a vivid description of the ancient technology that was used in mining precious metals and gemstones. Israel did not do a lot of mining (cf. 1 Sam. 13:19–22), because its natural resources were limited, but in Egypt there was extensive mining activity, beginning around 2000 BC. Typically, miners sank vertical shafts into the earth until they intersected with veins of ore or precious stones. Then they would use a variety of techniques, including fire and redirecting underground streams, in order to expose the desired objects. Later in history, horizontal shafts were drilled into the sides of mountains. Mining was a dangerous occupation in the ancient world, just as it is today.

Interpretive Insights

28:1–5 *Mortals put an end to darkness.* By describing miners toiling deep beneath the surface of the earth in their search for precious metals and gems, the narrator pictures how humans probe assiduously to the farthest limits in their effort to discover what they greatly value. In this effort they employ creative and risky techniques, even dangling precariously from ropes as they attempt to reach the treasures they crave (28:4). They use fire to crack open the subterranean rock in order to expose its ore and gemstones (28:5).

28:7–11 *No bird of prey knows that hidden path.* It is hard to imagine seeing better or farther than a falcon, but humans surpass even the keen-sighted birds of prey as they search for wealth. None of the four kinds of wild animals cited in verses 7–8 has gone to the lengths that humans have

in their attempt to find wisdom. Although humans seek throughout the whole world in their diligent search, they will inevitably return disappointed.

28:12 *But where can wisdom be found?* Although humans have been successful in finding the source of mineral treasure, that success cannot be transferred to their search for wisdom. In fact, the success that humans have achieved in so many other areas of life only makes their inability to find wisdom all the more vexing for them. Humans may understand how to find wealth, but no one seems to know where and how to find wisdom. The question in verse 12 is repeated in verse 20, and then it is answered in verse 23, when the narrator states that God alone understands the way to wisdom.

28:13–14 *it cannot be found in the land of the living.* Wisdom cannot be discerned in the human realm or even in the world of nature (28:14). This chapter makes it evident that the source of wisdom is not located within the physical creation but lies beyond the created

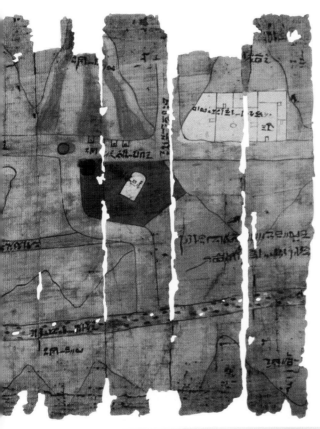

Job 28:1–11 gives an extensive description of mining. This map, drawn on papyrus, shows the gold mines in the Wadi Hammamat region of Egypt (twelfth to eleventh century BC).

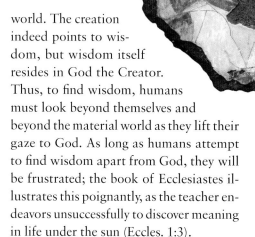

Gold was highly valued in the ancient world, but it could not buy wisdom. In this painting from the tomb of Sebekhotep (ca. 1400 BC), gold nuggets and gold rings are brought before the Egyptian king.

world. The creation indeed points to wisdom, but wisdom itself resides in God the Creator. Thus, to find wisdom, humans must look beyond themselves and beyond the material world as they lift their gaze to God. As long as humans attempt to find wisdom apart from God, they will be frustrated; the book of Ecclesiastes illustrates this poignantly, as the teacher endeavors unsuccessfully to discover meaning in life under the sun (Eccles. 1:3).

28:15–19 *It cannot be bought with the finest gold.* In ancient times, as today, gold was highly valued, so several words for gold are used in verses 15–17 to indicate that no amount of human wealth can purchase wisdom (cf. Prov. 8:10–11). In contrast to so many areas of contemporary life in which money talks, wisdom is not for sale to the highest bidder; it has to be received as a gift from God. The wise teacher in Proverbs 4:5–7 urges the youth to get wisdom at the price of everything he possesses, but even that may not be sufficient to procure it. One must come to God and receive wisdom from him on his terms.

28:21–22 *Destruction and Death say, "Only a rumor of it has reached our ears."* As in Job 26:6; 31:12; Proverbs 27:20; and Revelation 9:11, Destruction and Death represent the forces in the underworld. When verses 21 and 22 are read together,

no person, living or dead, has grasped wisdom, even though there are rumors that wisdom does in fact exist. These intimations of wisdom may be attributed to the sense of eternity that God has implanted in the human heart (Eccles. 3:11).

28:23–24 *God understands the way to it and he alone knows where it dwells.* This verse provides the answer to the question posed in verses 12 and 20 about where wisdom can be found. Neither Job nor the friends have found wisdom, because humans are limited in their knowledge. Only God knows where wisdom dwells, because his knowledge is unlimited (28:24). The way out of the impasse that Job and the friends have reached will come not from a human source (despite Elihu's valiant attempt in chaps. 32–37) but only from God himself, when he finally speaks in chapters 38–41.

28:25–27 *When he established the force of the wind and measured out the waters.* Verses 25–27 picture God's activity in creating and controlling aspects of the natural world that lie beyond human understanding (cf. Prov. 8:22–31). As Proverbs 3:19–20 declares, God's wisdom encompasses the whole sphere of his original creation of the world and his ongoing sovereignty over the world, so it is no wonder that finite humans cannot grasp it. Verses 25–27 foreshadow in brief Yahweh's extensive speeches to come in chapters 38–41.

28:28 *The fear of the Lord—that is wisdom, and to shun evil is understanding.* In this concluding verse of the interlude, the narrator indirectly breaks the divine silence by quoting God's words to the human race. By these words, the narrator points the reader toward the traditional definition of wisdom found in Proverbs 1:7 and 9:10. Wisdom is not discovered by knowing everything about the world, for that is beyond the range of human understanding. Rather, wisdom resides in God, and it is found in relationship with him as a person reveres and obeys God. True wisdom, then, is not total comprehension of how life works but faithful reverence for the Lord, who sovereignly controls the world he has created. When this verse is compared with Yahweh's description of Job in 1:8 and 2:3, it is evident that Yahweh regards Job as a truly wise man, because Job fears God and shuns evil.

Theological Insights

Job 28 concludes with the theme of the fear of the Lord, which is a prominent focus in Old Testament wisdom literature. The prologue of Proverbs highlights the fear of the Lord as the beginning of knowledge (Prov. 1:7) and of wisdom (Prov. 9:10), and the book ends with the extended portrait of the virtuous woman who fears the Lord (Prov. 31:30). After searching in vain for meaning in life under the sun, the book of Ecclesiastes concludes by saying that fearing God and keeping his commands is the

whole duty of humans (Eccles. 12:13). In the book of Job, the title character is described by both the narrator (1:1) and Yahweh (1:8; 2:3) as one who fears God. Each of these references has a slightly different nuance, but they all indicate the need for humans to revere God by their moral behavior. Thus, biblical wisdom is theological, as it teaches humans how to live in a way that honors God; it is not just secular counsel on how to succeed in the pragmatic affairs of life, as the other ancient Near Eastern cultures typically viewed wisdom.[1]

Teaching the Text

Job 28 is set up as a contrast between what humans can know and what God alone knows. We are well aware of how knowledge is exploding in the contemporary world. Nearly every day we hear about new discoveries across the broad range of research. Every year, college and high-school textbooks are enlarged and revised as students have an expanding field of information to learn. Despite all this learning, however, there is so much that humans do not know, so they must maintain a spirit of humility. Only the omniscient God truly understands life in its totality.

As the narrator illustrates the extent of human searching, he describes the processes used by miners in ancient times. In their pursuit of precious metals and gems, miners devised all sorts of creative and risky procedures. Their technology enabled them to probe deeply into the earth, far beyond where even the birds and animals go. If the narrator were to write on this subject today, he could detail the extensive research done in labs, with high-speed computers, and by space missions. In every age there is no shortage of human effort and ingenuity expended in the search for what people want to discover. Nevertheless, even the rapid advances of technology fail to answer the profound questions that people ask today.

Although humans can find many of the things they seek, they are not able by their efforts alone to find wisdom, which is skill in living according to God's way. Humans are successful in multiplying the facts they know, but they cannot understand how these facts all relate together in a meaningful life. No human apart from God can truly comprehend what makes life work as it ought. To discover that, we must turn to God, who is the author of true wisdom.

We live in a world in which just about everything is for sale. If someone has enough money, then there is usually a way to purchase valuable items, enjoy pleasurable experiences, and even attain powerful positions. There are, however, limits to what human wealth can purchase. As Job 28 teaches, wisdom cannot be bought even with the finest gold. Wisdom is not reserved for the highest bidder. It is not a commodity that can be sold and exchanged by those who are privileged. Rather, it is a gift given

by God to those who ask him for it (James 1:5–8).

Wisdom resides in God, who is the creator and sovereign of all. God has said to humans that if they want wisdom, then they must receive it from him. Wisdom is found in the fear, or reverence, of the Lord. By revering the Lord, a person chooses the path of life that honors him, and that choice leads to skill in living as God intends. To look at this from the other side, the person who possesses understanding is the one who shuns evil, because in revering God one also rejects the wickedness that is antithetical to what God values. Wisdom, then, is not the same as knowledge but is an approach to life that begins with humble submission to the Lord.

Illustrating the Text

Despite all the advances humans make, only God understands life in its totality.

Technology: The pace of research and discovery is increasing exponentially in every area of learning. For example, a standard

In spite of our advances in technology and engineering, we still do not fully understand the process by which the pyramids were built. Job also reminds us that we will never be able to grasp fully God's wisdom. Pictured here are the pyramids at Giza (twenty-sixth century BC).

laptop computer used by students today has far more capacity than the computers that guided the Apollo missions to the moon.

History: We so highly regard today's technological marvels that we fail to appreciate just how advanced ancient cultures were. The great pyramids of Egypt, the nautical expertise of the Phoenicians, and the roads and aqueducts in the Roman Empire, as well as the marvels of the Inca Empire as displayed at Machu Picchu, Peru—all these were amazing feats of engineering, especially when we consider that they were done without the aid of computers and modern machines. Some of the ways in which these wonders were undertaken continue to remain a mystery.

Wisdom, which comes only from submission to God, is superior to wealth.

Biography: Howard Hughes. Many people, such as Howard Hughes (1905–76), the Texan who became one of the world's richest men, cannot find meaning and happiness in life. Human wealth cannot produce what really matters in life. Hughes, a gifted movie producer and aviator, and a billionaire, was a hypochondriac with germ-phobia, finally becoming severely reclusive. Toward the end of his life, he lay naked in bed in darkened hotel rooms, considering them a germ-free zone. He wore tissue boxes on his feet to protect them, and he burned his clothing if someone near him became ill.

Quote: Ernest Hemingway. Today great emphasis is placed on education, and because of this, cities, states, and the federal government all devote vast resources to it. The assumption is that if people get more education, it will lead to a better quality of life for our whole society.

Ernest Hemingway (1899–1961), an intelligent and influential writer of the twentieth century, once wrote that "happiness in intelligent people is the rarest thing I know." Hemingway, who took his own life in 1961, knew many intelligent, unhappy people. He lived through two world wars, the Great Depression, four wives, and an unknown number of failed romantic relationships.

Job Recalls the Good Old Days

Big Idea *Before his adversity, Job enjoyed blessing by God and esteem from his community.*

Understanding the Text

The Text in Context

The silence of Job's friends following chapter 25 indicates that they have given up on their attempt to answer Job by their own wisdom. In chapter 27, Job began a formal testimony (*mashal*), in which he defended his innocence before God. After the narrator's interlude in chapter 28, reminding the reader that wisdom is rooted in the fear of the Lord (28:28), Job resumes his testimony in 29:1. In chapter 29, Job recalls his former happiness, before his adversity. During that delightful time, his life was amply blessed, just as the retribution principle teaches. In 29:2–6 Job describes his experience of God's blessing. In 29:7–17 Job portrays his esteem in his community. In 29:18–20 Job recalls expecting blessing on his life to continue unabated. The chapter closes in 29:21–25 with Job depicting his positive effect on others around him.

Historical and Cultural Background

In 29:7, Job speaks about taking his seat in the gate of the city. In the ancient Near East, the gate of the city played a role similar to the later Greek agora and the Roman forum. As the center of community life, the gate combined the activities of the commercial marketplace (2 Kings 7:17–18), the legal court (Deut. 21:19; Ruth 4:1), and the intellectual interchange of ideas (cf. Ps. 127:5). In Proverbs 1:21 and 8:3, personified Wisdom cries out in the gate as the master teacher of humans. To have a seat in the gate is to enjoy a privilege reserved for the most prominent citizens (Gen. 19:1; Prov. 31:23), so it reflects Job's lofty status as "the greatest man among all the people of the East" (Job 1:3).

Interpretive Insights

29:2 *How I long for the months gone by, for the days when God watched over me!* The terms "months" and "days" may indicate the general length of Job's ordeal. He counts the time not in hours or in years, but in days and months. His adversity, then, has been relatively brief, but very intense. As Job reflects on his time of past blessing before adversity turned his life upside down, he paints a beautiful picture of God's kindly care over him. During those halcyon days, God watched protectively over him (cf. Pss. 91:11; 121:7–8). Job is aware and appreciative of God's blessing, but he does not manifest a sense of entitlement, as though this is his right.

29:6 *when my path was drenched with cream.* Job's past life was so blessed that only the language of exaggeration is adequate to begin to describe it. Just as the land of Canaan is often depicted as a land flowing with milk and honey (e.g., Exod. 3:8), so now Job says that the festive delights of cream and olive oil flowed out all over his life. Even the barren rock burst out with oil, which is a picture of God's limitless blessing on him (cf. Yahweh's provision for Israel in Deut. 32:13). Without a doubt, Job's former experience was full of lavish celebration, all from God's hand.

29:11–16 *I put on righteousness as my clothing; justice was my robe and my turban.* In contrast to Eliphaz's false accusations in 22:6–9 about Job's mistreatment of vulnerable people, Job claims that his esteem was well deserved, because his

Key Themes of Job 29

- In the past, Job experienced God's protection, communion, and blessing.
- Job's past esteem in his community was unquestioned.
- Job used his exalted position to help the needy.
- Job was a channel of God's blessing to others.

behavior toward the needy was above reproach. Job has used his exalted position in the community to bring justice to the powerless, who are often oppressed by the powerful. "Righteousness" speaks of what conforms to a standard, specifically the standard of what God values as morally right. "Justice" refers to action that must be taken in order to make a situation righteous in God's sight. By his consistent commitment to righteousness and justice, Job has lived up to the divine standard for rulers (Ps. 72:1–2, 12–14), and he imitated the example of Yahweh's righteousness (Ps. 85:10–14).

29:17 *I broke the fangs of the wicked.* Job has done more than just have a compassionate feeling toward the needy. Job has taken on the risk of confronting and countering predatory evildoers as he actively opposed those who were oppressing the vulnerable people in his society. He did not merely utter abstract platitudes of support but struck at the source of the oppression,

snatching the victims out of the grasp of those who had mistreated them.

29:18–19 *I thought, "I will die in my own house."* Job was not being presumptuous or arrogant, but because he had lived according to God's way, he expected that his God-honoring life should result in divine blessing. During his past time of prosperity, Job assumed that the retribution formula ensured blessing for him. He was confident that God would continue to honor him because of his righteous life. Consequently, Job had every expectation of a long (28:18) and secure (28:19) life. The term translated "house" is the familiar word for a nest, so it paints a lovely picture of a peaceful end to a good life within a close-knit family.

29:20 *the bow will be ever new in my hand.* In addition to being a familiar weapon of the warrior, the bow is also used in the Bible as a picture of physical vigor and virility. In Genesis 49:24, it is used in parallel with strong arms. In his former state of blessing, Job anticipated that he would maintain the strength of his youth. He could not foresee anything that could make his glory fade but expected to remain active and influential throughout his life. Consequently, the severe adversity that he is experiencing has come as a great surprise to him.

29:23–24 *the light of my face was precious to them.* Despite what the friends have said, Job is not just interested in preserving his own affluence. Rather, Job sees himself as a channel of God's blessings to others. By his generosity, Job has brought joy and help to those in need. His joyful demeanor has buoyed and encouraged others. By his positive spirit, Job made those around him better.

29:25 *I dwelt as a king among his troops.* Job concludes his recollection of his past condition by describing how he lived in his community as though he were a deeply loved and well-respected king. He was influential in directing his community in good ways. His virtuous life benefited all who came into contact with him. Job comforted those who mourned, which is a stark contrast to the treatment he has received from his friends during his own adversity. When Job needs the same kind of comforting ministry, no one is willing or able to do for him as he has done for others who were hurting.

Theological Insights

Throughout the Old Testament, Yahweh's rule is characterized by righteousness and justice (Ps. 89:14), and in particular he protects vulnerable people, such as the poor, the stranger, the widow, and the orphan. Those who are godly are expected to share this same kind of compassion as the natural expression of a life committed to Yahweh and his values. In the Mosaic law, Yahweh condemns the oppression of the stranger, widow, and orphan (Exod. 22:21–24). More than that, Yahweh calls on his faithful people to serve as champions for those who are oppressed (Amos 5:14–15). This was how Job has ministered to the needy, as he relates in 29:11–17.

When Jesus began his public ministry in Nazareth (Luke 4:16–21), he read and then applied to himself the prophetic words of Isaiah 61:1–2. This oracle that Jesus fulfilled emphasized the arrival of God's good news for the needy and deliverance for the oppressed:

The Spirit of the Lord is on me,
    because he has anointed me
        to proclaim good news to the poor.
He has sent me to proclaim freedom
        for the prisoners
    and recovery of sight for the blind,
To set the oppressed free,
    to proclaim the year of the Lord's
        favor.

Teaching the Text

When we enter into hard times, we often find ourselves reflecting on how much better life used to be before adversity arrived. In Job 29, Job remembers the good old days when he was blessed by God and esteemed in his community. His opening words, "How I long," indicate that Job yearns for the return of those delightful days. In his relationships both with God and with other people Job found joy and fulfillment, and that is such a contrast to the sorrow and ridicule that have come to mark his life. The Bible often exhorts the people of God to remember God's past blessings, because in remembering the good that God has done in our lives we also remember that God himself is good even when life becomes difficult.

During those good days, life seemed to work just as the retribution formula said it should. Job was living a righteous life, and God rewarded him with protection, communion, and blessing. As a result, Job felt safe in God's care, fulfilled in his relationship with God, and blessed by God's goodness to him. In Job's words (1:21), Yahweh gave, and Job enjoyed his gifts in every area of life.

Many people who attain high position become self-centered and insensitive to the needs of others, but that did not happen in Job's life. Instead, Job used his position as a leader in the community to help the needy. He heard their cries for help. He took up the cause of those who had no position or voice. He intervened to rescue those who had become victims of wicked oppressors. By this means, Job is an example of the positive and practical difference that righteous, God-honoring people should make in their society.

Job recognizes that God has intended him to be a channel of blessing to other people. Because God had amply blessed him, Job was in the position to influence

Job dispensed justice in the city gate when he "rescued the poor who cried for help," assisted the fatherless, and "took up the case of the stranger" (29:12, 16). Here is the interior of a gate chamber at Beersheba showing the benches where the important men of the community would gather to hear legal cases.

many others for good. His wise counsel provided insight and direction to those who listened to him. His affirmation brought encouragement and joy to the downtrodden. His comfort lifted the sorrowful hearts of those who mourned. By his righteous life, Job helped and lifted all those around him, and he teaches us that God's blessings are not for spending on ourselves but for sharing with others.

Illustrating the Text

When adversity comes, memories of God's past faithfulness can sustain us.

Personal Stories: Remembering God's demonstrations of his faithfulness in the past can provide a powerful antidote to discouragement and can help us see beyond present circumstance. One biblical example is Psalm 63, in which the psalmist recounts his intense yearning for God in the face of threats and adversity. He declares,

> On my bed I remember you;
> I think of you through the
> watches of the night.
> Because you are my help,
> I sing in the shadow of your
> wings. (Ps. 63:6–7)

Through remembering, the psalmist moves from yearning to confident trust in God. Remembering God, who is his help and who he has powerfully experienced in the past (63:2–3), leads to confidence even in the face of murderous threats. This theme of remembering God's past faithfulness is integral to God's commands to Israel, seen, for example, in the establishment of the Sabbath (Deut. 5:15). Are there particular experiences of God's faithfulness that you draw on in difficult times? Recount a time when memory of God's past faithfulness provided encouragement or sustenance through times of difficulty when that faithfulness may have otherwise seemed more distant or where God's goodness may have been called into doubt.

There are people, like Job, who use their position and authority to do good.

Film: *To Kill a Mockingbird.* In this enduring, Academy Award–winning film (1962) based on the novel by Harper Lee, Atticus Finch, the main character (played by Gregory Peck), is a lawyer who chooses to defend a wrongly accused black man in a racist setting. When he had finished his final defense speech, he lingers in the courtroom, and when it is empty, he makes his exit. The black public, confined to the balcony, have waited, and as he leaves, they all rise to show their love and respect. Atticus Finch is the kind of man one imagines Job was.

Biography: Sam Walton. While it is very common to hear the rich as a group vilified and generalized as greedy, mercenary, and lacking in generous impulses, this is a great overstatement. Those qualities can mark anyone. On the other hand, particularly well known for his philosophy of helping his employees is Sam Walton, the founder of Walmart. His profit-sharing program helped those who worked for him to benefit from the store's success. He wanted to make sure that his employees knew he respected them. He wanted them to be encouraged, to be challenged to work hard through positive incentives, and he introduced innovative work strategies to make sure everyone felt appreciated and motivated.[1]

History: For many years the investment firm E. F. Hutton, one of the most respected financial firms in the United States, was so highly esteemed that its famous advertisements featured the line, "When E. F. Hutton talks, people listen." The confidence this firm inspired (or at least aspired to) parallels how Job was esteemed by people in his community.

Biography: Henri Nouwen. The well-known Catholic priest and writer Henri Nouwen (1932–96) left his brilliant teaching career at Harvard in order to minister to mentally handicapped men at the L'Arche community in Toronto. Similarly, Job actively cared for the needy of his day.

Biography: William Wilberforce. Wilberforce (1759–1833) was a British politician and philanthropist. He was converted to evangelical Christianity in 1785, an event that profoundly changed his life and introduced into his consciousness a great passion for reform. He used his position in the British Parliament in the early nineteenth century as the means to hasten the end of slavery throughout the British Empire. Until his resignation from Parliament because of failing health, he was part of the movement to completely abolish slavery. Through the life of this faithful Christian, God brought great blessing to millions of oppressed people.

From the Heights of Honor to the Depths of Humiliation

Big Idea *Job describes how he feels rejected by others and by God.*

Understanding the Text

The Text in Context

In general terms, Job 29 and 30 are an exposition of Job's words in 1:21. As he looks to the past, he sees that the Lord has given him so much blessing and honor (Job 29). In the present, however, the Lord has taken all of that away (Job 30). These chapters describe the jarring contrast between the delightful before and the dismal after pictures of Job's experience. The expressions "but now" (30:1) and "and now" (30:9, 16) signal the tragic reversal in Job's life from prosperity to pain, from honor to humiliation. In 30:1–15, Job laments the rejection he feels from his community. In 30:16–23, he complains about his apparent rejection by God. As Job looks ahead, he anticipates only despair without any prospect of relief (30:24–31).

Historical and Cultural Background

As Job decries the people who mock him, he uses strong language that implies they are dogs (30:1), and then his description of them in 30:2–8 represents them as so desperate that they live almost like animals. Apart from Egypt, in the ancient world dogs were not the lovable pets that we think of today. Rather, they were most often vicious scavengers, more like what we associate with coyotes and hyenas. They were typically seen in despicable situations, such as eating a human corpse (2 Kings 9:36) or licking up their own vomit (Prov. 26:11). The men who treat Job with great dishonor forage for whatever food they can find, even eating salt herbs that they gather in the brush (30:4). Living like animals (30:7), they eke out a miserable existence on the margins of society, much as Nebuchadnezzar does during the time of his insanity (Dan. 4:33).

Interpretive Insights

30:1–10 *But now they mock me.* The word translated "mock" in verse 1 is the same Hebrew term rendered "smiled" in 29:24, as Job in the past has brought blessings on others and made their lives better. This play on words marks the profound change that has transformed Job's prosperity in the past into pain in the present.

Previously, Job enjoyed respect and esteem in his community, from even the greatest citizens. Now the rabble are mocking and scorning him (30:8). Job's compassion (30:25) has been rudely rewarded with contempt, as the most disreputable people are treating him with disrespect. Job uses the literary pattern of tragic reversal, which also features prominently in the book of Lamentations, as he negatively contrasts his present situation with his past.

30:11 *Now that God has unstrung my bow and afflicted me, they throw off restraint.* The image of an unstrung bow indicates that Job's strength is gone (in contrast to the picture of vitality in 29:20; cf. Ps. 18:34). God has left Job defenseless in the face of his opponents, so the wicked swoop in to finish him off. His enemies are unrestrained, because they no longer feel awed by Job's high standing, which in the past was the indication of divine blessing and approval. If Job's adversity evidences that God is against him, then what would hold back his enemies? Consequently, they pile on Job when he is down.

30:12–14 *they build their siege ramps against me.* In 30:12–15, Job uses the image of a city under military attack to describe how he feels bombarded by those who mock and despise him (30:9–10).

Key Themes of Job 30

- Job feels mocked by those whom he used to help.
- Job believes that his adversity from God has prompted others to humiliate him.
- Job feels under attack from God.
- Job can see no hope for the future.

By this metaphor, Job expresses the sense of danger, fear, pain, and despair that has overwhelmed him. Those who mock him take pleasure in defeating and humiliating him. They are intent on destroying him so thoroughly that he can never recover (30:13). Instead of feeling compassion for Job, they exploit his calamity for their own advantage.

30:15 *my dignity is driven away as by the wind.* In contrast to the great honor he has enjoyed in the past, Job now feels deeply shamed. All of his prior dignity has blown away like chaff, which is the consequence that should come to the wicked rather than to a righteous man like Job (cf. Ps. 1:4). The evidence of his lofty

status—his children, wealth, health, and power—is gone, and he now feels totally humiliated by the basest of people.

30:16–19 *He throws me into the mud.* Job feels as though his life is ebbing away (30:16) as he endures constant pain (30:17) that strangles or chafes him (30:18). What is most painful is that in addition to his human oppressors, God also seems to be fighting against him. Job feels that God is employing his great power to humiliate Job by hurling him into the mire.

30:21–23 *You turn on me ruthlessly; with the might of your hand you attack me.* Like the psalmists, Job cries out to God, hoping that God will answer, but instead God seems to turn on him. There is a possible play on words in the Hebrew text. The word that Job uses for "attack" sounds much like the word for Satan, or the adversary, in Job 1–2, except that the final consonant is *m* rather than *n*. God's treatment seems sadistic to Job as it brings him down to what appears to be certain death (30:22–23).

30:24–26 *Yet when I hoped for good, evil came.* Job insists once again that he has ministered to others in their affliction (30:24–25), but God has not rewarded him or cared for him in his need. The retribution principle maintains that God blesses those who act righteously, but Job has received the opposite of what he expects from God. This is the same kind of mistreatment that the psalmist receives from sinful people in Psalm 35:11–16, but it is not what Job expects to receive from the righteous God.

30:27 *The churning inside me never stops; days of suffering confront me.* Job's suffering penetrates well beyond his physical pain. As he looks ahead, he can see nothing but the prospect of continued adversity. This psychological trauma has left him perplexed and confused.

30:28 *I go about blackened, but not by the sun.* Job's self-description may refer back to verse 19, where he says that his condition is so dire that he has begun mourning for his own death in dust and ashes. The ashes he placed upon his head have made his skin appear black. In verse 30 a different Hebrew term is used when Job says that his skin "grows black" and peels. This likely refers to a skin disease that darkens his skin and makes it shrivel up and fall off (cf. 2:7–8).

In 30:21, Job says of God, "with the might of your hand you attack me." The mighty arm ready to strike is one of the poses recorded for Egyptian pharaohs. In this relief at Medinet Habu, Ramesses III holds a weapon in his upraised hand, ready to smite the prisoners he holds with the other (Twentieth Dynasty, twelfth century BC).

30:29 *I have become a brother of jackals, a companion of owls.* Jackals and owls are noted for their solitary nature, but they also emit screeching sounds (cf. Mic. 1:8) rather than life-enhancing tones (30:31). Likewise, Job feels alone and isolated from other humans and from God. His adversity has profound physical, psychological, theological, and social repercussions that are deeply painful for him to bear.

Theological Insights

In 30:19, Job complains that God has reduced him to dust and ashes. This expression is used only a few times in the Old Testament, and it will function prominently in Job's final answer to Yahweh in 42:6. When God creates the first human in Genesis 2:7, he takes the dust of the ground and then breathes into it his life-giving breath. That combination of the material and the immaterial is what enables Adam to become a living being. In the ancient world, dust and ashes were commonly used as signs of mourning, because they were pictures that only the lifeless material body remained after the death of a person. Job's self-description indicates that he feels so humiliated that he is as good as dead. All that is left is his physical body, and even that is in a miserable state indeed (30:28, 30).

Teaching the Text

As Job shifts his attention from the past (Job 29) to the present (Job 30), his emotions change profoundly. In place of the joy he had in the past, his life now is consumed by sorrow. Instead of enjoying honor, he now endures humiliation. This is not an occasional down day; Job's whole life has been devastated. Job now feels rejected by everyone. Other people in his community have turned against him, and God no longer seems to care for him. No wonder Job feels such pain.

Several times in the book Job describes in detail how he has helped those in need. In particular, Job has been compassionate and generous to the poor and oppressed. Now, however, those very people whom Job assisted in the past have turned on him. They mock him, spit at him, and take advantage of his weakened condition. Even though they themselves are desperate people who do not fit into normal human society, they attack Job when he is down. This is deeply painful to Job because it strikes at his character and honor.

As Job considers their treatment of him, he believes that his adversity from God has caused others to humiliate him. Because God seems to have destroyed Job's power and position, others feel no restraint from treating him poorly. In essence, they think that God, by his example, has given them the green light to attack Job. Therefore, they do not hesitate to exploit Job's weakness. The adversary earlier complained that Yahweh had placed a hedge of protection around Job, but now that protective barrier is gone, and Job feels the onslaught of those who detest him.

Even more painful to Job is his sense that God is attacking him directly, not just indirectly through the human enemies. God seems to be strangling him and throwing him into the mud. Instead of answering Job's cry for help, God seems to turn on him ruthlessly, so Job is convinced that he is going to die. Job is confident that God is sovereign over all that happens in life, so Job has to conclude that what is happening to him must be attributed to God, even though it seems out of character for God to act this way. This is what makes Job's situation so painful and perplexing to him.

Because Job feels rejected by both humans and God, he can see no hope for the future. If he had only human oppressors, then he could count on God to intervene for him. But because God seems to be in on the attack, there is nowhere else to turn for help. Job therefore feels totally alone in his pain, like a solitary animal cut off from anyone who would assist him. All Job can do in his adversity is to mourn and wail.

This pathetic cry of Job presents some great challenges for the teacher. The book of Job is an honest record of how Job feels in his great affliction, and in that it parallels many of the lament psalms, which disclose the feelings of their writers. However, just as the lament psalms move from pain to praise as the psalmist takes the problem to the Lord, so Job 30 must be read in the context of the whole book. At this moment in the story, Job is hurting and confused, but at the end he will have a better understanding of God and his ways. Thus, Job's experience of pain in this chapter is an accurate snapshot of what he feels at this point in time, but it must be viewed in the context of the whole story of his experience of trusting God.

> Job's pain and distress cause him to wail and howl, making sounds such as this jackal would make.

Illustrating the Text

At times we may feel rejected by God and humans and see no hope for the future.

Literature: "A Job of the Plains," by William Humphrey. This short story, published in 1965 and set during the Great Depression, is a modern take on the life of Job. The main character, a simple but "blameless and upright" farmer named Dobbs, goes from having a successful farm and family to progressively losing everything to even becoming the victim of a cyclone. Finally, he says in his rough English, "What's it all for, will somebody please tell me? What have I done to deserve this? I worked hard all my life. I've always paid my bills. I've never diced nor gambled, never drank, never chased after the women. I've always honored my old mama and daddy. I've done the best I could to provide for my wife and family, and tried to bring my children up decent and God-fearing. I've went to church regular. . . . And what have I got to show for it?" Later, his discouragement is complete, and he "[sits] alternately wishing he were dead and shivering with dread lest his impious wish be granted."[1]

Film: *A Serious Man*. The directors of this movie, the Coen brothers, seem often to be interested in the fate of men and women left in a world without transcendence. In *A*

Serious Man (2009), the lead character, played by Michael Stuhlbarg, is Larry, a Jewish man whose life in every area, both personally and professionally, begins to fall apart. He starts to question his faith, turning to a number of rabbis with his questions. Instead of having helpful answers and engaging Larry in good discussions or even expressing genuine empathy, these religious men prove to be dense, incomprehensible, and indifferent. This surely represents how Job must feel when God seems distant.

Literature: *Ben Hur*, by Lew Wallace. In this story published in 1880, the title character, Ben Hur, is unjustly accused and sentenced to serve as a slave in the mines, a fate that at the time was the equivalent of a death sentence. Just as Job must have felt trapped by his fate, so too Ben Hur could only believe that he would die in the mines. However, by an unforeseen turn of events, he is released from slavery and elevated to a high position.

Job's Final Oath of Innocence

Big Idea *Job rejects the accusations against him and calls on God to issue his just verdict.*

Understanding the Text

The Text in Context

This chapter brings to a climactic conclusion the long dialogue between Job and his three friends in Job 3–27, followed by the narrator's interlude in chapter 28 and Job's final confession of his innocence in chapters 29–31. Despite all his adversity and all the accusations by the friends, Job is still convinced that he is innocent. Unwilling to follow the counsel of the friends and utter a contrived and insincere confession of sin just to get his suffering to cease, Job holds firmly to his integrity. In Job 31, Job rests his case after stating his final oath of innocence. To do this, Job pronounces a series of strong oaths by which he swears that both his actions and his attitudes are right before God. Job continues to think within the framework of retribution theology, even though he has noted that it does not always apply in life, so he claims that he is innocent and he demands justice from God. At the end of this chapter, the stage is set for Yahweh to render his verdict, but before he does, the young man Elihu will burst on the scene and have his say in chapters 32–37. Only after Yahweh eventually speaks does Job acknowledge that God's ways cannot be adequately explained by humans (42:2–6).

Historical and Cultural Background

In his final oath of innocence, Job employs the ancient legal strategy of negative confession, an approach also found in Egyptian and Hittite texts. Job lists the various accusations that have been raised against him, and then he denies them all. Several times, Job uses the form, "If I have done this crime, then let God punish me with this horrible consequence." Other times, Job states the condition, but he leaves the consequence undefined. By this means, Job as the defendant calls on God as judge either to condemn him to the full extent of the law or else to clear him of the erroneous charge. If Job is guilty, then he has invited God to strike him with horrific penalties. If God does not exact the punishment, then his failure to do so will tacitly acquit Job of the charges against him. By this legal procedure, even the silence of God the judge can exonerate Job.

Interpretive Insights

31:1 *I made a covenant with my eyes not to look lustfully at a young woman.*

Job begins his oath with a statement that establishes from the outset the extent of ethical innocence he is claiming. He declares that he has made a covenant, or a binding commitment, not to look at a young woman. The NIV reading reflects how this verse has often been taken as anticipating Jesus's exposition of God's law in Matthew 5:27–28, with Job committing himself not to gaze at a young woman with sexually impure intent. However, the adverb "lustfully" is not explicitly in the Hebrew text. Therefore, it may be better to read Job as not looking for young women to collect as wives from powerful families with which he wanted to build powerful alliances (cf. Deut. 17:17; 1 Kings 11:1–3).

31:5–8 *let God weigh me in honest scales and he will know that I am blameless.* Job is convinced that he has not diverged from God's path to stray into falsehood and deceit (31:5), so he challenges God to evaluate him accurately, confident that this

Key Themes of Job 31

- Job recognizes that God knows him thoroughly.
- Job longs for God to treat him justly.
- Job's blamelessness encompasses his entire life.
- Job is confident that God will decide in his favor.

will demonstrate that he is blameless. The reader realizes that God has already twice told the adversary that Job was blameless, in 1:8 and 2:3. If Job has transgressed God's way, then he invites God to give his crops to others (31:8; cf. Lev. 26:16; Mic. 6:15) or else to destroy his crops altogether.

31:9–10 *If my heart has been enticed by a woman.* Job's denial of adultery is especially shocking in its language. The terms "door," "grind," and "sleep" (31:9–10) were common euphemisms for sexual activity. Job proposes that if he has been guilty of adultery, then the fitting punishment for his sin is for his own wife to be sexually exploited by others. Job is not trying to shift the consequences of his sin onto his wife. Rather, he is so confident he is innocent of this charge that he expresses what would be the most humiliating punishment for a man in the ancient world to endure.

Job wants God to evaluate his life and find him blameless by weighing him on honest scales (31:6). This brings to mind the weighing-of-the-heart ritual that Egyptians believed occurred as the deceased passed through the netherworld. The heart was weighed to determine if it was pure. The ritual is depicted here in this drawing on papyrus (fourth to first century BC).

31:13–15 *Did not he who made me in the womb make them?* In the treatment of his slaves, Job has gone well beyond what is required in the Mosaic law (cf. Exod. 21:1–11; Lev. 25:39–55; Deut. 15:12–18). In the ancient Near East, slaves were typically regarded as property, but Job views his slaves as fellow humans made by God. Therefore, he has treated them humanely, as people possessing human rights, just as he does.

31:16–23 *If I have denied the desires of the poor.* Eliphaz earlier accused Job of mistreating the needy (22:7–9), so now Job emphatically denies the charge. He counters that he has taken a special interest in the plight of those who are dependent on the generosity of others. Job insists that he has treated the orphans and widows as though they were his own family (31:18). He has not abused his lofty status in the community to take advantage of the poor in legal proceedings (31:21). His care for the needy emerges from his reverence for God (31:23).

31:24–28 *If I have put my trust in gold.* In his earlier speech, Eliphaz insinuated that Job was materialistic (22:23–26), but now Job insists that he has not placed his confidence in his wealth (31:24–25; cf. Ps. 62:10). Job has not compromised his commitment to God either by materialism or by idolatry (31:26–28),

because he regards both of them as sinful acts that constitute unfaithfulness to God.

31:29–30 *If I have rejoiced at my enemy's misfortune.* It is natural for sinful humans to take pleasure in the defeat of their enemies (cf. Obad. 12), but Job says that he has not taken delight when his enemy has suffered disaster. In his words and in his attitudes, Job obeys God by not sinning even against those who have wronged him (Prov. 24:17–18). Only a man of impeccable blamelessness would dare to make a claim like this. By his oath, Job invites God to probe his inner motives and attitudes, not just his overt actions (cf. Ps. 139:23–24).

31:31–32 *my door was always open to the traveler.* In the ancient world, hospitality to strangers was viewed as a solemn

Job denies worshiping the sun and moon (31:26–27), which was a common practice in the ancient world. This stela shows Nabonidus, king of Babylon, with upraised hand before three divine symbols: crescent, winged disk, and star. These represent Sin the moon god, Shamash the sun god, and Ishtar or Venus (sixth century BC).

obligation (e.g., Gen. 18:1–8; 19:1–3), and God commands his people to be faithful in this grace (Lev. 19:34; Rom. 12:13; Heb. 13:2). Job is renowned for his generosity to strangers, even serving them meat (31:31), which was typically reserved only for special occasions of celebration. It is evident that Job has given from the heart, not grudgingly.

31:35–37 *I sign now my defense—let the Almighty answer me.* Job is steadfastly confident of his innocence, so he imaginatively signs his name to this final legal argument, and then he calls on God to break his silence and to rule in Job's favor. Job is so sure that God will exonerate him that he looks forward to proclaiming the verdict publicly. He envisions wearing the verdict of innocence proudly on his shoulder (cf. Isa. 22:22) or as a crown (31:36; cf. Zech. 6:9–15), so that everyone can read it.

31:38–40 *if my land cries out against me.* Job's words in verses 38–40 would seem to fit logically before his signature in verse 35, so it is possible that an early scribal error misplaced the last three verses of the chapter. Job claims that his righteous behavior extends even to how he has treated his land. He has been a faithful steward over God's earth, so his land has not cried out in complaint about how Job exploited it. For the last time, Job invites God to exact measure-for-measure judgment if Job has not acted as he has said. In this case, God should cause the land to produce briars and weeds instead of wheat and barley.

Theological Insights

Job's denial that he has mistreated the poor and the oppressed (31:16–23) reflects a widespread biblical theme. Throughout the Bible, God's people are commanded to care for the needy. The Old Testament prophets frequently pronounce divine judgment because of the people's failure to deal justly with the poor and the weak (Isa. 1:16–17; Jer. 7:5–7; Amos 4:1; Mal. 3:5). The New Testament also strongly condemns those who fail to show compassion and to seek justice for the needy (Matt. 25:41–46; James 2:1–7; 5:1–6). Yahweh is consistently presented as the father of the orphan and the protector of the widow (Pss. 68:5; 146:9), so humans who oppress the needy violate God's commandment, and they spurn his character by their unjust actions.

Teaching the Text

Throughout the book of Job, Job has been the target of numerous accusations. In the prologue, the adversary accuses Job of having selfish motives. Then, the three friends invent all sorts of sins that would justify Job's great adversities. Job knows in his heart that these accusations are false, so in his final oath in Job 31 he rejects all of them in the strongest possible language. In fact, Job goes so far as to say that if the accusations are accurate, then God should pour out horrific punishments on him. Job has not been intimidated by his accusers into making an insincere confession to sins that he has not committed.

Job clearly works from the realization that God knows all things. That means that God knows what Job has done and what he has not done. More than that, God knows what is in Job's heart, when others can only speculate about Job's motives and desires. To Job, the omniscience of God is a comfort because Job knows that he has been blameless before God. God's perfect knowledge will also enable God to reach a verdict that truly fits the facts of the case. Because God knows us thoroughly, we can be confident that he will always do what is right for us.

Job longs for justice from God. He is well aware of the many ways in which humans sin both publicly and privately in their actions and attitudes. As Job examines his own life for sin, he cannot discern how he may have missed God's mark. Like Job, we need to examine our lives carefully, so that we may honor the Lord in our actions, attitudes, thoughts, and motives. In the words of Psalm 19:14, our desire should be that the words of our mouth and the meditation of our heart are pleasing in God's sight.

As Job progresses through his confession of innocence, he addresses every area of his life. His blamelessness permeates his interaction with women, his business dealings, his treatment of his servants, his care for the poor, his use of money, his attitude toward his enemies, his hospitality to strangers, and his use of the land, as well as his commitment to God alone. All of the parts of life that are often regarded as secular pursuits are included in Job's blamelessness before God. Job demonstrates that there must be no distinction between what is sacred and what is secular—all of life must be lived in a way that honors and fears the Lord.

Job signs his final oath with confidence that God in his justice will decide in Job's favor. Job does not know why he has experienced this severe adversity, but he knows that God is just, and he knows that he has been blameless in all areas of his life. Like Job, we may face situations in our lives that we cannot understand. But we must always hold on to the certitude that the Lord is faithful and just, so that he will eventually bring all things to their proper end.

As Job employs his legal strategy of negative confession, he may be crossing the line when he attempts to manipulate God to answer him, even if only tacitly.

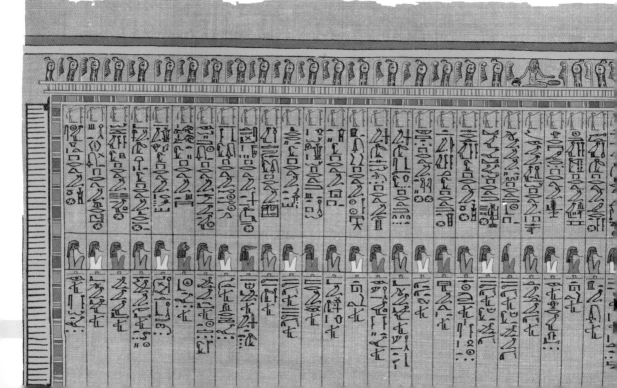

The author does not describe Job's inner thinking, so we cannot be sure if this is the case. Nevertheless, Job is at least very close to trying to put God in a box, as we also sometimes attempt to do by the promises or threats we make to him. In the end, God is not compelled by Job's strategy but remains free to do what he has sovereignly determined, despite what Job may desire or expect. We, too, must allow God to be God in our lives, rather than trying to dictate to him what he must do, how he must do it, and when our deadline is for his action.

Illustrating the Text

For a person of integrity, there is no disconnect between character and behavior.

Literature: *A Christmas Carol*, **by Charles Dickens.** In this beloved Christmas novella (1843), Ebenezer Scrooge is a wealthy man who dismisses the poor as merely surplus population, ignores the misery of those who work for him, and scoffs at all social expectation. After three visions that show him his terrible life and the consequences of his behavior, his heart is changed. After this transformation, Scrooge becomes unusually generous to those in need. In this generosity, he mirrors Job.

History: Abraham Lincoln was criticized for selecting Edwin Stanton, one of his political rivals, to be in his cabinet. Lincoln explained that the best way to defeat an enemy is to turn him into a friend.

When we long for God's justice, we must put our case in God's hands.

Literature: "A Job of the Plains," by William Humphrey. This short story is based on the story of Job, though it is certainly not identical to it in its philosophical conclusion. The main character, Dobbs, is an affluent, successful farmer and a simple, good man. He loses everything materially and finally wishes himself dead, except that he is concerned for the fate of his family. At one moment, sitting under the rubble of his house, he says to his family, in what looks like a surrender of his circumstances to God, "'Well, now, everybody, here we all are, all together, safe and sound. Let's be thankful for that. Now to keep our spirits up, let's sing a song. All together now, loud and clear. Ready?' And with him carrying the lead in his quavering nasal tenor, they sang: 'Jesus loves me, this I know, For the Bible tells me so.'"[1]

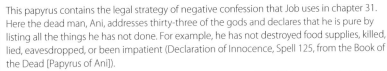

This papyrus contains the legal strategy of negative confession that Job uses in chapter 31. Here the dead man, Ani, addresses thirty-three of the gods and declares that he is pure by listing all the things he has not done. For example, he has not destroyed food supplies, killed, lied, eavesdropped, or been impatient (Declaration of Innocence, Spell 125, from the Book of the Dead [Papyrus of Ani]).

Elihu Makes His Appearance

Big Idea *The young Elihu claims to know the truth that has escaped Job and his friends.*

Understanding the Text

The Text in Context

After Job concludes his words in 31:40, the reader expects to hear Yahweh speak to resolve the debate between Job and his friends. Instead, a young man named Elihu bursts upon the scene, and for the next six chapters he holds the stage. In his long, uninterrupted speech, Elihu summarizes the points made by Job and the friends, often quoting or alluding to their specific words. He agrees with them that God sends suffering as his judgment on sin, but he adds that God can also use suffering to refine human character. Thus, for Elihu suffering is both punitive and formative. Elihu supposes that he has the final word in this discussion, but Yahweh will retain that prerogative in chapters 38–41. In the structure of the book, Elihu's speeches extend the dramatic tension as the reader keeps waiting for Yahweh to bring resolution to Job's case.

Job 32 begins with the narrator's description of Elihu (32:1–5). Then Elihu describes himself in 32:6–22. He claims to be inspired by God (32:6–10), he expresses impatience with the friends and with Job (32:11–16), and he articulates how intent he is on speaking (32:17–22).

Historical and Cultural Background

In 32:19, Elihu compares his urgent intention to speak to wine bottled up in new wineskins and ready to burst. In the ancient world, wine was typically stored in animal skins (Jer. 13:12), which could expand as the wine fermented. In the New Testament, Jesus uses the same image in Matthew 9:17 to explain how his teaching cannot be confined within old ways of thinking that have grown rigid and inflexible. Even new wineskins have to be vented, or else they will explode under the pressure of the fermented wine within them.[1]

Interpretive Insights

32:2 *Elihu . . . became very angry with Job for justifying himself rather than God.* The likely sense of the Hebrew is that Elihu perceives Job as regarding himself to be more righteous than God. As Elihu views it, when Job holds on to his claim of innocence, he is implying that his righteousness is superior to God's. Elihu cannot tolerate Job raising a question about God's righteousness. He feels that he must defend God's honor and character against Job's fallacious accusation.

32:3–5 *his anger was aroused*. The narrator repeatedly says that Elihu is angry (32:2, 3, 5). Elihu is angry with Job for justifying himself more than God (32:2). He also is angry with the friends, because they have not been able to refute Job, and they have given up the attempt to do so (32:3, 5). To Elihu, Job's situation seems clear enough, and he is agitated that things have reached an impasse rather than a resolution. The repeated emphasis on Elihu's anger and his youth may well be intended to alert the reader that Elihu, for all his commendable theology and good intentions, does not provide the final answer to Job's situation. That will await Yahweh's speeches at the end of the book.

32:6–7 *I am young in years, and you are old*. With these words, Elihu begins an extended prelude to his speeches (32:6–22). Traditional wisdom values the aged, because their long years have given them the opportunity to accumulate much observation of life

In Job 32, Elihu arrives on the scene and begins his speech. One can imagine this impassioned young man looking much like the ancient Greek orators who are well known for their eloquent speeches. Shown here is the figurine of an orator (first century BC to first century AD).

Key Themes of Job 32

- The narrator describes Elihu as angry against Job and the friends.
- Elihu claims to have received understanding from the Spirit of God.
- Elihu regards the arguments of the friends as ineffective.
- Elihu is ready to burst with what he wants to say to Job.

(Prov. 4:1–9), and therefore they can become expert in wisdom. In wisdom thought, the young are the learners, and they receive instruction from their elders (Prov. 1:8). Elihu says that he has deferred to the seniority of Job and the friends. Nevertheless, he is deeply disappointed in their answers, so he determines now to speak up for the truth.

32:8 *But it is the spirit in a person . . . that gives them understanding*. Elihu argues that the elders do not have a corner on wisdom. Although he is young, he too has the spirit of understanding within him. This expression could refer generally to the spirit that all humans have because they have been made in the image of God (cf. Gen. 2:7), but more likely Elihu is claiming that as he speaks, the Spirit of God is communicating through him (cf. 33:4). Understanding, then, is not the sole possession of the aged (32:9); Elihu has the same capacity for understanding as they. The insight that he has received from divine inspiration is not limited by his age or life experience. Elihu's claim here is similar to what Eliphaz maintained for himself in chapter 4.

32:9 *It is not only the old who are wise*. In making this observation,

Elihu identifies himself with teachings found elsewhere in the Bible. In Ecclesiastes 4:13–16 a poor but wise boy is regarded as better than an old and foolish king. In Psalm 119:98–100 the psalmist says that the word of Yahweh makes him wiser than the aged. Both Joseph and Daniel confound their elders by their God-given wisdom. In Luke 2:46–47 the boy Jesus amazes the scholars in the temple by his insightful questions and answers.

32:10–14 *Therefore I say: Listen to me.* In 32:10–14, Elihu addresses the three friends. He has waited and listened to them speak, but they have not been successful in refuting Job (32:11–12). They have claimed in vain to have found wisdom; what they have actually done is to punt to God to answer Job (32:13). Elihu resolves to answer Job more persuasively than the friends have done (32:14), and in fact he does come closer to the mark, but Yahweh alone will give the full and final answer.

32:15–20 *Must I wait, now that they are silent?* Beginning in verse 15, Elihu turns away from the friends to speak to Job specifically. In Elihu's opinion, the friends have failed, so he sees no need to wait for them to speak further. He determines to express his opinion that is welling up within him (32:17–20). His turgid language makes Elihu come off sounding pompous rather than as a serious teacher of wisdom.

In 15:2, Eliphaz asked rhetorically if a wise man should fill himself with windy knowledge. Elihu here seems to be doing just that, as he comically describes himself as a windbag who has to speak in order to get relief from the flatulence within him

(32:18–20). Elihu indicates that he is ready to explode and that his only relief is to speak right away. He is indeed full of words (32:18), but they come from his belly, which was regarded as the seat of the passions rather than of reasoned reflection. This appears to be another signal by the author that Elihu's aspirations in speaking to Job are better than the answers he gives him.

Elihu says he is so full of words that he is like a new wineskin ready to burst (32:19). Shown here is a servant carrying a wineskin or waterskin (Persepolis, Iran, 358–338 BC).

32:21–22 *I will show no partiality, nor will I flatter anyone.* Elihu claims that he is incapable of partiality, which makes him an unbiased observer or a judge who speaks only the truth (cf. Job's desire for an impartial arbiter in 9:33). Moreover, he says that God would take him away if he were to speak insincerely (32:22). After his long and promising prelude, Elihu's actual speeches are somewhat disappointing by comparison. When Yahweh finally speaks, he addresses Job and the three friends, but he says nothing about Elihu (42:7–9). Elihu is accurate in defending the justice of God, but in the larger context of the book, he may best be seen as an ironic figure. In his passionate and ornate words he at times says what he does not intend (32:18–20). He is repeatedly described by the narrator as angry (32:2–5), which in the wisdom tradition is a trait of a fool (Prov. 29:22). In his evaluation of Job, Elihu is ignorant of Yahweh's assessment of him as righteous (1:8; 2:3).

Theological Insights

Interpreters have viewed Elihu in a wide variety of ways, with some evaluating him positively as speaking for Yahweh and others dismissing him as intrusive and empty. In order to assess accurately his role in the book, several textual features must be considered. Elihu is not mentioned either before or after he speaks. In contrast to the other characters, Elihu has a genealogy included, and he seems to be related to Abraham, although he lives outside Israel in the area close to Dedan and Tema (cf. Jer. 25:23). Elihu's words look back to what the friends and Job have said already, but they also look ahead to foreshadow the entrance of Yahweh. Elihu is represented by the narrator as angry, and his introduction of himself seems to have a bombastic tone. When Yahweh speaks, he does not criticize Elihu, as he does the three friends, but he does not commend Elihu either, as he does Job. Elihu has no knowledge of the events narrated in the prologue, so he does not correctly discern the background to Job's adversity.

When all of this evidence is taken together, it seems that Elihu summarizes the arguments of both Job and the friends, and he points out their deficiencies. His own position assumes that the retribution formula applies to Job's case, but he adds the important point that suffering can be formative as well as punitive. Elihu aspires to the role of the judge who will decide the case, but his angry tone and his unintentional slips of speech suggest that the author wants the reader to construe him as a well-intentioned but ironic figure who sets the stage for Yahweh, the real judge.

Teaching the Text

While Job and the three wisdom teachers were speaking in chapters 3–31, a younger man named Elihu listened attentively to what they said. Finally the time has come when all the older men are silent, so Elihu jumps into the conversation. With great self-confidence, the young Elihu claims to know the truth that has escaped Job and his friends. When Job concludes his words in 31:40, the reader expects Yahweh to speak next, but Elihu postpones the divine resolution of the case. As Elihu begins to speak, the reader wonders if perhaps youth will succeed where the reasoning of the elders has failed. However, a self-confident tone is not necessarily an indicator of genuine wisdom.

The narrator describes Elihu much more fully than he does the other speakers in the book. In particular, he repeatedly portrays Elihu as angry—angry with Job, angry with the friends, and angry that the debate seems to have been abandoned rather than resolved. With this description, the narrator provides a lens through which Elihu should be viewed. It is true that anger can at times

Elihu claims that although he is young, his words contain wisdom given by God. This Egyptian figurine shows a scribe sitting at the feet of Thoth, the god of knowledge, science, and wisdom (1450–1280 BC).

be justified, if it is directed at those things that dishonor God, and that God himself is angry at sin (Exod. 4:14; Deut. 4:25; Ps. 7:6). However, in wisdom literature anger is the mark not of the wise person but of the fool, so Elihu's words must be evaluated with that in mind.

In traditional wisdom, wisdom resides in the elders, who have had the opportunity to observe life broadly. Elihu is well aware of his youth, so he claims that he has received his insight from the breath of the Almighty, who gives understanding to humans. Rather than competing head to head with the aged wisdom teachers, Elihu attempts an end run by insisting that he has received his insight directly from God.

Elihu brushes off the arguments of the friends as ineffective. He has listened attentively to them as they tried to prove Job wrong, but they have not been able to do so. Elihu insists that he will answer Job with different and better arguments, and he does

provide an important reaffirmation of the justice of God along with his observation that God may use adversity for formative reasons, not just as punishment for sin, as the friends have contended. However, much of what Elihu says repeats what has already been stated, and his new material does not fully explain Job's situation.

Elihu is almost comical when he says that he is full of words and that he must speak in order to find relief from the words that are ready to burst within him. For all of his good theology, which in many ways surpasses that of the three friends, Elihu mistakes his sense of passionate urgency for genuine understanding. There are many people like Elihu, whose confidence in their opinions is better than their comprehension of the situation. They are eager to speak, but they do not realize that many words do not necessarily equal sound wisdom. People like Elihu end up saying a lot, but they may contribute less of substance to the discussion than they suppose. When so many seem eager to offer their opinions, sometimes very passionately, we need to be careful to measure all that they say by the truths of God's Word, because true wisdom comes from God.

Illustrating the Text

Even when counselors and public figures are confident, they may be wrong.

Television: Late-night talk show hosts and comedians (e.g., David Letterman, Conan O'Brien, and Jon Stewart) are often witty, brash, and full of ridicule, but when not paired with constructive alternatives, their comments add little understanding to the issues of the day. Elihu is angry at all the previous speakers who have addressed Job; impatient with their arguments, he claims to offer better ones. He is, however, also short on wisdom.

Literature: *J.B.*, by Archibald MacLeish. In this existential version of the book of Job published in 1952, J.B. (the Job character) answers one of his accusers with the following words, which are appropriate in the face of wrong counsel:

> Yours is the cruelest comfort of
> them all,
> Making the Creator of the Universe
> The miscreator of mankind—
> A party to the crimes He punishes.[2]

Book: *In God's Waiting Room*, **by Lehman Strauss.** After preaching for many years on the Christian's response to suffering, Strauss (1911–97) learned firsthand about affliction and the pain of helplessness and despair when his wife, Elsie, suffered a severe stroke. He writes in his book *In God's Waiting Room* (1984) that there is a chasm between knowing truth intellectually and knowing it by personal experience. He asks himself if there is anything wrong with a minister and teacher of the Bible being "perplexed." He concludes that such perplexity makes one draw near to God, that God's adversity can be a gift to his child. This is the posture of a true counselor and not that of Elihu.

Quote: Blaise Pascal. Probably quoting from Isaiah 45:15, Pascal asserts, "A religion which does not affirm that God is hidden is not true. *Vere tu es Deus absconditus*— truly you are a hidden God."[3]

Elihu Urges Job to Listen

Big Idea *Elihu presents a simple explanation for Job's complex situation.*

Understanding the Text

The Text in Context

After his extended prelude in chapter 32, Elihu now launches into his speeches to Job. Chapter 33 is the first of four uninterrupted speeches (in chapters 33, 34, 35, and 36–37) by Elihu in chapters 32–37. Elihu talks more than anyone else in the book, with the exception of Job. In fact, Elihu speaks longer than Yahweh does in chapters 38–41. In Job 33, Elihu addresses Job directly, urging Job to listen to the wisdom that he intends to teach him. As Elihu's prelude has indicated, he is very confident that he understands Job's situation and that he can point Job in the right direction. It will become evident, however, that Elihu promises more than he can deliver.

Historical and Cultural Background

When Elihu declares to Job in 33:6, "I too am a piece of

Elihu says he is like Job before God because he is also formed from clay (33:6). Other ancient Near Eastern cultures speak about humankind being formed from clay. Shown here is a fragment from Tablet I of the Gilgamesh Epic, where the goddess of creation pinches off clay to form Enkidu.

clay," he alludes to an image that is found both within the Bible and in ancient Near Eastern literature. The creation narrative in Genesis describes the first human, Adam, as being formed by God from the dust of the ground (Gen. 2:7). Other biblical passages refer to humans as clay that God sculpts (Job 10:9; Isa. 45:9; 64:8; Jer. 18:6; Rom. 9:20–21). In the Mesopotamian Epic of Gilgamesh, the goddess of creation pinches off clay to form Enkidu. In the biblical texts, the image of humans as clay most often focuses on God's sovereign work in the lives of individuals and nations as he shapes them according to his plan. In all cases, clay suggests that humans are the recipients of God's actions as he molds and directs their lives.

Interpretive Insights

33:4 *The Spirit of God has made me; the breath of the*

Almighty gives me life. With these words, Elihu echoes what he said earlier, in 32:8, when he implied that he speaks by special revelation from God. He claims to possess a better source of wisdom than either Job or the friends have, because he has received his insight directly from God, not indirectly through observation of life. In effect, Elihu suggests that he is the voice of wisdom (cf. Prov. 8:7–8). By this means he seeks to establish his credentials as superior to Job in knowledge.

Key Themes of Job 33

- Elihu declares that he has the answer that Job needs to hear.
- Elihu sums up Job's speeches as he has heard them.
- Elihu explains how God communicates through dreams and pain.
- Elihu holds out the prospect of restoration for Job.

33:5 *Answer me then, if you can.* Elihu takes the tone of a prosecutor as he addresses Job directly. Job has been regarding himself as the plaintiff, but Elihu tries to compel him into the role of the guilty defendant. Elihu seems to be overly impressed with his own intellect, because the words "if you can" imply that Job in fact cannot answer him. There is no record in the book that Job does venture an answer to Elihu, but instead Yahweh speaks up when Elihu is finished at last at the end of chapter 37.

33:8–11 *But you have said in my hearing—I heard the very*

Elihu suggests that God may speak as he chastens people "on a bed of pain" (33:19) in order to bring them to repentance. Prayers of confession would then result in restoration. Other ancient Near Eastern cultures also believed that illness could have a supernatural origin, whether attributed to gods or demons. Amulets like the one shown here from Mesopotamia were created to ward off demon-induced sickness. The middle register shows special healers wearing fish-skin robes performing the prescribed ritual over the sick person in order to restore their health (Neo-Assyrian, ninth century BC).

Wisdom and God's Chastening of His Children

Elihu's discussion of God's use of chastening parallels the wisdom teaching found in Prov. 3:11–12:

> My son, do not despise the LORD's discipline,
>> and do not resent his rebuke,
> because the LORD disciplines those he loves,
>> as a father the son he delights in.

The Proverbs text is taken up in Heb. 12:5–11 to encourage Christians to embrace God's discipline as his process of producing a harvest of righteousness and peace in their lives. Similarly, James 1:2–4 teaches that trials should be welcomed, because they cultivate perseverance and maturity in God's people.

words. Elihu declares that he is quoting the very words of Job, but what Elihu says in verses 9–11 slants Job's position in a simplistic way that does not encompass Job's total way of thinking. Elihu depicts Job as saying that he is innocent (four times in v. 9) and that God has wronged him (four times in vv. 10–11). With this skewed summary of Job's speeches, Elihu expresses the friends' misconceptions of Job more than Job's actual position, which is much more complex than this.

33:12 *in this you are not right, for God is greater than any mortal.* This criticism of Job by Elihu rings hollow, because Job agrees with Elihu and the three friends about the greatness of God (cf. 9:19). Job's real question is not about God's transcendence but about God's justice toward him. Elihu conceives of Job's situation as a question of abstract theology, but Job is trying to comprehend how his experience of adversity can be reconciled with God's sovereignty and justice. Elihu has not heard Job nearly as well as he thinks he has.

33:13–14 *For God does speak—now one way, now another—though no one perceives it.* In verse 14 Elihu counters Job's complaint in verse 13 that God does not respond to humans when they cry out to him. Elihu insists that God speaks in a variety of ways to humans, even to sinners like Job. Elihu will go on in verses 15–22 to explain how God uses dreams and pain to communicate with people. The problem is not God's lack of communication but Job's inability or unwillingness to listen to God. According to Elihu, by wrongly insisting on his innocence Job has become deaf to what God has been saying to him all along.

33:15–18 *In a dream, in a vision of the night.* Elihu states in 33:15–18 that one of the ways that God communicates with humans is through dreams and visions. God uses these disquieting messages in order to warn sinners and to turn them away from their wrongdoing and pride. God's purpose is to prevent people from proceeding in their sin. Elihu's implication is that Job needs to heed the warnings he is receiving from God rather than dismissing them as not applicable to him.

33:19–22 *Or someone may be chastened on a bed of pain.* Elihu speaks in general terms of "someone" experiencing pain, but it is clear that he has Job specifically in mind. Elihu's description of the person in pain in verses 19–22 closely resembles Job's physical ailments in 3:24; 16:8; 19:20; and 30:17. By chastening people with pain, God gives them an opportunity to repent rather than to proceed into death (see the sidebar). Elihu suggests that Job should not reject his pain as an unwelcome intruder but should value it as

God's agent of conviction that can lead to his restoration.

33:23–28 *Yet if there is an angel at their side.* Earlier in the book, Job expressed his desire for a mediator to represent his case before God (16:19; 19:25). Elihu now raises the possibility of an angel who can restore a person to uprightness and intercede for that person before God. This requires, however, that the person confess any sins (33:27). Like the friends, Elihu thinks that Job's adversity has been caused by his personal sin. Thus, Elihu repeats their counsel to Job, even though Job has steadfastly maintained that he is innocent of any wrongdoing and has no sin to confess.

33:29–30 *God does all these things to a person . . . to turn them back from the pit.* Elihu concludes his first speech by summarizing what he has said in verses 13–28. He alleges that God's purpose in communicating to humans through dreams and pain is to bring them to repentance. God seeks to deliver sinners like Job from the precipice of divine judgment that looms before them. In Elihu's view, God is just, but he also is gracious in extending forgiveness to those who repent of their sins.

33:31–33 *Pay attention, Job, and listen to me.* Elihu pleads with Job to be attentive to him rather than brushing him off. Elihu is convinced that he has the wisdom that Job needs (33:33) and that what he has said will vindicate Job (33:32). Once again, Elihu seems to overestimate his ability to comprehend and counsel Job.

Theological Insights

Elihu's description of God's communication to humans through dreams and

Elihu tells Job that God is not silent but that God may speak through dreams or pain. This votive column was erected to thank the "supreme God" for protection because of a warning sent in a dream (late first century AD).

visions (33:15–18) fits into the larger theology of divine revelation in the Bible. Both in the Old Testament and in the New Testament God uses dreams to communicate with numerous individuals, including Joseph, Samuel, Daniel, Paul, and John. Dreams, then, are legitimate means by which God reveals his truth to humans. However, the Bible also warns against those who falsely claim to receive a dream from God when they have not. Charlatans like this are denounced in very strong language in Deuteronomy 13:1–5 and Jeremiah 23:25–32. Although no definitive judgment is made in the biblical text, Eliphaz's dream that he describes in Job 4:12–21 seems to be something other than a word from God.

Teaching the Text

In his first speech, in Job 33, Elihu presents a simple explanation for Job's complex situation. The prologue has revealed that Job's adversity is tied up with the dispute between Yahweh and the adversary, so it is not a standard case easily explained by the retribution formula. Job's earlier speeches have wrestled with numerous questions that have dominated his mind as he reflects on what has happened to him. Elihu, however, is confident that he has deciphered the puzzle that has baffled Job. The answer he gives would fit many cases, but it does not explain Job's specific situation.

At the beginning and the end of this speech, Elihu urges Job to listen to him, because he believes that he has the answer that Job needs to hear. No doubt, Elihu is sincere in his motives, and he is confident in his knowledge of the situation. However, sincerity does not always mean accuracy, and confidence is not the same as competence. As a counselor, Elihu wants to help, and he thinks he is helping, but in reality he misses the mark.

Before a cure can be prescribed, the disease must be diagnosed correctly. Elihu has listened to what Job has said, but his diagnosis of Job's condition is flawed. Elihu has heard Job say two things: he is innocent, and God has wronged him. Job has indeed said these things, but he has also said much more than that. In trying to comprehend Job's situation, Elihu oversimplifies what Job has said. Because of that, Elihu reduces Job's problem into an easily treated ailment rather than recognizing it as the complicated condition that it is. In a sense, what Elihu declares is analogous to saying that Job has a common cold when in reality Job is struggling with a serious case of pneumonia. It is tempting to reduce painful situations to simple answers, but Job's experience reveals that life is more complex than that.

Elihu is more hopeful for Job than the friends are, because he holds out the prospect of restoration for Job. He realizes that one of the most important functions of a comforter is to restore hope to one who is tempted to give up. Elihu's instinct in this is right, even though he does not fully understand Job's problem.

Illustrating the Text

Those who counsel others need to understand the situation before they speak.

Psychology: *Escape from Loneliness*, by **Paul Tournier.** Tournier (1898–1986) was a Swiss physician and psychotherapist. He describes what a doctor must do for his patient, a description that parallels what a counselor must do for those he or she counsels. He writes, "Often I have heard a patient tell me that he has been disappointed in his doctor, who yet had taken good care of him, 'because he didn't take me seriously.' The patient means that the doctor wasn't interested in detail, in particular problems that meant a great deal to his patient." Then he quotes a Dr. Dubois who said, "The patient must be much more than just an interesting case; he must become your friend."[1] To hear details is to begin to know the person one is listening to. This is what Elihu needed to do.

Those who counsel others need to be careful not to oversimplify the situation.

Literature: *J.B.*, by **Archibald MacLeish.** In this verse play based on the book of Job, MacLeish is responding to the horrors he saw in two world wars, the Holocaust, and the bombings of Hiroshima and Nagasaki. It tells the story of a twentieth-century American millionaire banker whom God allows to be stripped of everything. In scene 1, the members of a well-to-do family from New England, who are at the core of the story, are seated around a table having Thanksgiving dinner. The wife and mother wishes her children would be more thankful for their substantial gifts because she believes that such gratitude will earn God's pleasure and that He will punish ingratitude. She says, "If we do our part He does His, / He always has. If we forget Him / He will forget. Forever. In everything."[2] This is the kind of oversimplification Elihu is guilty of.

Elihu Argues That God Always Acts Justly

Big Idea *Elihu reasons that because God is always just, Job must necessarily be wicked.*

Understanding the Text

The Text in Context

In his second speech, in chapter 34, Elihu takes a tone that is more rigid than in his first speech (Job 33). Adopting the retribution theology of the three friends, Elihu argues deductively from the premise of the justice of God to the necessary conclusion that Job is a sinner. Because God is absolutely powerful and just, humans must not question his ways. By objecting to how God has treated him, Job is proving that he is not pious. Elihu views Job's situation strictly as a legal case to be adjudicated rather than as a painful personal tragedy. Thus, Elihu is long on rhetoric but short on compassion. In effect, Elihu functions as another prosecutor against Job as he defends God's just governance of the world. Elihu begins (34:1–9) and ends (34:31–37) this speech with appeals to the wise men, whom he believes he represents, and the central portion of his speech, in 34:10–30, is an extended argument that God always acts justly.

Historical and Cultural Background

In many modern governments, the executive branch is separated from the judicial branch. In ancient cultures, and even in some governments today, the head of state was also responsible for judging the people. This practice is reflected in the Old Testament when individuals appeal to the king for legal judgment or protection (e.g., 2 Sam. 15:2; 1 Kings 3:16–28; 2 Kings 8:5–6). In Psalm 101:8, the king pledges to bring timely judgment against the wicked of the land. Elihu assumes this legal arrangement when he speaks of the impossibility of God perverting justice (34:12) and of God's judgment of kings and nobles (34:18–19).

Interpretive Insights

34:2 *Hear my words, you wise men.* As Elihu speaks to Job, he also addresses a wider audience. His references to "wise men" (34:2) and "men of understanding" (34:10, 34) probably are broader than just the three friends who have already spoken, because Elihu has rejected their claim to wisdom (32:11–14). He wants to present a united front of wisdom against Job, and he is very confident that he has the answer that truly wise men understand.

34:5–8 *Job says, "I am innocent, but God denies me justice."* Elihu's quotation in verses 5–6 generally summarizes what Job has said before, especially in 9:15 and 27:2–6. However, Elihu selectively cites Job's words, and then he interprets them in a way that does not fairly represent Job's meaning (34:7–8). He also neglects to describe Job's conflicted feelings and thoughts about God and how Job cannot comprehend why God is treating him as he does. Elihu reduces all the evidence into two simplistic assertions that he puts into Job's mouth: Job is innocent, and God is unjust. But these assertions do not truly represent all that Job has said. The facts are a lot more complex than Elihu indicates.

34:9 *There is no profit in trying to please God.* Job comes close to saying these words in 21:14–15, but in that context Job is describing what the wicked cry out. Elihu insists that Job is indeed one of the wicked (34:8), and that Job's earlier sentiments in 9:29–31 are proof of his guilt. Elihu, however, fails to consider how these words were prompted by Job's pain and anguish as he felt abandoned by God. Instead of considering this factor, Elihu extrapolates Job's words into an outright dismissal of God as morally arbitrary.

34:10–15 *Far be it from God to do evil.* Elihu begins with the premise that the Sovereign God (34:13) is incapable of doing evil, so

whatever he does is just. This leads logically to the doctrine of exact retribution (34:11), by which God repays all people for what they have done. Any departure from divine justice is unthinkable to Elihu (34:12). Elihu, therefore, has no place in his tidy theological system for the possibility of a righteous man experiencing adversity, so he regards Job's contention that he is innocent as a theological impossibility. Elihu goes on in verses 14–15 to argue that God can do whatever he pleases, even causing the whole human race to perish. With these words, Elihu comes very close to affirming the deistic dogma that whatever is, is right.

34:16–20 *Can someone who hates justice govern?* In verses 16–20, Elihu describes God as all-powerful, ruling even over the kings of the earth. Elihu

Elihu asks the question, "Can someone who hates justice govern?" (34:17). In the ancient world, kings were charged by the gods to administer justice as they ruled. The top register of the Stele of Hammurabi shows Hammurabi being commissioned by the god Shamash to administer justice.

connects God's power with his justice, reflecting the widespread ancient notion that the king is the source, interpreter, and executor of the law. Within this framework of thought, one who exercises rule is by definition just, so God as the absolute ruler must be absolutely just in all that he does. Elihu's implication is that Job, by questioning God's justice, is also rebelling against his authority.

34:21–23 *God has no need to examine people further.* In verses 21–22, Elihu states

that God sees every step that humans take. Consequently, there is nothing that is hidden from the all-knowing God, a truth that Job also affirms (31:4). Unlike a human judge in a trial, God never has to acquire more information than he already possesses before he can make a just decision. Elihu concludes that Job cannot tell God anything that he does not know completely. Therefore, Job's request for a trial in which he can present his case before God is unnecessary.

34:24–27 *He punishes them for their wickedness.* Elihu is confident that he knows where Job must fit in God's just world. In Elihu's view, Job has turned from following God (34:27), so God has overthrown him (34:25), as God does regularly to evildoers. With these words, Elihu lumps Job's adversity into the general category of divine punishment of the wicked.

34:29–30 *But if he remains silent, who can condemn him?* Elihu grants that God may not always exact judgment immediately. This divine silence, however, should not be misconstrued as God's lack of sovereign control. Elihu's implication is that Job's previous prosperity, not his present

---

In 34:26, Elihu states that God punishes evildoers where everyone can see them. This brings to mind the actions of the victorious Assyrian army, who would impale the bodies of the captured enemy high on poles for all to view. The impalement scene shown here is from the larger Assyrian relief depicting the battle of Lachish and its aftermath (700–692 BC).

adversity, was the anomaly. The question that Job should be asking is why God allowed him to prosper before despite his wickedness. What Job is now receiving from God is the just retribution that he deserves for his sin.

34:33 *Should God then reward you on your terms, when you refuse to repent?* To Elihu, the next step is simple: Job needs to repent of his sin. In this, Elihu echoes what Eliphaz said earlier (22:21–30). Elihu perceives that the ball is in Job's court, not in God's court, as Job insisted at the end of his final confession of innocence in chapter 31. God, moreover, will not change his rules of justice, no matter how much Job complains to him.

34:34–35 *Men of understanding declare . . . , "Job speaks without knowledge."* As he comes to the end of his second speech, Elihu claims to speak for all men who truly understand. He is supremely confident of his analysis of Job's situation, and just as certain that Job speaks without knowledge and insight.

34:36–37 *To his sin he adds rebellion.* In verse 36, Elihu expresses his desire that God would exact his full judgment upon wicked Job. Elihu's rigid logic has led him to conclude that Job is not at all a victim as he has claimed. Rather, he is an obstinate fool, a scorner whose words against God are prompted by a spirit of rebellion.

Theological Insights

In Genesis 2:7, the creation of the first human is described as God forming the physical body out of the dust of the ground and then breathing into it his breath of life. This divine breath continues to sustain humans throughout the duration of their lives (Eccles. 3:19–21; 12:7), until it is withdrawn at the time of death. Elihu refers to this in 34:14–15, when he argues that if God intended to withdraw his spirit and breath, then all humanity would perish together. When that occurs, humans return to the dust from which they have been made (Job 21:26; Ps. 104:29). The Old Testament says little about a future resurrection (Dan. 12:2 is a rare exception), but in the New Testament the resurrection of Christ prompts revelation of the resurrection of humans, in which the present corruptible body is transformed into an incorruptible, glorified body (1 Cor. 15:42–57).

Teaching the Text

In Job 34, as Elihu answers Job he follows much the same line of reasoning that the three friends have taken. Although Elihu does acknowledge that God may not exact judgment immediately, he accepts the basic structure of retribution theology. Therefore, Elihu reasons that because God is always just, and Job is experiencing adversity, Job must be wicked. To Elihu's thinking, that is the only reasonable way to explain the situation. Elihu's theological system does not allow for the possibility of a righteous man experiencing adversity despite his innocence. Like the friends, Elihu demonstrates that reducing theology to a simple formula may not adequately represent all of God's truth about the subject.

Elihu begins and ends this speech by claiming to be the voice of wisdom. He calls on those who are wise to join with him in discerning what is right. He claims that wise men who truly understand agree with him that Job has spoken without knowledge. In his own mind, Elihu has attained wisdom, but what he concludes about Job will not be validated by Yahweh when he speaks in chapter 42. We may give answers that seem convincing to ourselves and to others, but they may actually be inaccurate and hurtful. Sometimes it is best not to give an answer but to point the person to God, who alone knows the answer.

Elihu reasons that because God is sovereign, he must be just. In other words, as the ultimate authority, God makes the rules, and he is always right. Elihu comes very close to saying that whatever happens in life is good and right, simply because it occurs in the world governed by the Sovereign God. This simplistic view of life, however, does not consider that there are incidents in life that grieve God and that there are human wrongs that deeply offend him.

God will triumph over all sin and wrong in the end, but in the meanwhile we live in a world that is contaminated by many evils. The death and resurrection of Christ are the down payment of the final victory that God will accomplish for those who are in Christ (1 Cor. 15:12–28).

Both Job and Elihu agree that God knows all things, including every step that Job takes. Job regards this as a promising basis on which to approach God with his case. Elihu takes the opposite view, for he insists that God already knows all the facts of Job's situation, so he has all the evidence he could possibly need to adjudicate Job's case. Job believes that God knows his heart is innocent, but Elihu

Job believes that God knows his heart is innocent. Elihu believes that Job deserves punishment because his heart is wicked. In Egypt the deceased's heart would be weighed against the feather of Maat, which symbolized truth and justice. So that their own hearts would not testify against them, mummies had heart scarabs enclosed in their chest wrappings. On the reverse side of this scarab, an inscription from the Book of the Dead, Spell 30, requests of the deceased's heart, "Do not stand up against me as a witness; do not contradict me in the court; do not be hostile to me in the presence of the Keeper of the Balance" (Heart Scarab of Hati-iay, ca. 1567–1085 BC; translation from http://art.thewalters.org/detail/19093/heart-scarab-of-hati-iay/).

counters that God knows Job is guilty. Elihu concludes that Job's insistence on bringing his case before God is really a demonstration of his rebellious attitude. As Elihu sees it, Job deserves punishment from God, because his heart is wicked and rebellious. In trying to analyze Job's situation logically, Elihu misreads Job's heart. Elihu gives a cold, theoretical answer when what Job needs is compassionate support. Elihu tries to solve a theological puzzle, but he fails to salve the pain of Job's heart. Although other people can and do misconstrue our hearts, the Lord always understands us perfectly, and his omniscience is a great comfort.

Illustrating the Text

God's promises to bless the faithful are not meant to be turned into litmus tests that judge the hurting.

Object Lesson: Use a telescope or binoculars to highlight this point. When viewed through one end, the optics can make something far away seem very close and clear; when viewed through the other end, they have the opposite effect, making something quite near seem much smaller and farther away. Explain that in the same way, proverbs and statements of truth about God's justice and desire to bless the righteous help us to see the character and heart of an immense and invisible God quite clearly; conversely, when we attempt to evaluate the cause of human suffering through those same promises, we end up looking through the same lens but in the wrong direction. In such cases, our view of things ends up distorted as God gets smaller and less immanent and people's value gets reduced to the sum of their works rather than the immensity of God's grace to them.

Even when no one else understands our hearts or our motives, God does and his omniscience is a great comfort.

TV Clips: Consider using a clip from an appraisal-based show in which antiques or memorabilia are evaluated by experts and items of great value are distinguished from fakes. This could be used as a springboard to discuss the notion of expert testimony. When the owner brings in his or her knickknack to the pawn shop or the antiques show, he or she may have an idea of what it is worth. But until the expert appraiser verifies the value of the object, the accuracy of the owner's evaluation is highly disputable. In the same way, human evaluation of our own motivations and intentions is highly disputable; on the last day, however, the omniscient God will give his appraisal and there will be public vindication for those who are righteous through Christ and public humiliation for the wicked.

Human Experience: Encourage reflection on the following questions: "If you were accused of a crime and thrown into jail, whom would you call with your one phone call? Who would trust you and believe in your innocence, even before they heard your side of events? Why would they do that? Are they blind, biased fans, or do they actually know your character that deeply? Who are the ones that would stay on your side, forgive you, and love you, even if you *did* do it?" Point out that God knows our hearts even better than we do. The Lord knows us and our motivations *completely* and still loves us whether we are innocent in a given situation or not, and he loves us enough to forgive and redeem us at the cost of his only Son, *even when* we have been guilty of trampling him underfoot in our ignorance.

Elihu Describes God as Too Distant and Detached to Listen to Job

Big Idea *Elihu regards God as absolutely transcendent and therefore unconcerned about human actions.*

Understanding the Text

The Text in Context

In his third speech, in Job 35, Elihu attempts to summarize Job's claims and then counters them. Elihu, however, has not really grasped Job's meaning, but instead he exaggerates Job's anguished words in passages such as 7:17–21 into a view of God as totally impervious to human actions. Following the lead of the three friends before him, Elihu so emphasizes God's transcendence that he concludes that humans cannot affect God either by their sins or by their righteous deeds. God is so far above humans that he does not pay attention to what they say and do. Elihu declares that Job has no grounds for his legal case against God and that his words are just empty talk. Although Elihu regards himself as wiser than Job and the friends, he does not offer any additional insight beyond what has already been suggested by the others.

Historical and Cultural Background

In Job 35:10 Elihu reasons that people who are oppressed cry out in pain, but they fail to pray to the God who made them. The God to whom they should pray is the one "who gives songs in the night." This reference has prompted a broad variety of interpretations, including viewing the songs as the clap of divine thunder (cf. Psalm 29) and the music of the heavenly spheres (Ps. 19:2–4). Some scholars appeal to a homonym that means "protection." Although the precise meaning of this phrase is not clear, the other biblical references to night as a time of peril and to singing in the night in anticipation of God's deliverance seem to fit Elihu's thought well (see further discussion of this verse under "Theological Insights" below).[1]

Interpretive Insights

35:2–3 *You say, "I am in the right, not God."* The final clause in this verse is ambiguous, and the earlier NIV edition renders it "I will be cleared by God." Elihu construes Job as saying that he is more righteous than God but that his righteousness brings him no profit (35:3). It is true that Job said in 10:7 and 27:5 that he is innocent, but Elihu here puts words into Job's mouth that Job did not intend. In 21:15 Job actually said that it is the wicked who complain that serving God brings them no gain, although in 9:21–23 he did perceive God as judging the innocent and the wicked identically. Elihu seems to view Job in the most negative light rather than taking into account the emotional trauma from which Job has spoken.

35:4 *I would like to reply to you and to your friends with you.* On the surface, Elihu appears polite, but once again he assumes the role of the master teacher explaining what he alone understands. With a condescending tone, Elihu is supremely confident that he has the answer that has eluded the others (cf. 32:11–22; 33:2). No one else can comprehend this situation, but Elihu can!

35:5–7 *If you sin, how does that affect him? . . . If you are righteous, what do you give to him?* Directing attention to the heavens (35:5), Elihu portrays God as so absolutely transcendent that there is a vast and impassable chasm between God and humans. This leads Elihu to agree with Eliphaz's words in 22:2–3 that God is so

high that his governing of the world is not affected either by human sin or by human righteousness. By this view, the transcendent God is distant and detached, and therefore unmoved by what humans do.

35:8 *Your wickedness only affects humans like yourself, and your righteousness only other people.* Elihu declares that human actions are significant only within the human sphere. Only humans suffer from oppression by other people, and only humans benefit from the goodness of others. All these human actions mean nothing good or bad to the transcendent God. From God's lofty perspective, what humans do is negligible. The implication of what Elihu says is that there is no way the high God could be concerned enough about a human situation to respond to Job's cry or to intervene on his behalf. This, however, clearly conflicts with the prologue of the book, in which Yahweh is very much aware of Job's life and concerned about his condition, as well

In 35:5, Elihu tells Job to look up at the heavens to realize how far away and transcendent God is. In this Assyrian stela, King Ashurnasirpal II (884–859 BC) in a typical pose has his hand raised toward symbols of the various gods he worships.

The Book of Job and Deism

Although the book of Job long predates the rise of Deism about three hundred years ago, there are some significant similarities between what Elihu propounded and what much-later Deists taught. Deism emphasizes the transcendence of God to the point that he is not actively involved in human life. Deists, similar to Elihu, employ strict cause-and-effect logical thinking to reason to conclusions. God's world, according to Deism, is like an intricate clock that keeps working mechanically without divine intervention. Although Deism does not now maintain the prominence it once held, it still has significant influence at the popular level, because many people, especially teens, live by the belief system that has been described as moralistic therapeutic deism.[a]

[a] For an insightful explanation of Deism, see Sire, *Universe Next Door*, 47–65. The term "moralistic therapeutic deism" was coined by Christian Smith and Melinda Lundquist Denton on the basis of their extensive research on the religious beliefs of American teens in *Soul Searching*.

as Psalm 8:4, where Yahweh is mindful of humans and cares for them.

35:9 *People cry out under a load of oppression.* Elihu is skeptical about human appeals to God, because to him they smack of self-interest. He says that God pays no attention to these cries (35:13), because he is not impressed by foxhole converts who only turn to him when their situation is dire. Elihu implies that Job's cries to God are not sincere expressions of his faith and devotion but rather insincere schemes to manipulate God to come to his aid.

35:10–11 *But no one says, "Where is God my Maker?"* Elihu argues that humans who cry out for relief from oppression (35:9) are not sincerely seeking God. What they need to do is submit themselves to God's

teaching (35:11), so that they can learn his wisdom. As it is, they want to enjoy the privileges of the graduate without having to undergo the regimen of the student.

35:12–13 *God does not listen to their empty plea; the Almighty pays no attention to it.* The reader realizes that Job's condition is complex, but Elihu instead offers only a trite analysis of it. In Elihu's thinking, all humans are sinful, so God does not listen to their cries. If this were the whole story, however, it would destroy any possibility of communication or relationship between God and humans. In addition, it would reduce God to a being who is thoroughly predictable.

35:14–15 *How much less, then, will he listen when you say that you do not see him.* In verses 14–15, Elihu twists words that Job has uttered previously. Job said in

Elihu explains to Job that the reason why God does not listen and answer petitioners is because of their wickedness (35:13). Ear tablets such as these were created to remind Egyptians that their gods heard all. But sometimes ears were added to paintings to remind the god to listen to a particular request.

9:11 that he cannot see God. He brought his legal case before God in 23:4 and 31:35. Job expressed his hope in God in 13:15 and 14:14. He complained in 9:24; 12:6; and 21:17 that God is not acting justly toward him. Elihu takes Job's words and spins them so that they sound like an arrogant rejection of God, but that is not an accurate sense of Job's spirit and intention.

35:16 *So Job opens his mouth with empty talk*. Taking the same harsh tone as the three friends before him, Elihu concludes that Job's words are empty. He uses the Hebrew term *hebel*, which is found repeatedly in the book of Ecclesiastes and is often translated "vanity." To Elihu, Job's words have no substance or value, so he dismisses them as worthless and insubstantial. In wisdom literature, the wise person is restrained in speech, but the fool speaks many words (Prov. 10:19; Eccles. 10:14). In effect, Elihu insists that Job is not at all wise but that his empty prattle evidences he is indeed a fool. How this charge must cut Job to the heart!

Theological Insights

In the Bible, the night is often depicted as a time fraught with danger (Song 3:8), so it can prompt discouragement and despair (Ps. 30:5). However, as 35:10 indicates, God can give songs in the night as he provides protection for his people (Ps. 121:6). In Psalm 42:8, Yahweh's song is with the psalmist in the night, as a parallel to the divine loving-kindness that ministers to the psalmist in the daytime. In Psalm 77:6, the psalmist remembers his song in the night, as his heart meditates on how God has helped him in the past. As Paul and Silas are imprisoned in the Philippian jail,

they sing praises to God at midnight (Acts 16:25), and at that time the Lord intervenes to release them from their bondage.

Teaching the Text

The Bible teaches that God is both transcendent and immanent. As the transcendent God, he is exalted over all of his creation. As the immanent God, he is involved in his creation. These theological truths are equally taught in the Scriptures, so they must be held together rather than pitted against one another, as Elihu does.

Elihu focuses so much on the absolute transcendence of God that he comes to the faulty conclusion that God is unconcerned about human actions. He pictures God as distant and indifferent to human matters. By neglecting to consider God's involvement in his creation, Elihu ends up with a distorted perception of God that causes him to misjudge Job.

Elihu also misconstrues Job's claim of innocence. He has heard what Job has said, but he does not grasp Job's intended meaning. Therefore, Elihu distorts Job's words to say Job insists that he is in the right and that God is not right. Elihu also concludes wrongly that Job has given up on the righteous life because there is no profit to be gained by not sinning. Instead of really hearing Job, Elihu filters what Job says through his own assumptions. This is not fair to Job, because it distorts what he truly means. Elihu demonstrates that one who comforts must first listen carefully and really hear the heart of a person in pain.

Because Elihu emphasizes God's transcendence, he views God as so far above humans that they do not affect him no matter what

In reality, God is both transcendent and immanent. God wants to be in a relationship with his creation. A similar understanding of the gods can be illustrated by this Mesopotamian tablet. Here, the sun god Shamash is pictured large in size and enthroned above the waters of the heavens to show his transcendence. However, he allows the approach of the Babylonian king and two lesser deities, three much smaller figures, to communicate his immanence (Sippar, 860–850 BC).

Illustrating the Text

God is both transcendent and immanent.

Human Metaphor: Invite your listeners to reflect on the relationship between a child in utero and his or her mother. The mother's experience and influence far transcend the child's; she sees, hears, understands, and interacts in matters that are not only beyond the child's senses but also vastly more complex than any reality the child has ever experienced. The mother's existence transcends the child's in innumerable ways about which the child could never even begin to guess. At the same time, however, there is no human relationship that is more immanent; the child literally lives and moves and has his or her being (Acts 17:28) within the mother's womb and draws everything necessary for life from organic connection to the mother through the placenta and umbilical cord. In the same way, God's ways and thoughts are higher than ours, and he exists in a reality that is so far beyond our reckoning that we cannot begin to imagine or describe it. Yet he is so immanently and intimately connected to us that apart from his providence and grace we could never draw a breath or live a day.

Christian Year: This is a great place to connect with the idea of the Incarnation and the story of Christmas. In many ways, God

they do. Whether humans sin or are righteous, it makes no difference to God, according to Elihu. God is distant and remote, and he does not concern himself with human matters. Elihu argues that because this is true of humans in general, it is even more true of an individual like Job. In Elihu's thinking, God created the world, but he is not actively concerned about the lives of the mere humans that he has made. However, the book of Psalms and the prophets repeatedly present God as attentive to the cries of his people and active in coming to their aid (see the sidebar "Why Pray?"). God is indeed great, but he is also good.

never answers all the questions raised in the book of Job until he sends his Son to become incarnate and to reveal the full redemptive character of righteous suffering. The idea that God is only transcendent is put to rest soundly in the manger, and the assumption that suffering only comes to sinners is fully refuted at the cross. Invite listeners to wonder what Elihu would think of Christmas, and what he might have to say about God's transcendence if he were kneeling beside Mary and Joseph in the Bethlehem stable. Ask how the name Immanuel (God with us) ministers to the hearts of hurting people like Job.

God is not detached; he listens to what we have to say and responds immanently with compassion and grace that flow from his transcendent holiness and perfection.

Bible: There are a variety of passages you can cite that confirm the passionate, present nature of God's heart for his people. Try looking at Isaiah 49:13–18, Zephaniah 3:17, and John 1:1–14. Feel free to prayerfully search the Bible and add your own passages to the list. Sharing such references with listeners will assure them that, no matter how

Why Pray?

Elihu's words to Job raise a question that plagues many Christians today. If God is all-powerful and all-wise, so that he will accomplish his will, then what is the purpose for our prayers? Can we compel God to change his mind, or to do something different from what he has already determined? If we cannot, then are our prayers just a waste of time and words?

The Bible does not explain how our prayers function within God's sovereign plan, but the Bible clearly commands us to pray to God, with the assurance that he will hear and answer us. Our part is to trust God and to obey his command by praying to him about our needs and concerns. God's part is to accomplish what he knows is best for his people and for his own glory. How that all works together is a mystery that the Lord has not disclosed to us, any more than he explained to Job all about his adversity. Prayer drives us toward the God in whom we can trust, even when we cannot comprehend his ways with us.

the Elihus of the world insist that God is detached, God's own revealed Word about himself begs to differ.

Testimony: Invite one or two individuals to share a brief testimony about a time they were certain that God was with them. It may have been a sense of his presence in a time of crisis, a supernatural intervention in answer to prayer, a direct response to a request for insight or direction, or in many other ways.

Elihu Points to the Corrective Benefit of Suffering

Big Idea *Elihu insists that God is seeking to correct Job.*

Understanding the Text

The Text in Context

Elihu's fourth and final speech is also his longest, for it encompasses chapters 36 and 37. His tone in this speech is more compassionate and constructive than it was in his previous three speeches. Elihu now considers the consequences of suffering rather than merely its cause. He discusses what suffering can produce, not what precipitates it. He reasons that suffering is God's discipline by which humans can be built up. The wise person will accept suffering and become better because of it, but the fool resists suffering and is destroyed by responding to it with hostility. Even though Elihu is not accurate in his assessment of why Job is suffering, what he says in this speech does help to set the stage for the appearance of Yahweh in chapter 38, with his resolution of Job's situation.

Historical and Cultural Background

In Job 36:14, Elihu states that godless people who reject God's correction will die young among the male prostitutes of the shrines. In Canaanite and in Mesopotamian fertility religions, both men and women were employed in cultic prostitution, as worshipers engaged in sexual acts in an effort to elicit the blessing of the gods on their crops. In the Old Testament, homosexual intercourse in general and its occurrence in ritual prostitution in particular are regarded as abominations to Yahweh (Lev. 18:22; 19:29; 20:13; Deut. 23:17–18; 2 Kings 23:7). The reference here to dying young could point to the disastrous effects of venereal disease (cf. Prov. 7:23). With this image Elihu paints the horrific and shameful end that Job will experience if he does not respond positively to God's correction of his sin.

Interpretive Insights

36:2 *Bear with me a little longer.* Elihu likely senses that Job and the friends are losing interest in what he has to say. After all, Elihu has spoken without interruption for a long time, so they are probably getting impatient for him to finish. In 35:16 Elihu accused Job of multiplying words, but he outdoes Job, sounding like a talking windup toy that will not quit. His "little longer" turns into his longest speech, encompassing chapters 36 and 37.

36:3 *I will ascribe justice to my Maker.* In 35:2, Elihu misconstrued Job as calling God's righteousness into account. Elihu now insists that he will champion the justice of God. Elihu claims that what he says is right, because he has received his knowledge from afar, from the God who is right.

36:4 *one who has perfect knowledge is with you.* Once again Elihu confidently touts his own credentials. In the prologue, Job was three times described as *tam*, perfect or blameless in his behavior (1:1, 8; 2:3). Now Elihu uses a closely related term to

Key Themes of Job 36

- Elihu is unduly confident of his perfect knowledge.
- Elihu teaches that God uses affliction to correct sinners.
- Elihu challenges Job to accept God's correction.
- Elihu views God as great and beyond human understanding.

describe the perfect knowledge he claims to have. Later, in 37:16, Elihu will affirm that God is perfect in knowledge. Thus, Elihu as much as says that because he has received his knowledge from God, he is the voice of God's knowledge. To disagree with Elihu, then, would be tantamount to disagreeing with God himself.

36:5–7 *He does not keep the wicked alive. . . . He does not take his eyes off the righteous.* Elihu again reasserts the legitimacy of the retribution formula. According to him, God destroys the wicked (36:6) and exalts the righteous (36:7). In 21:7–16, Job called into question the validity of the retribution formula by adducing substantial evidence that the wicked actually often prosper in life. Elihu, however, totally ignores those facts that disagree with his conclusion.

36:8–14 *He makes them listen to correction.* Elihu now develops a new point

Elihu asserts that if people find themselves bound in chains, it is because they have sinned and are being corrected by God (36:8–9). This relief from Medinet Habu, Egypt, shows Ramesses III holding chains that bind three groups of prisoners together (twelfth century BC).

that significantly qualifies the retribution formula. He says that God uses adversity to reveal to humans their sin (36:8–9). This is really God's severe mercy to them, because through the pain of adversity God challenges them to repent of their evil. If they respond to God's correction with repentance, they will enjoy his prosperity (36:11). If, however, they refuse to listen to God, they will perish (36:12–14). In Elihu's thinking, adversity is prompted by personal sin, but it may also have the positive effect of correction (cf. Prov. 3:11–12; Heb. 12:5–7), as well as the negative effect of punishment. How the sinner responds to God's adversity makes all the difference.

36:16–21 *He is wooing you from the jaws of distress.* In this verse, Elihu turns from expounding general principles (36:2–15) to speaking directly to Job about his specific situation. Elihu portrays God as seeking to allure Job, by adversity, back into a place of blessing (cf. Hosea 2:14). Job, however, has become preoccupied with his legal dispute against God (36:17). Job needs to respond

Elihu illustrates God's greatness by describing his control of a thunderstorm: "He fills his hands with lightning and commands it to strike its mark" (36:32). Other ancient Near Eastern cultures also associated storms with divine power. Here the Syrian god Hadad stands on a bull, with lightning bolts in his fists (744–727 BC).

positively to God's tender overtures rather than resist him. If Job does not respond to God, he will have to endure the judgment that is due to wicked people.

36:22–23 *God is exalted in his power. Who is a teacher like him?* Elihu depicts God as transcendent both in his power and in his pedagogy, echoing what Job said about God in 21:22. Elihu does not realize all that he is affirming as he describes God as the unrivaled teacher. When Yahweh speaks in chapters 38–41, he demonstrates what a master teacher he is, for his thoughts are high above all human thoughts (cf. Isa. 55:8–9; Rom. 11:33–34). What Yahweh teaches far surpasses what Elihu is able to comprehend.

36:24 *Remember to extol his work, which people have praised in song.* Elihu urges Job to stop complaining against God and instead to praise him. Praise would silence Job's objections and enable him to accept God's correction. By this counsel, Elihu echoes the lament psalms, in which the psalmists turn to God in their times of affliction and, by doing that, find that their pain is transformed into praise (e.g., Ps. 30:8–12). Elihu advises Job to take this well-worn path that is familiar to faithful worshipers of God.

36:27–30 *He draws up the drops of water.* In 36:26–37:5, Elihu graphically describes God's power in a thunderstorm (esp. 36:32–33). This storm, as also in Psalm 29, is a visible indication of the greatness of God, which exceeds human understanding (36:26, 29). With this illustration, Elihu begins a transition to Yahweh's speech out of a storm, which commences in 38:1.

36:31 *This is the way he governs the nations.* Elihu draws a parallel between how God directs the natural world and how he governs the world of humans. In both areas God is transcendent and in control, but he is also immanent. Just as God is actively involved in forming the thunderstorm, so he is involved in the affairs of humans. This claim actually undermines what Elihu said earlier, in 35:6–7, where he argued that God is unconcerned with what humans do, whether it is good or bad.

Theological Insights

Job 36:27 begins a colorful description of how God rules over the natural world. Throughout the Old Testament, nature bears testimony to the greatness of God. The nature psalms are especially clear in describing how the heavens declare the glory, or impressiveness, of God (Ps. 19:1).[1] As God demonstrates his power in nature, humans are prompted to praise him (Ps. 104:33–34) and to find their peace in him (Ps. 29:11). As powerful as the forces of nature are, nature is not independent of God but is firmly under his control. The natural world is one of the primary contexts in which God reveals himself to humans (cf. Rom. 1:18–20).

Teaching the Text

Elihu believes in the validity of the retribution principle, that God blesses the righteous and punishes the wicked. However, he adds a feature to what the three friends declared in their retribution theology. Elihu says that God endeavors to correct sinners, so they will turn away from their wicked ways and to his righteous way. This, Elihu insists, is what God is seeking to do in Job's life. In other words, God afflicts sinners in such a way that they may repent of their sin and obey him. Adversity, then, may be God's severe mercy that prompts sinners to turn to him and to accept his gracious forgiveness. In times of pain, people may be prompted to turn to God.

Although Elihu presents some important truths for Job to contemplate, his tone sounds proud and arrogant. He is unduly confident that he has figured out life in general, and Job's situation in particular. In fact, he goes so far as to say that he has perfect knowledge, an expression that he will use again in chapter 37 for God's knowledge. Even if Elihu were accurate in his analysis of Job's situation, it would be very hard for Job to accept counsel from one who seems so smug and sure. By failing to maintain a humble spirit, we can dilute whatever positive effect we want to have on those to whom we minister. That is why Galatians 6:1 warns us that in restoring one who has sinned, we must do so with gentleness.

Elihu emphasizes that God uses affliction to correct sinners. This is a principle that can be observed many times in the Bible, as well as in the experience of many Christians today. God in his grace does not write off sinners but continues to seek and to save those who are lost (Luke 19:10). God, then, goes beyond the retribution principle, as he graciously extends the opportunity for repentance and restoration to those who deserve only his judgment. In doing that, God provides an example for us to keep reaching out to those who have sinned rather than writing them off as hopeless.

Where Elihu errs is in applying this truth to Job's specific situation. He assumes that Job's adversity must be God's correction, so he challenges Job to respond with repentance. Elihu is unable to recognize that if God treats sinners better than they deserve, then perhaps it is possible for a righteous man like Job to experience adversity that is worse than what he deserves. In other words, if the retribution principle does not hold absolutely on one side, then maybe it does not hold absolutely on the other side either. God's way of working with humans is likely a good deal more complex than the simple retribution formula allows.

Illustrating the Text

God's work with humans is more complex than Elihu understands.

Literature: *Pride and Prejudice*, by Jane Austen. In this nineteenth-century British novel (1813), Elizabeth Bennet is convinced that Fitzwilliam Darcy is aloof and judgmental, while he is convinced that Elizabeth is not his social and intellectual equal. So each disdains the other. Later in the story, both come to realize that their perceptions have been partially or totally flawed. Like Elihu, they are not as perfect in knowledge as they initially suppose.

Film: *Groundhog Day*. In this movie (1993), the lead character, a lovable egocentric played by Bill Murray, is given repeated opportunities to change his actions until he finally gets things right. Elihu says rightly that God uses affliction so that people can repent of their sins, but he fails to recognize that God, like the reality Bill Murray's character comes to grasp, is more gracious and complex than we might first assume or deserve.

Quote: **Madame Jeanne Guyon.** Madame Guyon (1647–1717), often thought of as the leader of the Quietist movement (spiritual passivism—"let go and let God"), in what is probably an oversimplification, once wrote, "If knowing answers to life's questions is absolutely necessary to you, then forget the journey. You will never make it, for this is a journey of unknowables—of unanswered questions, enigmas, incomprehensibles, and most of all, things unfair."[2]

Hymn: **"God Moves in a Mysterious Way," by William Cowper.** This hymn by Cowper (1731–1800) has been a source of comfort and blessing to many of God's people. Yet few people know of the circumstances leading to its composition. As a Christian, Cowper was often in the depths of despair, having never recovered from the death of his mother when he was a child. In fact, he lived with deep depression, what today might be considered mental illness, while still writing his inspirational hymns. One foggy night he called for a horse-drawn carriage and asked to be taken to the London Bridge on the Thames River. Overcome by depression, he intended to commit suicide. But after two hours of driving through the mist, Cowper's coachman confessed that he was lost. Disgusted by the delay, Cowper left the carriage to find the bridge on foot. After walking only a short distance, he discovered that he was at his own doorstep. The carriage had been going in circles. Immediately convicted, he recognized the restraining hand of God. He realized that the way out of his troubles was to look to God, not to jump into the river. Deeply comforted, he sat down and wrote these enduring words:

> God moves in a mysterious way
> His wonders to perform;
> He plants His footsteps in the sea
> And rides upon the storm.
>
> Deep in unfathomable mines
> Of never failing skill
> He treasures up His bright designs
> And works His sovereign will.
>
> Ye fearful saints, fresh courage take;
> The clouds ye so much dread
> Are big with mercy and shall break
> In blessings on your head.
>
> Judge not the Lord by feeble sense,
> But trust Him for His grace;
> Behind a frowning providence
> He hides a smiling face.
>
> His purposes will ripen fast,
> Unfolding every hour;

> The bud may have a bitter taste,
> But sweet will be the flower.
>
> Blind unbelief is sure to err
> And scan His work in vain;
> God is His own interpreter,
> And He will make it plain.

Sometimes the righteous and obedient experience adversity worse than they deserve.

Missionary History: Paul Carlson. Many missionaries were killed in a single year during the Simba rebellion from 1964 to 1965. In fact, as Ruth Tucker reports it, "The terror unleashed on innocent Congolese Christians and foreign missionaries left thousands dead and even more to suffer from physical and emotional scars that would stay with them the rest of their lives." One of these missionaries, Paul Carlson, had only been in the Congo for two years. As a medical doctor, he had responded to a letter detailing a pressing need in the Congo. Leaving his wife and two children behind, he went; soon becoming convinced of the need, he made a radical commitment. Then came the rebellion. Carlson, who was attending to approximately two hundred patients a day in a remote region, was taken by the rebels and subjected to months of brutal torture before his death.[3]

Elihu Finishes with a Flourish

Big Idea *Elihu challenges Job to consider the implications that God's wonders in nature have for his life.*

Understanding the Text

The Text in Context

In Job 37, Elihu completes his final speech, which he began in chapter 36. Throughout chapter 37 he continues to employ the storm imagery that he started to develop in 36:27, as he uses this vivid language to picture God's awesome power and majesty. Elihu's animated description of God's work in the world of nature anticipates what Yahweh will communicate to Job when he appears in chapter 38. Elihu is a skilled orator who finishes with a brilliant rhetorical flourish. Although Elihu thinks that he speaks for God, Yahweh will speak for himself in chapters 38–41, and in the epilogue he will not refer to what Elihu has said.

Historical and Cultural Background

The storm imagery that Elihu uses in Job 37 was familiar in ancient Near Eastern

Elihu describes a storm as God releasing lightning and his voice thundering (37:3–4). In the mythology of the ancient Near East, Baal and Adad play the role of storm god. The relief on this stela portrays the Mesopotamian storm god known as Adad or Hadad (Babylon, ninth century BC).

texts. In the Canaanite myths, Baal is the storm god who thunders at his enemies, and in the Mesopotamian literature Adad plays the same role. In 1 Kings 18, the prophet Elijah stages a contest with the prophets of Baal, in order to demonstrate to the people of Israel that Yahweh is the only true God, who deserves their worship. After the prophets of Baal try but fail to get their god to send a lightning bolt to ignite their sacrifice, Yahweh answers Elijah's prayer in a dramatic and undeniable fashion. In Psalm 29, a thunderstorm is portrayed as the voice of Yahweh, clearly countering and rejecting the false claims of the adherents of Baal and Adad.

Interpretive Insights

37:1 *At this my heart pounds and leaps from its place.* As Elihu observes God's mighty display of power in the storm, he has a strong emotional response. This strong rush of adrenaline is similar to what Habakkuk (Hab. 3:6) and the psalmist in Psalm 29 feel as they view the awesome power of God evidenced in the natural world. In 37:8, the storm has a comparable effect on the animals, which scurry to take cover in their dens.

37:5 *he does great things beyond our understanding.* Earlier, in 36:4, Elihu presumed that he was perfect in knowledge, but here he has to acknowledge that God's deeds exceed what humans can understand. This naturally prompts a question for the reader: if what God does in the natural world is beyond human understanding, then could not Job's situation also lie beyond what humans can comprehend? Elihu expresses the theological truth that God's ways are inscrutable, but he does not seem

to grasp the possible implications of what he is saying for Job's situation. He is moving in the right direction, but he doesn't take his line of thought far enough.

37:6–13 *He brings the clouds to punish people, or to water his earth and show his love.* By his inscrutable actions, God accomplishes a variety of purposes. In contrast to the simplistic retribution formula that the friends and Elihu have expounded, there is no single purpose that governs all that God does in the world. Sometimes God acts in order to correct evil, as he did when delivering the people of Israel from bondage in Egypt. Sometimes God acts for the benefit of his creation apart from any human consideration (cf. 38:26). Sometimes God acts out of his loyal love for his people. This range of divine purposes is much broader than the retribution principle will allow, and yet Elihu's direct entreaty to Job in verse 14 suggests that he believes he knows what God is doing in Job's particular situation.

37:14 *Listen to this, Job; stop and consider God's wonders.* Once again, Elihu appeals to Job to consider God's wonders in the natural world. Using the familiar teaching strategy of traditional wisdom (e.g., Prov. 6:6), Elihu calls on Job to observe and be wise. Elihu follows this entreaty with a string of rhetorical questions in verses 15–20 that suggest how little Job really understands of God's ways and how much he needs to learn. Elihu's implication is clear: if Job cannot understand God's dealings in the world of nature, then how can he reasonably expect to comprehend how God works with humans like him? What Elihu fails to consider, however, is that the same question could be posed to him. In his effort to prove that Job cannot understand God's ways, Elihu has managed to indict himself for the same inability to comprehend what God is doing.

37:16 *those wonders of him who has perfect knowledge.* Elihu describes God as having total knowledge, and this corresponds to what the psalmist says in Psalm 139:1–6. Elihu, however, has also claimed that he himself is perfect in knowledge (36:4), and that is where he has missed the mark. Elihu does not know all that he thinks he knows. He has criticized Job for speaking beyond what he knows, but Elihu is guilty of doing that very thing as well. Elihu is critical of Job, but he is not critical of himself. In trying to remove the speck from Job's eye, Elihu has neglected to consider the beam in his own eye (cf. Matt. 7:3).

In 37:18, Elihu asks Job if he can join God in "spreading out the skies, hard as a mirror of cast bronze." This reflects the ancient view of the sky as a solid dome. The bronze mirror seen here is from Egypt (ca. fourteenth century BC).

37:21–22 *Now no one can look at the sun.* In verses 21–24 Elihu describes the breaking of a storm as the sunlight streams through the clouds. This vivid picture from nature is a fitting illustration of the awesome majesty of God Almighty. Humans are warned against looking at the sun, even during a solar eclipse, because its light is so intense that it can easily cause blindness. In the same way, no human can comprehend the majesty of God. At best, God's majesty can be glimpsed only in part, because finite humans do not have the ability to understand the full measure of the greatness of God. He is beyond human comprehension.

37:23 *The Almighty is beyond our reach and exalted in power.* Humans cannot comprehend God in his greatness, and neither can they by their efforts manipulate what God does. They can, however, be certain that God is always just and righteous in his dealings. God, then, does not expect humans to comprehend all that he does, but he does want them to trust him to do what is just and right. With these words, Elihu anticipates—more than he realizes—the conclusion of the book, when Job will acknowledge that he cannot understand God's ways, and yet he will submit to him (42:2–6).

37:24 *Therefore, people revere him.* Elihu's final words in this verse are ambiguous, and various translations have rendered them in disparate ways. The NIV reads the final line in this way: "For does he not have regard for all the wise in heart?" Francis Andersen in his commentary on Job adapts the Septuagint reading: "Surely all wise of heart fear him!"[1] The general point of the verse is that wise humans will revere God even when they cannot comprehend all that he does. This links back to the statement in 28:28, which affirmed the basic tenet of traditional wisdom, that the fear of the Lord is wisdom (cf. Prov. 9:10; Eccles. 12:13). Being wise does not mean that one knows everything, but that one reveres and trusts the Lord who does know all things perfectly.

Theological Insights

In the ancient world, nature was often regarded as inhabited by a vast range of deities. The Bible is distinct, however, in its insistence that there is only one God, Yahweh, who created the world by himself, and who rules over the world and all that is in it. In the Old Testament, and especially in the wisdom literature, the natural world is one of the contexts in which God reveals himself and his wisdom to humans. Elihu calls upon Job to listen and consider God's wonders (37:14). In Psalm 8, the psalmist exclaims that the God who has displayed his splendor in nature has also taken thought of humans and placed them in a position of great responsibility in ruling over the works of his hands. The book of Proverbs frequently points out aspects in the natural world that illustrate principles of God's wisdom. In the New Testament, Jesus uses God's care of the birds and the flowers as the rationale for trusting him to supply every need rather than being anxious (Matt. 6:25–34).

Teaching the Text

Elihu concludes his speeches with a dramatic description of a thunderstorm. With this image he emphasizes God's wonders in nature. How God rules in nature, however, also has profound implications for humans like Job. Elihu speaks directly to Job as he urges him to stop and consider God's wonders. It is one thing to observe God's power in nature, but quite another to live in the light of that observation. All around us God gives tangible evidence of his greatness, and we need to consider how the great God who has revealed himself in the physical world can fully meet the needs of our lives.

Elihu accurately portrays God as ruling over the natural world in order to accomplish his varied purposes. What God chooses to do cannot be reduced into a single purpose that fits every situation. Rather, sometimes God works in his world in a way that punishes evildoers. Other times he works in the physical world for purposes that do not directly affect humans. Sometimes, God's actions are intended to bring blessing on humans as the expression of his love and commitment to them. The specific purpose of God in any particular action may well be difficult or even impossible for humans to discern. But we can be confident that what God is doing fits into his overall plan.

Elihu seems firmly convinced that Job is ignorant of God's ways, so he urges Job to consider God's wonders. To consider means to think carefully or to meditate on the significance of what God has done. If Job would ponder the rhetorical questions that Elihu has posed to him, he would realize that he does not comprehend how God controls the world of nature. This realization should naturally prompt Job to admit that he does not understand what God is doing in his life either. In the same way, this pattern of thinking will move us in the right direction toward greater trust in God.

In his final words, Elihu states that God's majesty, as demonstrated in nature, is beyond human reach. When humans like Job recognize God's transcendence, they should respond to him in reverence. God's mighty acts should lead humans to respect and fear God all the more. When the book ends in chapter 42, this is precisely what happens in Job's life, as his fear of Yahweh moves into a deeper level through what he learns about God from his experience of adversity. As James 1:2–8 teaches, trials can develop our faith, just as they do for Job.

God's power and majesty are revealed in nature. Elihu uses examples of snowstorms and rainstorms that obey God's command (37:6). This picture shows the aftermath of a rare snowstorm in Israel.

Illustrating the Text

God rules over the natural world to accomplish his varied purposes.

Nature: A video clip of the sights and sounds of a vivid thunderstorm would capture the force of the imagery that Elihu describes and get your audience's attention.

Nature: Storms are most often considered destructive forces, but sometimes they can have marked beneficial effects. For example, the rare storms that come to desert regions can cause flowers to germinate after many years of apparent barrenness. Pictures or videos of a desert in bloom can illustrate 37:13, in which one of God's purposes for the storm is watering the earth.

Nature: Elihu uses the light of the sun to portray how humans cannot observe the full majesty of God. It is dangerous to view the sun directly, but watching a video of a solar eclipse can provide a good sense of how awe-inspiring the light of the sun is. This natural phenomenon only points to the greater awesomeness of God's unrivaled power and knowledge. Our response to him should be one of reverential awe and worship.

Elihu is rigid and limiting when he applies God's rule to humans.

Book: *Your God Is Too Small*, by J. B. Phillips. Phillips (1906–82) was a British preacher and writer who was encouraged in his writing by C. S. Lewis. In his book *Your God Is Too Small* (1952), Phillips discusses the various ways in which inadequate views of God are detrimental to people's spiritual lives. Some of these are seeing God as a policeman, a parental hangover, a grand old man, God-in-a-box, managing director, and so on. Some of these categories fit well the views of God expressed by Elihu and the other friends of Job. The author concludes this book by saying, "We can never have too big a conception of God."[2]

Yahweh Speaks as the Master Teacher

Big Idea *Yahweh poses questions about the physical world to demonstrate that Job's knowledge is too limited to explain how God works in his world.*

Understanding the Text

The Text in Context

Throughout the speeches in chapters 3–37, the various human speakers claim to know what Yahweh thinks about Job's situation, but in chapter 38 Yahweh finally breaks his silence and speaks for himself. Yahweh addresses Job in 38:1–40:2, focusing on his design for the world (38:2), and then Job replies briefly in 40:3–5. Yahweh resumes speaking in 40:6–41:34, stressing his justice in the world (40:8), and then Job utters his final response in 42:1–6. These divine speeches are the rhetorical climax of the book as Yahweh speaks in vivid and brilliant poetry.

As the master teacher, Yahweh poses more than seventy unanswerable questions to Job. These questions are meant not to humiliate or intimidate Job but rather to disclose to him the many inexplicable wonders of God's workings in the world. Yahweh makes use of a skillful pedagogical technique by asking questions to help Job discover what he does not know (cf. Isa. 40:12–31). As Job comes to realize how much he does not comprehend about God's world, he is willing to accept a humble position before Yahweh, who does know all things. Yahweh does not answer the questions that Job has been asking, but instead he points Job in an altogether different direction. He wants Job to learn that the divine wisdom is superior to even the best human understanding. Yahweh knows what he is doing in his world and in Job's life.

Historical and Cultural Background

The words in 38:36 have been rendered in many ways by various translations, but the NIV is probably accurate in speaking of two birds, the ibis and the rooster. Yahweh asks Job, "Who gives the ibis wisdom or gives the rooster understanding?" In Egyptian thought, these birds were noteworthy because of their ability to signal changes coming in the weather. The ibis predicted when the Nile River would rise, and the rooster crowed to indicate the approach of morning or of rain.[1] The innate instincts of these birds could not be explained by humans; they were given to them by Yahweh, their creator.

Interpretive Insights

38:1 *Then the* LORD *spoke to Job out of the storm.* In 31:35, Job challenged God to answer him, but then Elihu began speaking instead. In chapter 38, Yahweh breaks his silence. Bypassing Elihu, who has been speaking for the previous six chapters, Yahweh addresses Job directly. This very act of communication is in itself evidence that Job's relationship with Yahweh is still intact. Yahweh speaks out of a storm, as

Key Themes of Job 38

- Yahweh takes the role of the teacher toward Job.
- Yahweh asks Job about his knowledge of the creation of the earth.
- Yahweh asks Job about his understanding of how the weather functions within God's order of the world.
- Yahweh asks Job about his ability to control the heavens.

he does elsewhere in the Old Testament. At times, a storm pictures divine wrath (Zech. 9:14), but it can also suggest the arrival of Yahweh as he speaks to his people (Exod. 19:16–20:21). Earlier, a storm was the cause of Job's pain (1:19; 9:17), but now it is the setting for Yahweh's communication to him.

38:2 *Who is this that obscures my plans with words without knowledge?* Yahweh's opening words, "Who is this?" introduce the central theme of his speeches. Yahweh wants Job to understand who Yahweh is and who Job is. Job has been speaking beyond what he truly knows, because he, as a finite human, is in no position to speak accurately about Yahweh's plans for the world or for him personally. Yahweh has a design that surpasses anything that Job can fathom or describe.

38:3 *I will question you, and you shall answer me.* In chapter 31 Job thought that his legal strategy of negative confession would put God on the defensive and compel him to rule at least indirectly on Job's innocence, but Yahweh will not be manipulated so easily. Yahweh takes the initiative by posing the questions and requiring Job to answer him. By this rigorous interrogation, Yahweh will demonstrate how inadequate Job's understanding is. Yahweh knows all the answers to the questions that he poses, but Job has no answer to even a single divine query.

38:4–7 *Where were you when I laid the earth's foundation?* Yahweh describes the moment of the creation of the earth, when the stars sang together and the angels shouted for joy (38:7). As Proverbs 8:22–31 states, wisdom was present at creation, but no human was there to observe it. Not even the first human was there to see how Yahweh constructed the earth, and certainly Job was not there to witness it. Yahweh presses Job in verse 5 by asking him, "Who marked off [the earth's] dimensions?" This question compels Job to admit what he does not know, but what Yahweh does know perfectly, and it implies that Yahweh is going to lead Job into new frontiers of understanding beyond anything he has comprehended before.

38:8–11 *Who shut up the sea behind doors when it burst forth from the womb?* Yahweh here uses the image of childbirth to picture the taming of the sea. In ancient Near Eastern thought, the sea was often the personification of chaos, but in the Bible the sea is securely under divine control (Gen. 1:2; Rev. 21:1). Yahweh places firm limits on the sea (38:10–11; cf. Ps. 104:5–9), with the sandy shore as its boundary (Jer. 5:22). Yahweh paints a lovely word picture of using the clouds and darkness as the cloths with which he swaddles the sea (38:9).

38:12–15 *Have you ever given orders to the morning, or shown the dawn its place?* In the creation narrative, God says, "Let there be light," and light comes into existence (Gen. 1:3). With his light, God thwarts the malicious people who work their evil under the cover of darkness (Job 24:13–17). Yahweh's question demands a negative answer from

Job, even though Job has vainly attempted to curse the day in 3:3–10. As a human, Job cannot assume Yahweh's prerogative to give orders to the morning.

38:16–18 *Have the gates of death been shown to you?* In 3:16–19 and 14:13–15, Job expresses a longing for Sheol. Nevertheless, Yahweh's questions in 38:16–18 indicate that Job does not truly understand death and the subterranean region, so his desire for the grave is born out of ignorance rather than knowledge

38:22–30 *What is the way to the place where the lightning is dispersed?* In 38:22–30, Yahweh asks Job about meteorological phenomena that he can observe. Job can see the effects of Yahweh's work, but he cannot understand how Yahweh accomplishes what he does in the weather. Job has to admit that his knowledge of snow, hail, lightning, wind, rain, and ice is profoundly deficient. Even what Job experiences he cannot comprehend or explain.

In directing Job's attention to the desert, Yahweh indicates that he sends rain to places where there are no humans to profit from it (38:26–27). Humans may perceive this as unnecessary or even a waste of resources, but Yahweh's purposes for the earth go far beyond specifically human concerns. His ways are higher than the ways of humans, and his thoughts surpass human insight (cf. Isa. 55:8–9). From Yahweh's perspective, the earth belongs to him, and though he causes it to function for human beings, it exists for his own divine purpose (Ps. 24:1). Humans are indeed an important part of his plan, but they are not the exclusive focus of his interest and his lavish grace. As the interchange between Yahweh and the adversary in the prologue indicates, there are aspects of Yahweh's plan and activity that may include human involvement, but they transcend merely human concerns.

38:31–33 *Can you bind the chains of the Pleiades?* In verses 31–33, Yahweh asks about Job's ability to control the celestial phenomena, which were often used for omens in the ancient Near East. Is Job able to direct the movements of the constellations and thus determine the course of history? Can he trace the laws that govern the movements of the heavenly bodies? The implied negative answers to these questions affirm that the stars are under Yahweh's control (cf. Isa. 40:26) and far beyond Job's grasp.

38:39–41 *Do you hunt the prey for the lioness and satisfy the hunger of the lions?* Yahweh now turns from asking about the non-living physical world (38:4–38) to direct Job's attention to the animal world (38:39–39:30), a transition that has actually begun in verse 36 with the reference to the ibis and the rooster (see the discussion under "Historical and Cultural Background"), thus shifting the focus closer to Job himself. There are countless aspects of the zoological domain in which Job has to admit his lack of knowledge and control. Both the predatory lions (38:39–40) and the ravens, which feed on carrion (38:41), receive their food apart from human enablement (cf. Ps. 147:9). Once again, Yahweh implies that his wise ordering of his world is not restricted to what the retribution principle predicts or regards as just and necessary.

Theological Insights

Yahweh's main point in his speeches is that the world must be understood in

In 38:32, Yahweh asks Job, "Can you bring forth the constellations in their seasons?" The arrangement and movement of the stars were much studied in the ancient world. The heavily restored circular cuneiform tablet shown here is a planisphere that charts the heavens (eighth century BC). It divides the night sky into eight sections, and the constellation Gemini and the Pleiades have been identified.

terms of what he is doing in it. Job's inability to answer the divine questions demonstrates that he cannot understand how Yahweh governs the world of nature. Consequently, Job should not expect to comprehend how Yahweh works with humans like him. Finite humans are in no position to call Yahweh to account, any more than a piece of pottery can dictate to the potter (Isa. 45:9; Rom. 9:20–21). Job and the friends have been asking why Job has experienced adversity, but this is the wrong question. The real question is "Who is Yahweh, and can he be trusted in what he is doing in his world?"

Teaching the Text

When Yahweh at last speaks in Job 38, he does not answer the questions that Job has raised previously. Rather, Yahweh takes the role of the teacher, and he asks questions of Job. By the time he finishes, Yahweh, the master teacher, poses more than seventy questions, and Job is unable to answer a single one. When Job concluded his confession of innocence in chapter 31, he thought that the Almighty God would have to render his verdict about Job's innocence or guilt. Yahweh, however, is not compelled by Job's legal strategy. Instead of following what Job has set out for him, Yahweh has his own lesson plan by which he instructs Job. As the book of Proverbs demonstrates, like Job we are students in God's school of wisdom. In his school, we need to be attentive to what God says, we need to accept his teaching eagerly rather than insist on our own way, and we must assimilate his lessons so that they affect every area of our lives.

Yahweh's purpose in posing so many questions to Job is to demonstrate to Job the limitations of his knowledge. Yahweh's questions all relate to the physical world that Job has observed for all his life. As Job considers each question, he has to admit in his own mind over and over again that he does not know the answer. By the time he has made that mental admission more than seventy times, Job cannot escape the conclusion that his knowledge is woefully inferior to what Yahweh possesses. With this humbling realization, Job has to accept the fact that he is finite in his knowledge but that Yahweh is infinite in what he knows. If that is true about the physical world, then it must also be true of Job's experience. Job does not understand what has happened to him, but Yahweh does understand it completely.

"Do you hunt the prey for the lioness?" is a question that Yahweh asks to help Job become aware of how little he really understands (38:39). This register from the Black Obelisk of Shalmaneser III (858–824 BC) shows a lion pursuing a stag.

As readers, we are aware of the factors in the prologue that Job is unable to discern. Because we now have the full Bible, we have more of God's revelation than was available when the book of Job was written, long before Christ's death and resurrection. However, even today there is much that God knows that he has not made known to us humans. So, like Job, we need to place our trust in God, who knows all, rather than expect to understand all of the puzzling paradoxes in our lives.

Yahweh's questions about the physical world lead Job to trust and worship him more. In the same way, the Lord has placed before us in nature a constant stream of evidence to convince us of his power and wisdom. By gazing at God's world, we have our attention directed toward him, and we are encouraged to appreciate his greatness in the world and for our lives.

Illustrating the Text

God teaches us that his knowledge is infinite while ours is finite.

Television: Perry Mason. In the old television series *Perry Mason*, based on the novels by Erle Stanley Gardner, the title character (played by Raymond Burr) was renowned for his keen ability to use questions during his cross-examination to destroy the legal argument presented by the prosecuting attorney. His skillful interrogations illustrate Yahweh's approach to Job, bringing in a right perspective.

Art: William Blake. The fourteenth engraving in Blake's (1757–1827) picture book on the book of Job is commonly called *When the Morning Stars Sang Together*, and it illustrates Job 38:7: "while the morning stars sang together and all the angels shouted for joy." In this engraving, Blake portrays the angels and God above, while humans are beneath them in a posture of humility. This illustrates the humble position of humans, who were not present at creation to witness God's handiwork.

Nature: On rare occasions, rain can cause a desert to burst forth in bloom. For example, in 2005 winter rain caused the Atacama Desert in Chile to become a giant meadow of beautiful, bright-colored flowers.

Nature: The constellations and their movements, the turbulence of the seas, and other natural phenomena—all are under God's control and visually illustrate the marvels about which God speaks to Job.

Literature: *The Silmarillion,* by **J. R. R. Tolkien.** This book, which was published posthumously in 1977 by Tolkien's son Christopher, presents a poetic depiction of the creation of the world. This description is imaginative and also speculative, because no human was there to observe God's creative work.

When God speaks, he may not directly answer our questions.

Book: *On Asking God Why,* by **Elisabeth Elliot.** Elliot (b. 1926) lost her husband, Jim, in Ecuador in 1956. Their only daughter was ten months old. Elliot understands suffering and talks about it often. She writes, "The psalmist often questioned God and so did Job. God did not answer the questions, but he answered the man—with the mystery of himself. He has not left us entirely in the dark. We know a great deal more about his purposes than poor old Job did, yet Job trusted him. He is not only the Almighty—Job's favorite name for him. He is also our Father, and what a father does is not by any means always understood by the child."[2]

Yahweh Asks Job about Animals

Big Idea *Job's limited understanding and control of animals demonstrate the inability of humans to grasp how Yahweh has ordered his world.*

Understanding the Text

The Text in Context

In chapter 39, Yahweh continues to pose questions to Job. After considering features of the non-living physical world in 38:4–38, in 38:39 Yahweh began to focus his queries on the animal realm, and this topic continues throughout the entirety of chapter 39. All the animals that Yahweh cites live beyond the control of humans. Most of them are totally wild, and even the war-horse is tamed only partially. Job does not comprehend the various features of the lives of these animals, but the chapter clearly implies that Yahweh knows them thoroughly. There is much going on in Yahweh's world that escapes the notice of humans, so these aspects of his purpose do not hinge upon human interests. Job, therefore, needs to view what is going on in his life in terms of Yahweh's much bigger and broader plan. This chapter leads directly into Yahweh's challenge to Job to answer him, in 40:1–2.

Historical and Cultural Background

In ancient times, as early as the Paleolithic period, cave art featured pictures of the wild ox. Ugaritic literary texts speak of the god Baal hunting for a wild ox in the upper Galilee region. In Egyptian and Mesopotamian literature and art, kings are depicted as hunting wild animals, including the aurochs (NIV: "wild ox") referred to in Job 39:9–12. The aurochs was never tamed before it became extinct about four hundred years ago, but it became the ancestor of the domesticated cattle of today.

Interpretive Insights

39:1–4 *Do you know when the mountain goats give birth?* The mountain goat here is the ibex that today can be seen in the En Gedi area of Israel. It is an elusive animal that can be observed only from a distance, and it resists domestication by humans. With telephoto lenses humans can now learn some of the habits of animals like the ibex, but until recent times little was known of its patterns of life. Job cannot detect even the gestation period for its offspring, in contrast to the knowledge of animal husbandry he must have for his domesticated animals (1:3). Nevertheless, even though it is not bred by humans, the ibex is able to manage very well by the instinct that God has given to it. Job, however, has virtually no knowledge of even the most basic details of the ibex.

39:5–8 *Who let the wild donkey go free?* It is evident from Yahweh's questions about the wild donkey that he has set this animal free from human control. The wild donkey is skillful in surviving in the wasteland, even thriving in places where humans rarely venture. It avoids the commotion and confinement of town life, happy to keep away from humans, who would distract it and try to domesticate it for their own purposes. This independence comes at a cost, because the wild donkey must forage for food in the barren wilderness.

39:9–12 *Will the wild ox consent to serve you?* The wild ox, or aurochs, is now extinct, but in the Old Testament it is a familiar image for strength (e.g., Deut. 33:17; Ps. 92:10). Its power and remoteness caused it to be the prize game for royal hunts in ancient Egypt. No doubt, this animal was viewed by many humans as a great potential

Key Themes of Job 39

- Yahweh asks about the ibex, which Job can see but about whose habits he knows little.
- Yahweh directs Job's attention to the wild donkey, which thrives in places that humans do not frequent.
- Yahweh made the ostrich act in ways that do not make sense to humans.
- Yahweh inquires if Job can control the mighty warhorse.

resource for activities such as plowing and transporting materials. The aurochs, however, would not surrender its freedom for a life of domesticated labor. As much as humans might have wanted to harness its prodigious strength for their own purposes, the aurochs would not be tamed by them. From the human perspective, this is a rich energy source going for naught, but that is how the aurochs functioned within Yahweh's world. Once again, Job has to realize that life as Yahweh has designed it does not revolve around human concerns, so humans like Job are not in a position to speak definitively about how Yahweh must govern his world.

Yahweh's questions help Job to realize how little he understands about the animal world. In 39:1–4 Job is asked when and how the ibex gives birth to her young. Pictured here is an ibex with her young kids.

Horses in the Ancient Near East and in the Old Testament

Horses were likely first domesticated in Central Asia around 4000 BC, and the first written record of tamed horses in Mesopotamia dates from around 2300 BC. From 1600 BC on, chariots drawn by horses are attested as being used by the Hittites and the Egyptians.

As the Israelites left Egypt, they were pursued by Pharaoh and his chariot forces (Exod. 14). Later, after the Israelites settled in the promised land, they were afflicted by the Canaanites, who had the distinct military advantage of iron chariots (Josh. 11:4–9; Judg. 4:1–3). The first Israelite king to employ horses and chariots was Solomon, whose military buildup disobeyed the command by Yahweh in Deut. 17:16. Both Israel and its enemies used horses extensively in their battles.

Frequently, the Lord warned his people against placing their trust in military resources such as horses (Isa. 30:16; 31:1). Instead, they were to rely upon the Lord for their defense (Ps. 20:7; 33:16–19).

39:13–18 *she cares not that her labor was in vain.* Yahweh's description of the ostrich in 39:13–18 reveals a bird that seems so bent on inefficiency that it makes us laugh.[1] The mother ostrich lays her eggs in the sand, which can place her young at risk (39:14–15; cf. Lam. 4:3). She is easily distracted, so she appears to neglect her young (39:16), although this could also be construed as a strategy to draw predators away from them. The ostrich has not been given wisdom or good sense by God (39:17), for reasons

that only he knows. It does, however, have great speed, which enables it to run away from a horse. In fact, ostriches have been timed running at fifty miles per hour, and they also have great maneuverability. These enigmatic features of the ostrich cause humans to scratch their heads and wonder why Yahweh made it as he did. The apparent inefficiency of the ostrich is a contrast to the tidy system of retribution theology, in which everything in life is explained in simple, logical terms.

39:19–25 *Do you give the horse its strength?* In 39:19–25, Yahweh paints a magnificent word picture of an awesome warhorse. This is the one animal in this section that is not wild, but even though it has been trained by humans for use in battle, it is still terrifying to behold (see the sidebar). In the heat of conflict, the warhorse is not completely mastered by its rider, because it can become reckless in its eagerness for battle (cf. Jer. 8:6). Its powerful features are

In 39:21–22, Yahweh describes a warhorse as charging into the fray, "afraid of nothing," like the image captured in this Assyrian relief of a horse-drawn chariot heading into battle (palace at Nineveh, 645–635 BC).

not the result of its training by humans, because humans can harness only in part the power that Yahweh has given to this animal. No human can take credit for the effectiveness of the warhorse.

39:26–30 *Does the hawk take flight by your wisdom?* Job 39:26–30 features the hawk and the eagle, which soar far above the domain of humans. No human, like Job, has taught them to fly, but rather their superb ability comes from Yahweh. These birds of prey live in inaccessible places that humans cannot approach (39:28), and no human can tell them when to fly or where to nest (39:27). The hawk and the eagle demonstrate that there is much in Yahweh's design for the world that humans do not know or control. Job, then, must realize that there is much that he must leave with Yahweh, in the realm of mystery.

Theological Insights

In the Bible, wisdom teachers often point to aspects of nature from which the learner can discover patterns for understanding life. In Proverbs 6:6–11, observation of the ant reveals that humans need to be diligent rather than slothful. In Matthew 6:26–34, Jesus directs attention to the birds and the flowers in order to teach that God provides for all the needs of those who seek first his kingdom and righteousness. When Yahweh instructs Job, however, he uses nature in a different way. His questions compel Job to look at nature and recognize what he does *not* know. As a result, Job has to admit the limits of his understanding, so that he will trust Yahweh, who does understand all things, including what he is doing in Job's life.

Teaching the Text

In chapter 39, as Yahweh questions Job about several animals, it becomes increasingly evident that Job as a human understands little about each of the animals cited by Yahweh, and he is even less able to control them. All of the animals can be observed at a distance by Job, but his comprehension of how they live is very limited. Yahweh's persistent interrogation and descriptions of the animals compel Job to acknowledge that he is virtually ignorant about considerable portions of God's world. In addition, Job has no ability to control what the animals do, because they function apart from humans. Even when humans have tamed animals for their own use, the animals retain the potential to assert their own will and do as they please.

Job may well have seen the mountain goat, or ibex, leaping upon the cliffs. The ibex, however, keeps its distance from humans, so Job cannot watch when it bears its young, or even calculate how long the gestation period is. Although Job can observe some of this animal's actions, he knows little about its habits. How its young are born, how they mature, and when they set out on their own are all mysteries to Job, but these things are totally understood by Yahweh.

Some of God's creatures make little sense to humans. People look at the ostrich and laugh, because they perceive it to be unthinking, careless, and foolish. That is indeed the case, because God has not endowed the ostrich with wisdom and good sense. In the divine plan, not everything has been designed to work with efficiency, as the ostrich demonstrates well. However, God has also enabled the ostrich to evade

significant limits to what we can know and control in our lives. Rather than assuming that we understand even our own experience perfectly, we must be willing to trust Yahweh, who alone knows and controls all things.

Illustrating the Text

Yahweh's plan encompasses more than just human concerns.

Bible: Make a reference to some passages in the Bible that mention sparrows and birds of the air, like Psalm 84:1–4; Matthew 6:25–26; or Matthew 10:29–30. Point out that we usually read these passages to assure ourselves that we are of value to God, and the

Yahweh uses examples from the animal kingdom to show Job that it is Yahweh alone who understands and controls all things. This idea of exerting control over the animal world is illustrated in scenes known as the "master" or "mistress of animals." This vessel from the mid-third millennium BC shows a female figure standing between two large cats while grasping a large serpent in each hand. Whether this represents a deity, a hero, or a priest is up for debate, but it is clear this figure is exerting dominion and power.

predators and humans intent on capturing it, by giving it unusual speed and expert maneuverability. The ostrich is God's object lesson to us that he works in ways that may escape our understanding, but that he knows what he is doing. Therefore, we need to trust him even when we cannot comprehend all of his ways.

These examples from the animal world teach Job, and they teach us, some key truths that we need to have clarified in our minds. Yahweh's plan includes more than just human concerns. There are many aspects of life that we humans can understand only in part. The ability of humans to control life is limited, because Yahweh has not placed everything under our mastery. Therefore, we must realize that there are

passages clearly carry that as their primary message. However, these passages also show that even the welfare and worship songs of these smallest creatures matter to God and have a place in his plan for creation. His wisdom and providence manage seasons and harvests for them, too, and he hears their groans along with all creation for the redemption he will bring in Christ (Rom. 8:9). The good news is that if God perfectly and brilliantly cares for such small creatures, we are certainly assured that he will do abundantly more for us. The very humbling news, however, is that his response to our needs isn't merely about us; it also takes due consideration of sparrows, ibex, nations, and distant nebulae, all giving glory to him. God will never reject us by telling us he has bigger fish to fry, but he will also never tell us that the world revolves around us.

Even a cursory glance around the created world ought to let us know we are not in charge or fully "in the know."

Science: Take time to share an interesting scientific fact or two about the hidden levels of complexity behind even a seemingly simple natural phenomenon that is relevant to your listeners. For example, about two hundred muscles are involved in taking a single step; or consider that twenty amino acids combine to form more than fifty thousand different proteins in the human body. Remind listeners that Jesus said that even the hairs of our heads are numbered (Luke 12:7) and that science estimates this number to be well over one hundred thousand on the average young adult head. If there are so many things we don't know about what's happening with our own bodies, how much more is going on in the world around us or in spiritual realms that is beyond our grasp and yet fully known to God? Challenge listeners to spend some time watching shows or reading books to find similar examples of the wonder of nature and the magnificent complexity of the systems we find in the created world.

Personal Stories: Take time to tell about a time when you were forced to stare into mystery and admit how little you truly understood about what God was up to in your life. Talk about what it was like to admit your own ignorance and your feelings of loss and panic that were related to this sort of helplessness. Then share a testimony about how you have discovered that dependence on God, who is omniscient and good, has shaped you, and how accepting mystery and resting in the hands of the Ancient of Days is a constructive experience, especially in times of suffering or loss like Job's.

Yahweh Directs Job's Attention to Behemoth

Big Idea *Job is in no position to call Yahweh's justice into question.*

Understanding the Text

The Text in Context

After posing to Job numerous questions about his knowledge of the non-living physical and animal domains (Job 38–39), Yahweh asks if Job is qualified to instruct him (40:1–2). Job responds with a tentative and evasive answer (40:3–5). Yahweh then challenges Job to listen again to him (40:6–14). He directs Job's attention to Behemoth as an especially amazing example of the divine creative work (40:15–24). In chapters 38 and 39, Yahweh focused on a great number of unknowable features in the natural world.

Now, beginning in 40:6, Yahweh zooms in to view intensively two creatures, Behemoth (chap. 40) and Leviathan (chap. 41). In Yahweh's first set of questions, Job learned that he cannot comprehend Yahweh's order in the world. As he considers Behemoth and Leviathan, Job comes to realize that Yahweh totally controls all threats to his order.

Historical and Cultural Background

The description of Behemoth in 40:15–24 has a number of parallels to artifacts in Egyptian and Ugaritic (Canaanite) art and literature. In Egypt, there are many ancient pictures and literary references to the hippopotamus, and this massive animal was also known to exist in Palestine at that time in history. Many of the features contained in Yahweh's words to Job would fit the hippopotamus well, especially its life in the water

Yahweh's description of Behemoth (40:15–24) contains many features of the hippopotamus, which was considered a very powerful and dangerous animal. Hippopotamus amulets, like the one shown here (1800 BC), were placed in Egyptian tombs to allow the deceased to exert control over this beast.

(40:21–23). In the Ugaritic literature, Leviathan (which Yahweh will discuss in chap. 41) is a mythological beast, so some scholars have regarded both Behemoth in chapter 40 and Leviathan as mythological symbols of chaos rather than as literal animals like those in chapters 38 and 39. In either case, Yahweh states clearly that he is in control even of these beasts, which no human can master.

Interpretive Insights

40:2 *Will the one who contends with the Almighty correct him?* This question echoes Yahweh's previous words to Job in 38:2. Yahweh refuses to be put on the defensive by replying to Job's charges and complaints. Rather, he places the burden of proof squarely on Job, as he asks if Job is qualified to instruct him. If Job cannot answer Yahweh's questions, then he has no standing to reprove Yahweh. Job then must either answer the questions that Yahweh poses to him, and by that means show that he has sufficient understanding to call Yahweh to account, or else he must admit that he cannot answer the divine questions. If that is the case, then Job will be obligated to concede to the superior wisdom of Yahweh, instead of finding fault with him.

40:4–5 *I am unworthy—how can I reply to you? I put my hand over my mouth.* Interpreters have taken Job's reply to Yahweh in 40:4–5 in two contrasting ways.[1] Some view this as Job's humble acknowledgment that he has been wrong. This rendering would imply that Yahweh agrees with the friends that Job has sinned. However, in 42:7–9 it is evident that Yahweh affirms Job as right against the friends, who are wrong. Other interpreters rightly contend that Job says that he is "small" rather than that he has

sinned, as the friends have insisted. This view sees Job as beginning to turn away from arguing against Yahweh and starting to accept what Yahweh has done in his life. Because Job's answer is only tentative, Yahweh follows up with a second round of questions and observations in 40:6–41:34, which prompts Job's final response in 42:1–6.

Job describes himself as unworthy or insignificant, rather than as right or wrong. He does not reiterate his earlier claim of innocence, but neither does he retract what he has said before. He says that he will not add to what he said previously, but he does not take it back either. Job is starting to feel the cumulative effect of Yahweh's questions, which he cannot answer, and this is moving him toward humility. Job is beginning to realize that there are many aspects of Yahweh's world that he does not understand, and it is likely dawning on him that his own experience lies in this area of mystery as well. Job's response at this point does not yet resolve the issue, but it is a step in that direction.

40:7 *Brace yourself like a man; I will question you, and you shall answer me.* As in 38:3, Yahweh again challenges Job to man up, to prepare for strenuous activity. This renewed interrogation will require every effort that Job can muster, as Yahweh has enrolled him in a graduate course in the divine school of wisdom. Using the familiar biblical image of girding up one's garment by inserting it in the belt (cf. Exod. 12:11; 1 Kings 18:46;

Jer. 1:17; 1 Pet. 1:13 KJV), Yahweh exhorts Job to prepare himself for a formidable intellectual and theological challenge.

40:8 *Would you discredit my justice? Would you condemn me to justify yourself?* Job earlier said (27:2; cf. 9:24) that God has denied him justice, apparently arguing from the assumption of retribution theology that his innocence does not deserve the adversity he has received. Yahweh now calls into question the legitimacy of Job's contention. If Job is innocent, is it necessarily the case that Yahweh has been unjust? Is there another alternative? Yahweh poses the central issue: does he have to be unjust in order for Job to be justified? Implicitly, Yahweh is saying that Job may be puzzled by what Yahweh is doing, but that Job is in no position to reprove him.

40:9–13 *Do you have an arm like God's, and can your voice thunder like his?* In Exodus 15:16 and Psalm 44:3, the arm of God is an image for his power. Yahweh's question here implies that Job can no more exercise moral judgment than he can control the natural world. Chapters 38 and 39 have already shown that Job is inadequate in his knowledge of the natural world, and he is unable to control it. In 40:10–13, Yahweh challenges Job with impossible commands that no human can fulfill. The logical conclusion is that Job is totally unqualified to fault Yahweh. Job is not Yahweh, and he cannot do what the Sovereign Lord does.

40:14 *Then I myself will admit to you that your own right hand can save you.* Assuming that Job cannot accomplish what the divine commands in verses 10–13 require, Yahweh concludes that he will

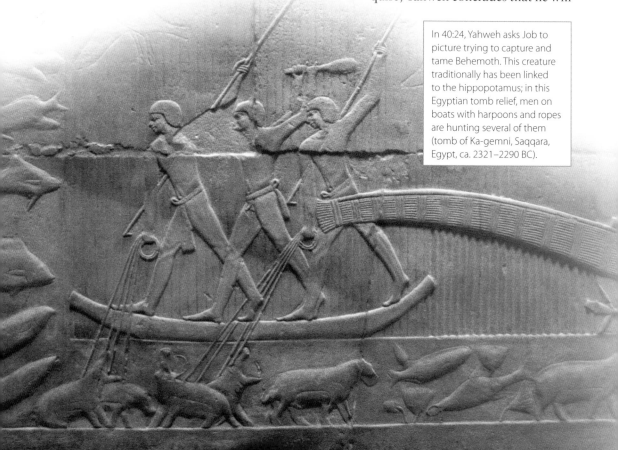

In 40:24, Yahweh asks Job to picture trying to capture and tame Behemoth. This creature traditionally has been linked to the hippopotamus; in this Egyptian tomb relief, men on boats with harpoons and ropes are hunting several of them (tomb of Ka-gemni, Saqqara, Egypt, ca. 2321–2290 BC).

not defer to Job. Job cannot govern the world by justice, because he is not Yahweh's equal. Job cannot exercise authority in the physical world, so he should not take it upon himself to dictate to Yahweh how to run the moral realm of life. Job has no ground for faulting Yahweh for choosing not to act as the retribution formula demands. Yahweh maintains that he alone is in control, and he has no intention of ceding his authority to Job or to any other human.

40:15–24 *Look at Behemoth, which I made along with you.* Scholars have debated extensively the identity of this animal. The term "Behemoth" is the plural form for the generic Hebrew word for an animal. The plural number likely has an intensive force, making it mean "the great beast." The language in 40:15–24 describing Behemoth parallels in many respects how literal animals are portrayed in Job 38–39. Behemoth has powerful physical features (40:16–18), it exercises dominion over other animals (40:19–22), and it is fearless before raging rivers (40:23) and humans (40:24). It has often been taken to picture the hippopotamus, but other suggestions include the water buffalo, the elephant, or a mythological sea monster. Even though Behemoth cannot be controlled by humans, Yahweh made it and securely controls it, so that it is no threat to the divine order in the world (40:19). Only Yahweh has sufficient power to master this formidable part of his creation. Behemoth, like Job, is a creature that functions within Yahweh's world and under Yahweh's authority.

Theological Insights

The Bible frequently uses the literary device of personification to communicate, in terms understandable to humans, aspects of God's being and activity. For example, Yahweh asks Job in 40:9 if he has an arm like God's and if his voice can thunder like God's. The arm or hand of God speaks of his power (Exod. 6:6), and his voice represents his communication. In a similar way, the eye of the Lord is an image for his knowledge (Ps. 33:18). His ear indicates his openness to listen (Ps. 17:6). The shoulder of the Lord is a picture of his acceptance of responsibility (Isa. 9:6). These personifications all make use of familiar aspects of the human body in order to communicate how Yahweh, who is not confined by a physical body, acts.

Teaching the Text

As the book rapidly proceeds toward its conclusion, it becomes increasingly evident that Job is in no position to call Yahweh into question. Earlier, in the dialogue section, Job made several statements about God as he viewed him through the lenses of retribution theology and his own experience of adversity. As Job maintained his innocence, he came to complain that God had not rewarded him with the blessing that he deserved. Yahweh is not yet ready to pronounce his verdict about Job's claim of innocence, but he does counter Job's implication that if he is innocent, then God must be unjust to him. By his persistent questioning, Yahweh demonstrates that Job knows much less than he thinks he knows and that Job can control very little in the world. When we are tempted to complain against God or to question his ways in our lives, we must remember that we too are limited in our

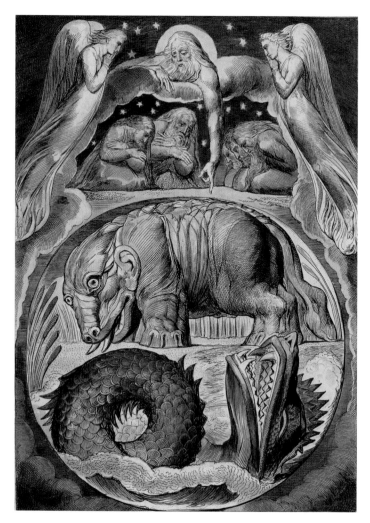

Behemoth and Leviathan, from the *Book of Job* by William Blake (plate 15, ca. 1793, hand-tinted line engraving)

he has been, then Yahweh has not been just to him. By asking Job, "Would you discredit my justice? Would you condemn me to justify yourself?" Yahweh opens up the possibility that there may be another alternative that Job has not considered to explain this situation. This would require that the retribution principle be amended. Perhaps Job's adversity is due to some other reason that transcends the retribution formula. Just as we will give someone we trust the benefit of the doubt, so we need to be careful not to jump to judgment against the Lord. There may well be more going on in God's wise plan than what we can understand and appreciate at the time.

Yahweh makes it painfully evident that Job is unable to control the world, because that is Yahweh's prerogative alone. Because Job cannot do what Yahweh does, Yahweh does not have to yield to Job's demands. It is Job who will need to bend to Yahweh, and not the other way around. We are always creatures who live within the Creator's world, so we must humbly accept our place in God's sovereign design for his world.

Yahweh compels Job to look at Behemoth, an unspecified but awesome animal. This powerful beast cannot be overcome by other animals or by humans, and even the raging rivers do not thwart it. This animal is again a vivid reminder to Job of just how limited he is in Yahweh's world. He is the greatest of all the men in the East, but compared

knowledge. Because we cannot comprehend all that God is doing, we must trust him to act according to his righteous and wise character.

Yahweh defines the central issue for Job and for the reader. Job, working within the framework of retribution theology, has linked the justice of Yahweh to his own righteousness. To Job's thinking, if he has been righteous, and he is confident that with the Lord, Job has paltry knowledge and feeble power. As we glimpse the grandeur of God's world, we too must acknowledge that we are dependent upon him.

Illustrating the Text

Even the greatest people are feeble when compared to the living God.

Film: Reference a popular superhero movie that will be familiar to your listeners. You might want to try a classic hero such as Superman, Spiderman, or Captain America. Take time to list some of the attributes that the hero has that are noble, and how those are amplified by the hero's superhuman powers and responsibilities. Then note that most heroes and gods from all the ages of this world are really just bigger versions of humanity. They may have abilities, stature, powers, and longevity beyond what is natural for humans, but they are, nonetheless, governed by basically the same motives, needs, flaws, and instincts that plague humanity. Contrast this with the God of the Bible, who is obviously *not* an invention of human imagination. Reflect on the ways in which the Lord's wisdom, power, and justice quantitatively and qualitatively differ from ours. Contrast the miracles of God with the exploits of the hero in question and show how the God of the Bible is not even on the same playing field with the heroes and gods of this age.

Hymn Text: Read aloud the text of the hymn "Immortal, Invisible" to the congregation, pausing to exposit the meaning of certain lines or to let their meaning sink in. Ask if the God described by the hymn writer is anything like the God they have come to worship and experience. If not, ask why humans are tempted to water down the majesty of God and what we miss out on when we lose sight of his unspeakable might and greatness.

Even moral innocence does not give a human the right to judge God's justice.

Bible: Consider Jesus's response to the Father's will in the garden of Gesthemane and in the passion. Unlike all other humans, Jesus truly was without sin and was fully above any moral reproach. However, he did not use this innocence as the basis of any complaint against his Father's will in sending him to the cross. Instead, he submitted his will to the Father's three times and obediently offered his body for undeserved punishment without complaint or grumbling. If ever there was an innocent person whose integrity endowed him with the right to complain about undeserved suffering, it was Jesus. Yet even he refused to malign his Father's justice or question his Father's right to insist that he carry a cross he had not earned.

Bible: Reflect on the text of the Lord's Prayer, paying special attention to the words "Thy Kingdom come, Thy will be done, on earth as it is in heaven." Remind listeners that Christians submit to the kingship of God and agree to live under the rule of his justice, however unsearchable it may seem at times. Invite them to join you in praying the prayer, perhaps with pauses for reflection. Ask them to consider if they have been grumbling against God's will or judging his justice by their own standards, and invite them to include that in the "forgive us our debts" section of the prayer.

Yahweh Points Job to Leviathan

Big Idea *Leviathan cannot be controlled by Job but is under Yahweh's control.*

Understanding the Text

The Text in Context

Yahweh's long-awaited speech to Job in chapters 38–41 climaxes with Yahweh's stirring description of the sea creature Leviathan (Job 41). After the barrage of unanswerable questions by Yahweh, this final object lesson at last wilts the remaining vestiges of Job's resistance, so that he responds humbly to Yahweh in 42:1–6. All that remains after Job's answer is the epilogue (42:7–17), in which Yahweh will affirm Job's innocence and restore a full measure of blessing to Job.

Historical and Cultural Background

In the Ugaritic (Canaanite) mythological literature, Lotan was a twisting sea creature with seven heads that was defeated by Baal. The description of Leviathan in Job 41, as well as references to it in Psalm 74:14 and Isaiah 27:1, likely borrows this familiar ancient image to refer to any factor that threatens to bring disorder to Yahweh's world. The

In the ancient world, Leviathan was viewed as a monster that threatened to unleash chaos in the world. This shell carving depicts a seven-headed monster with flames shooting from its back. A deity kneels before the mighty creature, ready to do battle.

Bible, however, is very clear that Yahweh has triumphed over Leviathan and even has made it to play in the sea (Ps. 104:26). In Revelation 12:3–9, the defeat of Satan is portrayed with the same kind of imagery, as a great dragon with seven heads is cast down from heaven by the angel Michael. Consequently, in the history of Christian biblical interpretation, the antichrist as he wreaks havoc on the earth is often depicted as riding upon Leviathan.[1]

Interpretive Insights

41:1 *Can you pull in Leviathan with a fishhook or tie down its tongue with a rope?* Once again, Yahweh asks a rhetorical question that expects a negative answer from Job. Leviathan is not a trout or bass

Key Themes of Job 41

- Yahweh teaches that because Job cannot tame or subdue Leviathan, he certainly cannot control what Yahweh does in his world.
- Yahweh describes Leviathan as impervious to all human attempts to control it.
- Yahweh discloses the formidable features of Leviathan.
- Yahweh's authority encompasses all creatures under heaven, including Leviathan and Job.

that can be caught with a hook and line. This fierce sea creature featured in ancient Near Eastern mythological literature is far too strong for any human to defeat. Leviathan is clearly beyond the range of Job's control.

41:3–5 *Will it keep begging you for mercy?* In verses 3–5, Yahweh uses humor to reinforce in Job's mind how ridiculous and futile it would be for any human to suppose that he could tame Leviathan. This powerful creature would scarcely entreat Job to be gentle with it (41:3). There is no chance that it would submit itself willingly to becoming a bond slave (41:4; cf. Exod. 21:6). Would Job be so silly as to think that he could train it as a pet for a little girl to lead around on a leash (41:5)? No, Leviathan is much too powerful for a human like Job to control.

41:10 *No one is fierce enough to rouse it. Who then is able to stand against me?* Yahweh here argues from the lesser to the greater. No human can tame Leviathan (cf. 3:8), so how could anyone ever expect to compel Yahweh to act in a particular way? In chapter 31, Job laid out his legal defense, and then he challenged Yahweh to answer him. Yahweh now states that no one is able to present a case against him in court (cf. 33:5), not even Job. Yahweh's authority is so

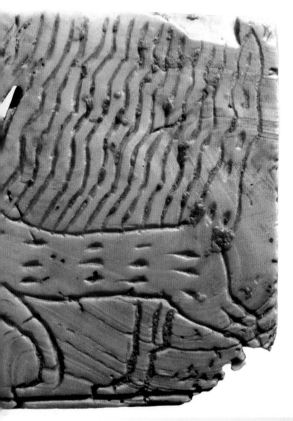

Mythological Language in the Bible

The extended description of Leviathan in Job 41, with its evident allusions to ancient mythological literature, raises some important theological and interpretive questions. In the ancient world, Leviathan was widely viewed as a mythical monster that threatened chaos, but was defeated by the Canaanite god Baal. When Yahweh and others in the Bible refer to Leviathan, they are not alleging that the Canaanite myths were factual accounts; rather, they used this creature as a familiar literary symbol of resistance to divine rule. In this way, they were able to make their point understandable to people in the ancient Near East.

In a similar way, preachers today may cite a character in a fictional book or movie in order to make a powerful rhetorical point. Even though they may refer to fictional characters such as Cinderella, Darth Vader, or Frodo, everyone realizes that they are not claiming that these literary characters actually existed as real people. Rather, effective speakers use vivid language to increase the rhetorical effect of their messages.

supreme that he is not obligated to submit to any subpoena that humans can render against him. Job, therefore, will not be able to succeed in forcing Yahweh into indicating his innocence through his strategy of negative confession. Job's best-laid plans will come to naught before the Sovereign God.

41:11 *Everything under heaven belongs to me.* As formidable as Leviathan is, it comes under Yahweh's rule, because everything under heaven belongs to him (cf. Pss. 24:1; 50:10). Job is unable to tame Leviathan (41:1–9), but Yahweh controls it completely. Clearly, then, Job is not the equal of Yahweh, so he will have to submit before the Lord of the whole world, just as Leviathan must.

41:12 *I will not fail to speak of Leviathan's limbs.* With these words, Yahweh begins an extensive, detailed description of the amazing features of Leviathan. In some respects, Leviathan appears like the crocodile, but other details suggest a more fantastic animal, like the fire-breathing dragons of myths. This vivid portrayal in verses 12–32

produces shock and awe in Job, and even readers today cannot fail to be impressed by the grandeur and power of this amazing creature. No other animal can match it.

41:15–17 *they cling together and cannot be parted.* In verses 15–17, the scales of Leviathan are described as impenetrable, like a row of shields that are sealed together. No one is able to plunge a sword between the scales in an effort to kill it. Later, in verses 23–29, Leviathan is depicted as having no vulnerability that can be exploited as humans try to defeat it. Clearly, it will take supernatural power and skill to take down this creature. Only Yahweh is up to this challenge.

41:18–21 *Its breath sets coals ablaze.* The description of Leviathan in verses 18–21 as breathing fire is not suitable for any literal animal. For this reason, it seems better to view Leviathan as a literary allusion to a fantastic creature like a dragon. This creature would be completely beyond Job's range of experience or control.

41:26–29 *it laughs at the rattling of the lance.* Just as the wild donkey laughs scornfully at the town (39:7) and the ostrich laughs at the horse and rider that seek to catch it (39:18), so Leviathan laughs at the warrior who tries to attack it. All human efforts to tame or defeat this animal are ineffectual and ludicrous. However, even though Leviathan is impervious to human efforts to control it, it is firmly under Yahweh's sovereign control (41:11).

41:33 *Nothing on earth is its equal—a creature without fear.* Leviathan is fearless, because it has no predator and no equal on earth. It is evident, then, that Job must be inferior to this powerful animal. Nevertheless, Leviathan is a creature

that is under the authority of Yahweh, its creator. If Yahweh is Lord over Leviathan, then he certainly is Lord over Job's life as well. Just as Job must acknowledge his inferiority before Leviathan, so he must accept his subordinate status before Yahweh. Yahweh's ordered world includes even unruly creatures, like Leviathan, that Job cannot control. Yahweh, however, is fully in control, so Job must accept humbly his subordinate place before God.

41:34 *It looks down on all that are haughty; it is king over all that are proud.* Leviathan has no match in the created world. It is more powerful even than humans, who take pride in their own accomplishments, and it will not submit to their

> Yahweh describes Leviathan's back as being like rows of shields tightly fastened together (41:15–17). This relief, which shows Assyrian bodyguards positioned with their shields making an impenetrable defense, is a picture of the impregnability of Leviathan (palace at Nineveh, 640–620 BC).

control. However, mighty Leviathan must bow before Yahweh, to whom everything belongs (41:11).

Theological Insights

In the ancient world, pagan gods were typically viewed as ruling over specific local areas. For example, in 1 Kings 20:23 when the Syrian army is defeated by Israel, they assume that the god of Israel must control the mountains, so they plan to attack

Israel the next time in the plain, where they supposed that the god of Israel would not have jurisdiction. Yahweh, however, is not like the false deities of the nations, because everything under heaven belongs to him (Job 41:11). The universal rule of Yahweh is maintained consistently throughout the Bible, both in the Old Testament (Exod. 19:5; Pss. 24:1; 47:2; Isa. 40:22–26; Dan. 2:20–21) and in the New Testament (Matt. 28:18–20; Rev. 19:15–16). The God of the Bible is Lord of all, and he will not share his glory, authority, or worship with anyone else. That is why every knee will bow and every tongue confess that Jesus is Lord (Phil. 2:9–11).

Teaching the Text

The final chapter of Yahweh's speeches focuses exclusively on the great sea animal, Leviathan. As Yahweh directs Job's attention to Leviathan, describes the animal in detail, and asks Job questions about it, it is clear that though Leviathan cannot be controlled by Job, it is firmly under Yahweh's control. Job wanted God to answer his legal complaint, and he expressed his desire for an umpire to adjudicate between him and God. This chapter, however, reveals that Job does not have the status to make these demands of Almighty God. As a human, Job is inferior to Leviathan, and Leviathan is inferior to Yahweh, so Job must take a submissive stance before the Creator. Like Job, we must let God be God, and we must live in faithful submission to him rather than demand that God do what we think is right.

As Yahweh describes the protective scales that cover the powerful body of Leviathan, it is evident that this animal is impervious to human attack. Human weapons can find no vulnerability to exploit, so they bounce harmlessly off Leviathan. This fierce animal seems to have its own way, even making the sea churn like a boiling cauldron. It is totally beyond the control of any person. Similarly, there are factors in our experience

that we cannot control and adversities that we cannot avoid. However, all these things that can alarm us are under the Lord's control, who in all things works for the good of those who love him (Rom. 8:28).

As powerful and unrivaled as Leviathan is on earth, it is a creature that is subordinate to Yahweh, the Creator to whom everything under heaven belongs. Leviathan lives under Yahweh's authority, even though what it does is well beyond the control of humans. Since Job cannot control Leviathan, but Leviathan is controlled by Yahweh, Job must accept the undeniable conclusion that he too lives under Yahweh's authority. His proper response must be to acknowledge Yahweh as Lord of all and to submit to Yahweh's authority over his life. Like Job, we too must recognize that we are limited and finite creatures who must humbly yield to the Lord's sovereign control over our lives. That is what it means to hope in God (cf. Rom. 5:3–5).

Illustrating the Text

God points to Leviathan to show how everything is under God's control.

Nature: It is not possible to determine conclusively what specific animal Leviathan represents. Because the crocodile and the whale share some characteristics with the Leviathan, seeing these animals in action gives a sense of the great power of the creature portrayed in Job 41.

> Leviathan is under God's authority and control even though "arrows do not make it flee; slingstones are like chaff to it" (41:28). Even the Assyrian army, with its expert slingers and archers, could not subdue this beast. This register of a larger Assyrian relief illustrating the attack on Lachish is from the palace at Nineveh (700–692 BC).

Literature: *Moby Dick*, by Herman Melville. In this epic nineteenth-century novel, the great whale of the title is often referred to as Leviathan, an allusion to the powerful animal in Job 41. The following description shows some of that power:

> As if to strike a quick terror into them, by this time being the first assailant himself, Moby Dick had turned, and was now coming for the three crews. . . . But ere that close limit was gained, and while yet all three boats were plain as the ship's three masts to his eye; the White Whale churning himself into furious speed, almost in an instant as it were, rushing among the boats with open jaws, and a lashing tail, offered appalling battle on every side; and heedless of the irons darted at him from every boat, seemed only intent on annihilating each separate plank of which those boats were made.[2]

Later, "both jaws, like enormous shears bit the craft completely in twain."

Literature: As mentioned in this unit, dragons feature prominently in many pieces of fantasy literature. For example, in *The Hobbit* (1937), by J. R. R. Tolkien (1892–1973), the dragon Smaug has many attributes and behaviors (great age; winged, fiery, and reptilian form; a stolen barrow within which he lies on his hoard; disturbance by a theft; and violent airborne revenge on the lands all about) that are derived directly from the unnamed old "night-scather," the monster Grendel in *Beowulf*, the old English epic. *The Voyage of the Dawn Treader* (1952), by C. S. Lewis (1898–1963), also features a vivid picture of a dragon. In many ways, these legendary dragons echo Yahweh's description of Leviathan.

Job Comes to a Good End

Big Idea *Job realizes that Yahweh's ways are more wonderful than he has known before, and he comes to enjoy Yahweh's renewed blessings on his life.*

Understanding the Text

The Text in Context

After Yahweh speaks to Job in chapters 38 and 39, Job replies tentatively to him in 40:3–5. Yahweh's second round of questions, in 40:6–41:34, with his detailed descriptions of Behemoth and Leviathan, then evokes a more definitive response from Job in 42:1–6. In his second reply, Job acknowledges that he has come to a more accurate understanding of who Yahweh is and also of who he himself is as a finite mortal living under Yahweh's authority.

In the epilogue (42:7–17), Yahweh brings resolution to Job's situation. Yahweh affirms Job's innocence against the charges of the friends, instructs the friends to ask Job to pray for them, and restores Job's family and fortune. The epilogue contains many textual links back to the

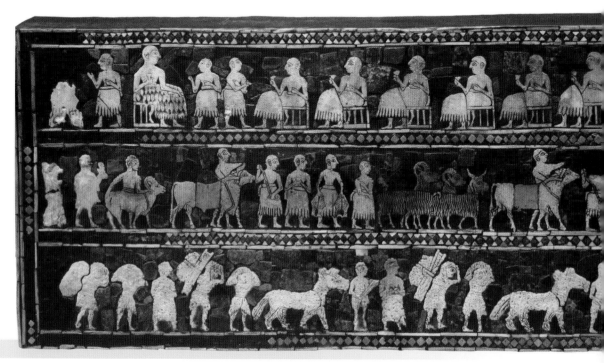

prologue (chaps. 1 and 2), so together they form the literary framework for the book. Job is not given an explanation for his adversity, and the dispute between Yahweh and the adversary is not disclosed to him. Even after his restoration, apparently Job has to live within the bounds of this divine mystery.

Historical and Cultural Background

The narrator speaks in unusual detail about the three daughters who are born to Job after his adversity is concluded. First, he names them (42:14), even though the names of Job's sons are not stated. Their names all reflect their exceptional beauty (cf. 42:15): Jemimah means dove (cf. Song 2:14), Keziah refers to cinnamon, or cassia (cf. Exod. 30:24; Ps. 45:8), and Keren-Happuch speaks of a bottle that holds black coloring used for eye shadow (cf. 2 Kings 9:30; Jer. 4:30; Ezek. 23:40). It is also mentioned that Job gives his daughters an inheritance along with their brothers. In Israel, daughters usually did not inherit property unless there were no living sons in the family (Num. 27:1–11; 36:1–12). In early Greek and Canaanite literature, there were some cases of daughters inheriting property, but it was not the norm in the ancient world.

In the epilogue, Yahweh returns Job to his former prosperity. Both his livestock and his offspring are restored, and his life is blessed more than it was before. The scene on the side of the Standard of Ur shown here is reminiscent of Job's new situation. Here banqueters dine to the music of singer and harpist, while the bounty of the land in livestock and other goods parades before them (Mesopotamia, twenty-fifth century BC).

Key Themes of Job 42

- Job acknowledges that he previously spoke beyond what he truly knew.
- Job changes his mind and humbly accepts his finite status as a creature before Yahweh.
- Yahweh commends Job and reproves the friends.
- Yahweh restores Job's fortune and family.

Interpretive Insights

42:2 *I know that you can do all things.* In verses 2–3, Job five times uses terms that refer to knowledge, plans, and understanding. This language evidences that Job has come to an enlarged recognition of the wisdom and power of Yahweh as he has contemplated the questions Yahweh posed to him in chapters 38–41. Job now knows in a better way how much more Yahweh understands than he does. Job realizes that his adversity must fall within the purpose of Yahweh, which cannot be thwarted by any force (cf. Dan. 4:35). Yahweh sovereignly directs history to his own ends, which may well be inscrutable to humans (Prov. 16:9; 20:24; 21:1).

42:3–4 *Surely I spoke of things I did not understand.* Job restates Yahweh's question to him in 38:2, but now he answers by admitting that in the past he spoke beyond what he truly understood. Job does not confess that he has sinned, as the friends have insisted that he must (cf. Zophar's words in 11:13–15). Instead, he acknowledges that previously he spoke too confidently about matters that in fact exceed the range of his knowledge. Yahweh's questions have changed Job's understanding, so that he now realizes how much he did not know.

42:5 *but now my eyes have seen you.* In verse 4, Job restates Yahweh's words of cross-examination in 38:3 and 40:7. Earlier, in 19:25–27, Job expressed his desire to see God. Now, Job's increased understanding of Yahweh's superior knowledge has dramatically enhanced his perception of Yahweh, so Job says that his eyes have seen him. Everything Job knew before was just so much hearsay when compared with what he has come to know of Yahweh.

42:6 *Therefore I despise myself and repent in dust and ashes.* This verse is the key to understanding the entire book of Job, but it has been rendered in many diverse ways.[1] This cannot be Job's repentance of sin, or else the friends would be right in their assessment of him. In verse 7 Yahweh makes it very clear that the friends have not spoken the truth, and he instructs them to offer a burnt offering and to ask Job to intercede for them in prayer. The term "despise" here can better be translated "recant" or "retract," and thus it refers to Job's withdrawal of his legal claim against God. Job repents in the sense of changing his mind, as he comes to the realization that he is just dust and ashes (cf. Gen. 18:27), a mere human before the transcendent Yahweh. Before the Sovereign Lord, Job is a finite creature who is limited in his knowledge. Because Job now recognizes how little he truly knows compared to the omniscient Yahweh, he retracts his insistence that Yahweh answer him (31:35). Job submits to Yahweh, without any knowledge that Yahweh will restore blessing to him in the epilogue.

42:7–9 *you have not spoken the truth about me, as my servant Job has.* In the epilogue, Yahweh assesses each of the major characters (except for Elihu, whom he totally ignores), and what he says about them is determinative for interpreting the book.

The friends have tried to protect Yahweh's reputation by insisting that Job must have sinned, but by extrapolating the retribution principle into an indictment of Job they have reduced Yahweh to a predictable deity who is confined by a fixed formula. Yahweh particularly singles out Eliphaz for criticism, which is ironic, because in 22:23–27 Eliphaz said that Job can intercede for others only if he first repents of his sins. Yahweh now calls on Job to reprise his role of a mediator and to intercede in prayer for his friends, who have angered Yahweh by not speaking the truth (42:8–9), just as previously he offered sacrifices for his own children in case they had sinned against God in their hearts (1:5).

It may seem startling to hear Yahweh imply that Job has spoken the truth, in contrast to what the friends have said wrongly. Numerous times in his speeches Job asks hard questions about God's justice and fairness, and he often complains that he has been mistreated by God. How Job addresses God can be compared with the lament psalms, in which the psalmists in their pain frequently express their doubts, fears, and questions to the Lord (e.g., Ps. 13:1–2). As humans, we assess others by what we hear them say and see them do, but the Lord knows completely what is in the hearts of his people, and he has evaluated Job on that basis of perfect understanding.

42:10 *the Lord restored his fortunes and gave him twice as much as he had before.* These restored divine blessings are not contingent on Job's confession of his own sins (contrary to what Bildad predicted in 8:7) but are granted by Yahweh after Job obediently intercedes for his friends. After all their harsh words to him, this could be a bit painful for Job to do, but nevertheless he overcomes their evil with good (cf. Rom. 12:21). In this, Job is not motivated by self-interest, as the adversary has wrongly charged in 1:9–11.

42:11 *everyone who had known him before came and ate with him in his house.* Yahweh has restored the vertical relationship between Job and him, and he has healed as well the horizontal relationships between Job and other people who were once close to him. During his time of need, Job's family and closest friends abandoned him (19:13–19), but now they return to fellowship with him. Even though his crisis is over, Job still has to deal with the considerable loss that he has incurred, especially the death of his children. His solitude and pain are replaced by community and rejoicing, as Job receives belated consolation and encouragement.

42:12–17 *And so Job died, an old man and full of years.* Yahweh doubles Job's animals over what he had before his calamity (42:10, 12). He also gives to Job seven more sons and three especially lovely daughters (42:13–15). Job goes on to live 140 years (double the typical life expectancy cited in Ps. 90:10), and he sees his great-grandchildren (42:16). With language that echoes the experiences of Abraham (Gen. 25:8), Isaac (Gen. 35:29), and David (1 Chron. 29:28), Job is described as living out a very good and satisfying life. The long life he enjoys is one of

the blessings offered by wisdom in Proverbs 3:2, 16; 4:10; 9:11; 10:27.

Theological Insights

In the final section of the book, Job receives renewed blessing by Yahweh, so the book as a whole confirms the general legitimacy of retribution theology. However, it also clearly teaches that the retribution principle must not be pressed into a rigid formula that must hold for every specific case. Within the world that is ordered and governed by Yahweh, there are factors that appear anomalous to humans, such as the ostrich, which seems to have little sense (39:13–18). There are observable cases when evildoers prosper (Job 21; cf. Pss. 49 and 73), and Job's adversity evidences that bad things can happen to righteous people. Nevertheless, the all-powerful and all-wise Yahweh accomplishes his inscrutable purpose, which transcends all that the human mind can comprehend. The book of Job does not answer all our questions, but instead it draws attention to Yahweh, who alone knows all the answers, even though he does not always choose to

Job's friends return to fellowship with him and each bring him a piece of silver and a gold ring (42:11). Before coins, payments of silver were made by cutting off pieces from coils, such as the one shown here.

make those answers available to humans. Job compels us to trust the character of Yahweh even when we cannot comprehend all his ways.

Teaching the Text

In chapter 42, the long and complex book of Job comes to a satisfying conclusion. After the long dialogue section, in which Job becomes increasingly perplexed and agitated, he at last realizes that he must withdraw his legal complaint against Yahweh. Job is not given answers to all his questions, but he is willing to trust Yahweh, who does know all the answers. Job demonstrates that the person of faith must find answers in the character of the Lord, even when there are many questions left about why God does what he does.

The lengthy questioning by Yahweh in chapters 38–41 had its intended effect upon Job. As Job considers all of the unanswerable questions that Yahweh has posed to him, he comes to the realization that Yahweh knows vastly more than he does. Previously, Job spoke confidently about things that he now recognizes he did not really know at all. Before, Job viewed Yahweh through the lens of what he thought he understood, but now he views himself through the lens of what Yahweh actually understands fully. When Job looks through the lens of Yahweh, he acknowledges that he himself is very limited in his own knowledge but that Yahweh is omniscient. If we insist on viewing God through the lens of our experience, our understanding of God will be small and distorted. What we need to do is to view our experience through the lens of the Lord as the Bible reveals him, one who is all-powerful, all-wise, and ever good and who controls those things we cannot understand.

In the epilogue, Yahweh makes it clear that Job has not sinned, as the friends have charged repeatedly. Rather, Yahweh is angry with the three friends because they have not spoken the truth, as Job has. Yahweh directs them to offer burnt offerings and to ask Job to pray on

Job is to pray for his friends as they present burnt offerings of seven bulls and seven rams before the Lord (42:8). This register shows a scene from the offering chamber of Merib, where a bull is being sacrificed and other animals are being brought as offerings (twenty-sixth century BC).

their behalf. By this means, Yahweh clarifies that Job is indeed the righteous man whom he commended in the prologue. The all-knowing Yahweh knows the pure heart of Job. As we struggle with adversity, we, like Job, may ask questions that seem dangerous, and we may even express feelings that are raw, but we can be sure that the Lord searches our hearts and knows our thoughts (Ps. 139:23–24) and that he will lead us in his good way.

Illustrating the Text

Having seen God's omnipotence, Job yields to God in great humility.

Book: *In God's Waiting Room*, by Lehman Strauss. In this book, Strauss writes, "I expect to meet Job one day. I will thank him for his rich legacy. He has helped me to regard my trial, not as the fiery darts of Satan (Eph. 6:16) but as 'the arrows of the Almighty' (Job 6:4). He who sent the arrows has bound up and dressed the wounds. In His own time and for His good purpose, He will heal them perfectly."[2]

Hymn: "O Love That Will Not Let Me Go," by George Matheson. These words could well have been the exhausted cry of Job's heart:

> O Love that will not let me go,
> I rest my weary soul in thee;
> I give thee back the life I owe,
> That in thine ocean depths its flow
> May richer, fuller be.
>
> O light that foll'west all my way,
> I yield my flick'ring torch to thee;

> My heart restores its borrowed ray,
> That in thy sunshine's blaze its day
> May brighter, fairer be.
>
> O Joy that seekest me through pain,
> I cannot close my heart to thee;
> I trace the rainbow through the rain,
> And feel the promise is not vain,
> That morn shall tearless be.

Yahweh vindicates Job, making it clear that he is a righteous man.

Church History / Biography: **John Knox**. John Knox (ca. 1514–1572), who headed up the Protestant Reformation in Scotland, suffered greatly in the process of obeying God's calling on his life. He was once made a galley slave for the French; at another time, he was exiled in Germany and Switzerland. After Protestantism became the state religion of Scotland in 1560, Knox chaired the committee that produced the foundational document for the Scottish Church. He was described as having had "a sore fight of an existence, wrestling with Popes and Principalities; in defeat, contention, life-long struggle. . . . A sore fight: but he won it!" "'Have you hope?' they asked him in his last moment, when he could no longer speak. He lifted his finger, pointed upward, and so died! Honor to him! His works have not died. The letter of his work dies, as of all men's; but the spirit of it, never." That is God's vindication of a man whose text was John 17:3: "And this is life eternal, that they might know thee the only true God, and Jesus Christ, whom thou has sent."[3]

Notes

Introduction to Job

1. For a succinct summary of the history of interpretation of the book of Job from biblical times up to the time of John Calvin, see Joel S. Allen, "Job 3: History of Interpretation," 361–71.

2. Kidner, *Wisdom*, 75–89, provides a helpful discussion and evaluation of the variety of arguments raised against the unity of the book of Job.

3. Ryken et al., *Dictionary of Biblical Imagery*; Walton, *IVP Bible Background Commentary*; Walton, *Zondervan Illustrated Bible Backgrounds Commentary*, 5:246–301.

4. Longman and Enns, *Dictionary*.

Job 1

1. Michael S. Heiser has presented an excellent brief discussion of the divine council in ancient religious thought in Longman and Enns, *Dictionary*, 112–16.

2. Milton, *Paradise Lost*, 1.34–48.

Job 3

1. Balentine, *Job*, 87, provides a succinct discussion of Leviathan in ancient thought and later literary interpretation.

2. Hopkins, *Poems and Prose*, 67.

Job 4

1. Tournier, *Escape from Loneliness*, 109.

Job 5

1. Clines, *Job 1–20*, 142, presents a helpful discussion of Resheph in Job 5:7, along with additional bibliography for further study.

Job 6

1. Two important studies on Yahweh as a warrior are Miller, *Divine Warrior*, and Longman and Reid, *God Is a Warrior*.

2. Melville, *Moby Dick*, 161.

Job 7

1. Walton, *IVP Bible Background Commentary*, 498–99.

2. Manning, *Abba's Child*, 27.

Job 8

1. See Dickens, *Hard Times*, xi.

2. Lewis, *Reflections on the Psalms*, 112–13.

Job 9

1. John Walton, email message to author, November 4, 2011.

2. Yancey, *Disappointment with God*, 9.

Job 10

1. Wiesel, *Trial of God*, xxv.

Job 12

1. For a brief discussion of descriptive praise psalms, see Estes, *Handbook*, 155–58.

2. Elliot, *These Strange Ashes*, 129, 131.

Job 13

1. Walton, *IVP Bible Background Commentary*, 501.

2. Yancey, *Disappointment with God*, 35.

Job 15

1. Further explanation and bibliography concerning the Adapa myth is found in Balentine, *Job*, 236.

2. Lincoln, *Speeches and Letters*, 235.

3. Pascal, *Pascal's Pensées*, 4, no. 9.

Job 16

1. Yancey, *Disappointment with God*, 163, 173.

Job 17

1. Karaagac, *John McCain*, 92.

Job 18

1. Clines, *Job 1–20*, 416–19, elucidates the ancient Near Eastern background for the reference to death in Job 18:13–14.
2. Hardy, *Tess of the D'Urbervilles*, 323.
3. Herbert, "Affliction (IV)," lines 19–30.

Job 19

1. Ten Boom, *Hiding Place*, 217.

Job 20

1. Estes, "Like Arrows."

Job 21

1. Dickinson, *Complete Poems*, 646, 662.

Job 22

1. Crane, "Open Boat," 25.
2. Bunyan, *The Pilgrim's Progress*, 111.

Job 23

1. Wolterstorff, *Lament for a Son*, 69.

Job 24

1. Clines, "Quarter Days Gone," compares Job's language to the long-standing English quarter days on which accounts are settled.

Job 25

1. Balentine, *Job*, 382, briefly discusses several prominent scholarly views on the speakers in Job 25–27, and he provides additional bibliography on the subject.
2. Tozer, *Renewed Day by Day*, April 20.

Job 26

1. Kushner, *When Bad Things Happen to Good People*.

Job 27

1. http://mickydee.hubpages.com/hub/The-Falsely-Accused-And-Wrongly-Imprisoned.

Job 28

1. Richard S. Hess presents an excellent discussion of biblical wisdom in conjunction with other ancient Near Eastern conceptions of wisdom in his article "Wisdom Sources," in Longman and Enns, *Dictionary*, 894–901.

Job 29

1. http://www.evancarmichael.com/Famous-Entrepreneurs/591/Lesson-1-Motivate-Your-Workers.html.

Job 30

1. Humphrey, "Job of the Plains," 128.

Job 31

1. Humphrey, "Job of the Plains," 128.

Job 32

1. For additional discussion of the significance of Elihu's language comparing himself to a full wineskin, see Clines, *Job 21–37*, 722–23.
2. MacLeish, *J.B.*, 126.
3. Pascal, *Pascal's Pensées*, 242.

Job 33

1. Tournier, *Escape from Lonliness*, 34.
2. MacLeish, *J.B.*, 30.

Job 35

1. Clines, *Job 21–37*, 790, 798–99, provides detailed discussion on the interpretive alternatives in Job 35:10.

Job 36

1. For a brief description of the nature psalms, see Estes, *Handbook*, 159.
2. Guyon, *Spiritual Torrents*, 48.
3. Tucker, *From Jerusalem to Irian Jaya*, 426–27.

Job 37

1. Andersen, *Job*, 268.
2. Phillips, *Your God Is Too Small*, 135.

Job 38

1. Balentine, *Job*, 657.
2. Elliot, *On Asking God Why*, 18.

Job 39

1. A succinct description of the peculiar habits of the ostrich is given in Walton, *IVP Bible Background Commentary*, 510.

Job 40

1. Clines, *Job 38–42*, 1139–40, discusses several of the leading interpretations of Job's reply to Yahweh in 40:4–5.

Job 41

1. Balentine, *Job*, 687.
2. Melville, *Moby Dick*, 400.

Job 42

1. For a detailed summary of the exegetical issues and interpretive alternatives for Job 42:6, see the lucid discussion in Clines, *Job 38–42*, 1218–23.
2. Strauss, *In God's Waiting Room*, 38.
3. Frank Boreham, "John Knox (1514?–1572)," in *A Frank Boreham Treasury*, 25, 31.

Bibliography

Recommended Resources

Alden, Robert L. *Job*. The New American Commentary 11. Nashville: Broadman & Holman, 1993.

Andersen, Francis I. *Job: An Introduction and Commentary*. Tyndale Old Testament Commentaries. Downers Grove, IL: IVP Academic, 2008.

Atkinson, David. *The Message of Job*. The Bible Speaks Today. Downers Grove, IL: InterVarsity, 1991.

Balentine, Samuel E. *Job*. Smyth & Helwys Bible Commentary. Macon, GA: Smyth & Helwys, 2006.

Clines, David J. A. *Job 1–20*. Word Biblical Commentary 17. Dallas: Word, 1989.

———. *Job 21–37*. Word Biblical Commentary 18A. Nashville: Thomas Nelson, 2006.

———. *Job 38–42*. Word Biblical Commentary 18B. Nashville: Thomas Nelson, 2011.

Estes, Daniel J. *Handbook on the Wisdom Books and Psalms*. Grand Rapids: Baker Academic, 2005.

Habel, Norman C. *The Book of Job*. Old Testament Library. Philadelphia: Westminster, 1985.

Hartley, John E. *The Book of Job*. New International Commentary on the Old Testament. Grand Rapids: Eerdmans, 1988.

Kidner, Derek. *The Wisdom of Proverbs, Job and Ecclesiastes*. Downers Grove, IL: InterVarsity, 1985.

Longman, Tremper, III, and Peter Enns, eds. *Dictionary of the Old Testament: Wisdom, Poetry and Writings*. Downers Grove, IL: InterVarsity, 2008.

Murphy, Roland E. *The Book of Job: A Short Reading*. New York: Paulist, 1999.

Ryken, Leland, James C. Wilhoit, and Tremper Longman III, eds. *Dictionary of Biblical Imagery*. Downers Grove, IL: InterVarsity, 1998.

Smick, Elmer B. "Job." In *The Expositor's Bible Commentary*, edited by Frank E. Gaebelein, 4:843–1000. Grand Rapids: Zondervan, 1988.

Walton, John H., ed. *Zondervan Illustrated Bible Backgrounds Commentary*. Grand Rapids: Zondervan, 2009.

Walton, John H., Victor H. Matthews, and Mark W. Chavalas, eds. *IVP Bible Background Commentary: Old Testament*. Downers Grove, IL: InterVarsity, 2000.

Wilson, Gerald H. *Job*. New International Biblical Commentary: Old Testament Series 10. Peabody, MA: Hendrickson, 2007.

Zuck, Roy B. *Job*. Everyman's Bible Commentary. Chicago: Moody, 1978.

Other Works

Allen, Joel S. "Job 3: History of Interpretation." In Longman and Enns, *Dictionary of the Old Testament*, 361–71.

Bernardin, Joseph Cardinal. *The Gift of Peace*. Chicago: Loyola, 1997.

Boreham, Frank. *A Frank Boreham Treasury*. Compiled by Peter Gunther. Chicago: Moody, 1984.

Bunyan, John. *The Pilgrim's Progress*. 1678. Reprint, Chicago: Moody Press, 2007.

Clines, David J. A. "Quarter Days Gone: Job 24 and the Absence of God." In *God in the Fray: A Tribute to Walter Brueggemann*, edited by Tod Linafelt and Timothy K. Beal, 242–58. Minneapolis: Fortress, 1998.

Crane, Stephen. "The Open Boat." In *The Open Boat and Other Tales of Adventure*, 1–63. New York: Doubleday & McClure, 1898.

Dickens, Charles. *Hard Times*. Oxford World's Classics. Oxford: Oxford University Press, 2006.

Dickinson, Emily. *The Complete Poems of Emily Dickinson*. Edited by Thomas H. Johnson. Boston: Little, Brown, 1960.

Elliot, Elisabeth. *On Asking God Why*. New Jersey: Fleming Revell, 1989.

———. *These Strange Ashes*. New York: Harper & Row, 1975.

Estes, Daniel J. "Like Arrows in the Hand of a Warrior (Psalm CXXVII)." *Vetus Testamentum* 41 (1991): 304–11.

Guyon, Jeanne. *Spiritual Torrents*. Augusta, ME: Christian Books, 1984.

Hardy, Thomas. *Tess of the D'Urbervilles*. 1891. Reprint, New York: Airmont, 1965.

Herbert, George. "Affliction (IV)." In *George Herbert and the Seventeenth-Century Religious Poets*, edited by Mario A. Di Cesare, 39. New York: W. W. Norton, 1978.

Hopkins, Gerard Manley. *Poems and Prose*. New York: Penguin, 1985.

Humphrey, William. "A Job of the Plains." In *Story and Structure*, edited by Laurence Perrine and Thomas R. Arp. 6th ed. Chicago: Harcourt Brace Jovanovich, 1983.

Karaagac, John. *John McCain: An Essay in Military and Political History*. Lanham, MD: Lexington, 2000.

Keller, Timothy. *The Prodigal God*. New York: Dutton, 2008.

Kushner, Harold S. *When Bad Things Happen to Good People*. New York: Schocken, 1981.

Lewis, C. S. *The Pilgrim's Regress*. 1933. Reprint, Grand Rapids: Eerdmans, 1977.

———. *Reflections on the Psalms*. New York: Harcourt, Brace, Janovich, 1958.

Lincoln, Abraham. *The Speeches and Letters of Abraham Lincoln: 1832–1865*. Everyman's Library. New York: E. P. Dutton, 1907.

Longman, Tremper, III, and Daniel G. Reid. *God Is a Warrior*. Studies in Old Testament Biblical Theology. Grand Rapids: Zondervan, 1995.

MacLeish, Archibald. *J.B.* Boston: Houghton Mifflin, 1958.

Manning, Brennan. *Abba's Child: The Cry of the Heart for Intimate Belonging*. Colorado Springs: NavPress, 1994.

Melville, Herman. *Moby Dick*. Edited by Luther S. Mansfield and Howard P. Vincent. New York: Hendricks House, 1952.

Miller, Patrick D. *The Divine Warrior in Early Israel*. Harvard Semitic Monographs 5. Cambridge, MA: Harvard University Press, 1973.

Milton, John. *Paradise Lost*. New York: Penguin, 2003.

Pascal, Blaise. *Pascal's Pensées*. Introduction by T. S. Eliot. New York: Dutton, 1958.

Phillips, J. B. *Your God Is Too Small*. New York: Macmillan, 1954.

Sire, James W. *The Universe Next Door*. 5th ed. Downers Grove, IL: IVP Academic, 2009.

Smith, Christian, and Melinda Lundquist Denton. *Soul Searching: The Religious and Spiritual Lives of American Teenagers*. New York: Oxford University Press, 2005.

Strauss, Lehman. *In God's Waiting Room*. Chicago: Moody Press, 1985.

Ten Boom, Corrie. *The Hiding Place*. New York: Bantam, 1971.

Tournier, Paul. *Escape from Loneliness*. Translated by John S. Gilmour. Philadelphia: Westminster, 1977.

Tozer, A. W. *Renewed Day by Day: A Daily Devotional*. Compiled by G. B. Smith. Camp Hill, PA: Fleming H. Revell, 1950.

Tucker, Ruth. *From Jerusalem to Irian Jaya*. Grand Rapids: Baker, 1983.

Wiesel, Elie. *The Trial of God*. New York: Schocken, 1995.

Wolterstorff, Nicholas. *Lament for a Son*. Grand Rapids: Eerdmans, 1987.

Yancey, Philip. *Disappointment with God*. Grand Rapids: Zondervan, 1988.

Image Credits

Unless otherwise indicated, photos, illustrations, and maps are copyright © Baker Photo Archive.

The Baker Photo Archive acknowledges the permission of the following institutions and individuals.

Photos on pages 32, 52, 198 © Baker Photo Archive. Courtesy of the Aegyptisches Museum and Papyrussammlung, Berlin, Germany.

Photos on pages 42, 44, 54, 64, 83, 99, 104, 113, 117, 124, 152, 158, 172, 190, 208, 213, 216, 226, 233, 234, 238, 242, 252, 254 are © Baker Photo Archive. Courtesy of the British Museum, London, England.

Photo on page 196 © Baker Photo Archive. Courtesy of the Metropolitan Museum of Art, New York.

Photos on pages 4, 21, 57, 95, 106, 143, 207, 220 © Baker Photo Archive. Courtesy of the Musée du Louvre; Autorisation de photographer et de filmer. Louvre, Paris, France.

Photos on pages 87, 129, 189, 200, 257 © Baker Photo Archive. Courtesy of the Oriental Institute Museum, Chicago / University of Chicago.

Photo on page 50 © Baker Photo Archive. Courtesy of the Pergamon Museum, Berlin.

Photo on page 59 © Baker Photo Archive. Courtesy of the Skirball Museum, Hebrew Union College–Jewish Institute of Religion, 13 King David Street, Jerusalem 94101.

Photo on page 224 © Baker Photo Archive. Courtesy of the Turkish Ministry of Antiquities and the Istanbul Archaeological Museum.

Photo on page 16 © Baker Photo Archive. Courtesy of the Vatican Museum.

Additional image credits

Photo on page 119 © Bisitun, Iran / The Bridgeman Art Library.

Photo on page 246 © Blake, William (1757–1827) / Fitzwilliam Museum, University of Cambridge, UK / The Bridgeman Art Library.

Photo on page 212 © Carol M. Highsmith Archive, Library of Congress, Prints & Photographs Division [reproduction number, LC-DIG-highsm-13921].

Photo on page 195 © Croquant courtesy of the Musée historique et archéologique de l'Orléanais, France / Wikimedia Commons, CC-by-sa-3.0.

Photo on page 39 © Daniel Baránek / Wikimedia Commons, CC-by-sa-3.0.

Photo on page 62 © Dr. James C. Martin and the Israel Museum. Collection of the Israel Museum, Jerusalem, and courtesy of the Israel Antiquities Authority, exhibited at the Israel Museum, Jerusalem.

Photo on page 162 by E. A. Wallis Budge (1857–1937) / Wikimedia Commons.

Photo on page 171 © Egyptian Museum, Turin, Italy / De Agostini Picture Library / The Bridgeman Art Library.

Photo on page 78 © Egyptian National Museum, Cairo, Egypt / The Bridgeman Art Library.

Photos on pages 13, 108 by Gustave Doré / Wikimedia Commons.

Photo on page 31 from the Horniman Museum, London, UK / Photo © Heini Schneebeli / The Bridgeman Art Library.

Photo on page 34 © Jim Henderson / Crooktree.com.

Illustration on page 135 © John H. Walton; drawing by Alva Steffler.

Photo on page 144 © Kathryn Hooge.

Photo on page 90 © Kim Walton.

265

Contributors

General Editors	*Interior Design*
Mark L. Strauss	Brian Brunsting
John H. Walton	Michael Williams
Associate Editor, Illustrating the Text	*Visual Content*
Rosalie de Rosset	Kim Walton
Series Development	*Cover Direction*
Jack Kuhatschek	Paula Gibson
Brian Vos	Michael Cook
Project Editor	
James Korsmo	

Index

nations, 77
nature, 224, 229, 239, 253
    analogies from, 50, 54, 86, 89–90
    evidence from, 76, 160, 235
    God's power over, 57, 60
    as revelation of God, 227–28
nature psalms, 221
negative confession, 56, 188, 192,
    231
night, 215
Noah, generation of, 136
noonday sun, 70

observation, 28, 30, 34, 146
Odyssey, 85, 98
offspring, 112
Old Testament prophets, 191
olive trees, 93
oppression, 63, 65, 136, 146,
    147–48, 150, 177–79, 186,
    191, 213, 214
order in heights of heaven, 152
orphans, 41, 146, 191
ostrich, 238, 239–40
outcasts, 18
owls, 185

pain, 23–24, 99, 102, 186, 201,
    202–3
papyrus plant, 51
partiality, 197
Pascal, Blaise, 97, 199
patriarchal age, 1
Perry Mason (TV program), 84,
    235
perseverance, 93, 202
personification, in the Bible, 245
pestilence, 32
physicians, 80–81, 84
Pilgrim's Progress, 97, 139
plant, uprooted and withered, 52
Pleiades, 60, 233
poetry, 6, 113
polytheism, 101, 152
poor, 146, 147–48, 149, 150, 190–91
praise, 215, 220–21
prayer, 138, 217
preaching Job, 6–7
preaching to wrong audience, 136
pride, 93, 94, 123, 160
problem of evil, 3, 29, 76, 101, 125
prologue, to Job, 8, 14, 65, 154,
    197, 203, 213, 219, 255, 259
prosperity, 95, 137

protection, 212
"proverb of ashes," 80
Proverbs, 4, 5, 17, 234
providence, 63, 114, 240
purity, 154

Ra, 134
racial discrimination, 169
rahab, 160
Rahab, 56
rain, 33, 235
raised hands, 68
Ramesses III, 219
ravens, 233
rebellion, 209
redeemer, 116, 118, 119
refining of impurity, 140–41, 142,
    143
remembering God, 53
repentance, 70–72, 74, 100, 209,
    221, 256
repetition and variation, 14
Resheph, 32
rest, 22
resurrection, 22–23, 86, 87–88, 90,
    101, 118–19, 209
retribution principle, 4, 5, 17, 79,
    168, 245, 238, 257
    Bildad on, 50, 51, 53–54, 111,
        112, 113, 152–53, 155
    Elihu on, 204, 206, 219–20,
        221–22, 225
    Eliphaz on, 27–28, 35, 94, 95,
        96, 137–39
    of friends of Job, 26, 38, 40–41,
        84, 105–6, 128–29, 142, 146
    Job on, 42, 47, 59, 65, 74–79,
        105, 130–32, 149, 166, 178,
        179, 184, 188, 246
    Zophar on, 71, 122–23, 126
revelation, 28, 68
rich man and Lazarus, 125
righteous, adversity of, 113, 136,
    168, 207
righteousness, 177, 178
rooster, 230–31

sackcloth, 100
sarcasm, 33, 75, 93, 135, 159, 161
satan, 8
Satan, 9, 249
scales, 38, 189
sea, 160, 232
sea monsters, 44, 46, 160

seeing God, 256
self-examination, 144
serpent, tempting of Adam, 93
sexual impurity, 189
Shaddai (title), 34
shadow of death, 21
shalom, 35
Shamash, 134, 216
shame, 123, 183
Sheol, 44, 161, 232
Shu, 162
silence, of friends of Job, 14, 15,
    152
sin, 47
    Eliphaz on, 94
    of humanity, 96
    of Job, 82, 93, 96
    and suffering, 3, 112, 142, 220
skin disease, of Job, 16, 18, 70,
    110, 184
slave driver, 22
slaves, 190
sleep, 46
soap, 59
Sodom and Gomorrah, 112, 115
songs in the night, 212, 215
"sons of God," 8, 9
sparks, 32, 33
spider, 52
stars, 56, 154, 233
stillborn, 64
stoicism, 12, 21, 33, 43, 47
storms, 58, 137, 221, 224–25, 229,
    231
Strauss, Lehman, 199, 259
streams, 38
suffering, 2, 120
    perseverance through, 93
    as punitive and formative, 194,
        197, 218–22
    of righteous, 73, 113, 136
    and sin, 3, 30, 68
    See also pain
Suffering Servant, 73
suicide, 40
sulfur, 112
sun, 226, 229
sword, 33

tambourine, 128
Tannin, 44, 56
tears, 101
technology, 173, 174–75
ten (number), 116
Ten Commandments, 137

tent, 35, 111, 112
terror, 142
theodicy, 29
theology
    collision with experience, 60
    as open and flexible, 132
    See also retribution principle
thunderstorm, 221, 225, 227
Tiamat, 44
Tolkien, J. R. R., 48, 235, 253
tongue of the crafty, 93
Tournier, Paul, 30–31, 204
tradition, 50, 51, 53, 54, 68, 76
trusting God, 17, 24, 42
turmoil, 22

unanswerable questions, 3, 5, 23,
    160, 230, 248, 255, 258
understanding, 52
under the sun, 173
underworld, 44

vanity, 12, 215
venereal disease, 218
vengeance, 43, 168
virtuous woman, 173

wadis, 38, 39
warhorse, 238–39
washing, 59
wasteland, 77
water buffalo, 245
water vapor, 159
weakness, 29
wealth, 95, 136, 167, 190
weather, 232
whale, 253
"why" questions, 20, 21, 161
wicked Job as, 129, 209
    prosperity of, 75, 76, 128, 132, 136
    punishment of, 59, 87, 90, 112,
        113–14, 124–25, 126, 168, 208
    temporal happiness of, 123–24,
        126, 129, 130
    See also evildoers
widows, 146, 191
wife of Job, 16, 18, 22, 189
wild donkey, 69, 237, 250
wild ox, 236, 237
wine, 194
wisdom, 1–2, 3, 4
    and circumstances, 36
    Elihu on, 206–7

human search for, 171–74
resides in God, 173–74
way of, 22
wise men, 206–7, 209
womb, 64
world
    complexity and ambiguity of,
        33
    as temple, 160
worms, 45, 106, 148, 154, 156, 158,
    159, 161
worship, 10
wrath of God, 231

Xerxes, 74, 75

Yahweh (name), 76. See also God
Yamm, 44, 56
Yancey, Philip, 61, 84–85, 103
youth, wisdom of, 196, 198

Zaphon, 159
Zion, 159
Zophar, 50, 68–72, 122–26, 146,
    152, 165, 167

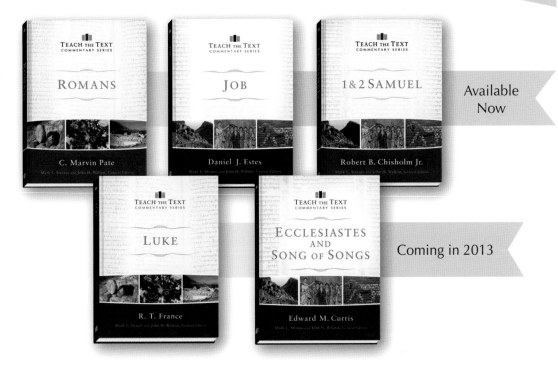